SPEARTHROWER OWL
A Teotihuacan Ruler in Maya History

STUDIES IN PRE-COLUMBIAN ART AND ARCHAEOLOGY
NUMBER FORTY-ONE

SPEARTHROWER OWL
A Teotihuacan Ruler in Maya History

DAVID STUART

DUMBARTON OAKS, TRUSTEES FOR HARVARD UNIVERSITY
WASHINGTON, D.C.

© 2024 Dumbarton Oaks
Trustees for Harvard University, Washington, D.C.
All rights reserved.
Printed in the United States of America by Sheridan Books, Inc.

LIBRARY OF CONGRESS CATALOGUING-IN-PUBLICATION DATA

NAMES: Stuart, David, 1965–, author.

TITLE: Spearthrower Owl : a Teotihuacan ruler in Maya history / David Stuart.

OTHER TITLES: Teotihuacan ruler in Maya history | Studies in pre-Columbian art and archaeology ; no. 41.

DESCRIPTION: Washington, D.C. : Dumbarton Oaks, Trustees for Harvard University, [2024] | Series: Studies in pre-Columbian art and archaeology ; 41 | Includes bibliographical references and index. | Summary: "Nearly twenty-five years ago, David Stuart published an article titled 'The Arrival of Strangers,' in which he proposed that 'Spearthrower Owl,' a prominent historical figure cited in the Early Classic inscriptions of Tikal, might be a ruler of Teotihuacan. Stuart expands on this provocative argument in *Spearthrower Owl: A Teotihuacan Ruler in Maya History*, offering evidence that Spearthrower Owl was a historical individual whose political legacy reverberated for generations in the Maya Lowlands and Central Mexico. Many of the epigraphic, iconographic, and historical particulars surrounding his life are presented here for the first time; these varied lines of evidence point to him being a powerful foreign individual in the history and dynastic politics of the Maya Lowlands as well as a ruler of Teotihuacan from 374 to 439 CE. To contextualize this examination of Spearthrower Owl, the volume looks more closely at the Entrada of January 16, 378, especially in light of newer archaeological discoveries, epigraphic readings, and historical interpretations. The resulting historical framework, even vague as it sometimes is, highlights the complexity and nuance of the Teotihuacan-Maya relationship in the Early Classic period"—Provided by publisher.

IDENTIFIERS: LCCN 2023039171 | ISBN 9780884025023 (paperback)

SUBJECTS: LCSH: Mayas—Guatemala—Petén (Department)—Kings and rulers. | Indians of Mexico—Mexico—San Juan Teotihuacán—Kings and rulers. | Mayas—Guatemala—Petén (Department) —Politics and government. | Inscriptions, Mayan. | Tikal Site (Guatemala) | Petén (Guatemala : Department)—Antiquities. | Teotihuacán Site (San Juan Teotihuacán, Mexico)

CLASSIFICATION: LCC F1435.3.P7 S78 2024 | DDC 972/.52—dc23/eng/20231025

LC RECORD available at https://lccn.loc.gov/2023039171

GENERAL EDITOR: Frauke Sachse

MANAGING EDITOR: Sara Taylor

ART DIRECTOR: Kathleen Sparkes

DESIGN AND COMPOSITION: Melissa Tandysh

COVER PHOTOGRAPH: Detail of the Tikal Marcador, showing the name of Spearthrower Owl. Photograph by Kenneth Garrett.

www.doaks.org/publications

CONTENTS

	Acknowledgments	vii
	Introduction	ix
1	The Entrada of 378 and the Early Classic Peten	1
2	Interpreting Spearthrower Owl	47
3	The Tikal Marcador: A Monument of Conquest	71
4	Eagles and Emblems	91
5	Hints of Teotihuacan History	117
	Appendix 1 Key Dates of the Entrada	
	and Early Classic Peten History (250–450 CE)	127
	References Cited	129
	Index	147

ACKNOWLEDGMENTS

IT WAS TWENTY-FIVE YEARS AGO THAT I FIRST BEGAN WORKING ON THE historical aspects of Teotihuacan-Maya relations, analyzing a pattern of events and actors cited in the Maya inscriptions of Tikal, Uaxactun, and nearby centers. A quarter century is a long time, and over the years I have benefited from the help and inspiration of a great many people, indeed too many to name. But some I must single out for their help and inspiration.

The seeds for these ideas were planted during my early work on the archaeological projects at Copan, where questions about Teotihuacan relations always seemed to be in the air, as more and more discoveries were made. My interest in the topic found fertile ground in many conversations at Copan in those years, either at the site or at the old Tunkul Bar, with friends including Will Andrews, Ricardo Agurcia Fasquelle, Ellen Bell, William Fash, Barbara Fash, Robert Sharer, and Loa Traxler. My colleagues in Maya epigraphy were also instrumental in spurring my interests and refining my ideas over the decades, and I would especially like to thank Stephen Houston, Simon Martin, Dmitri Beliaev, Alexander Safronov, Karl Taube, Alexandre Tokovinine, Sergei Verpetskii, and Marc Zender. My students at Harvard University and the University of Texas, Austin, have been of great help in developing these ideas, some of which were first presented in seminars and brown-bag talks in Cambridge and Austin. Recently Edwin Román-Ramírez, my former student at the Univeristy of Texas, has renewed archaeological investigations at Tikal, with the study of Teotihuacan and the Entrada foremost in his research, with great results and with my own deep appreciation and interest.

For their help and encouragement over the years, I would like to thank Barbara Arroyo, Tim Beach, Fred Bove, Marcello Canuto, David Carballo, Nicholas Carter, Michael Coe, Clemency Coggins, George Cowgill, Patrick Culbert, Arthur Demarest, Hector Escobedo, Francisco Estrada-Belli, Federico Fahsen, James Fitzsimmons, Antonia Foias, David Freidel, Thomas Garrison, Stanley Guenter, Nikolai Grube, Peter Harrison, Heather Hurst, Chris Jones, Juan Pedro Laporte, Rudy Larios, Sheryl Luzzader-Beach, Mary Miller, Enrique Nalda, Olivia Navarro-Farr, Philippe Nondédéo, Rene Ozaeta, Astrid Runggaldier, William Saturno, Linda Schele, Juan Antonio Valdés, Evon Vogt, and Gordon Willey. J. Dennis Baldwin of the Department of Geography at the University of Texas, Austin, kindly provided the illustrated map of the central Peten, shown in Figure 2.

The staff and editors at Dumbarton Oaks were of infinite help, and I thank them and the manuscript reviewers for improving nearly everything I submitted. Sara Taylor patiently saw the manuscript through to the published end, and Frauke Sachse has been a wonderful coordinator of the whole effort. Her comments on an earlier draft of the manuscript led to many much-needed improvements.

Finally, my family deserves so much thanks for all of their support and patience over the many years that led up to this work, including my late father George Stuart, my sister Ann Stuart, and my three wonderful boys, Peter, Richard, and George. And I dedicate this book to Carolyn, my wife and partner in all things, with love.

INTRODUCTION

REVISITING ONE'S OWN OLD IDEAS AND INTERPRETATIONS CAN BE tricky, especially in the ever-changing world of Maya archaeology and epigraphy. New finds over the years inevitably bring to light previous errors of interpretation or off-base assumptions, both large and small. So it was with some trepidation that I recently read over a paper that I wrote over twenty years ago on the nature of Teotihuacan-Maya relations (Stuart 1998b, 2000) while organizing my graduate seminar on the art and archaeology of Teotihuacan. That old chapter had probed what I saw as the deep historical foundations of Teotihuacan's presence in the Classic Maya world, using Tikal and Copan as sources for understanding what the Maya had to say about the great city in highland Central Mexico. A few specific ideas did not stand up well on my rereading, but several broader interpretations of the paper seemed fairly resilient in retrospect. One, built on the remarkable insight made earlier by Tatiana Proskouriakoff, proposed that a "foreigner" named Sihyaj K'ahk' conquered Tikal on January 16, 378 CE, on behalf of Teotihuacan in some capacity.[1] I used the term "Entrada" (borrowed from Peten's colonial history) to refer to his arrival from afar, passing through El Peru (Waka') on his way eastward to the heart of the Maya world. Today, this singular event is considered a turning point in Teotihuacan's involvement in the history, art, and archaeology of the Maya Lowlands. In my chapter, I also presented a related idea, but with far less certainty: Maya texts referred to a prominent historical figure of the same era who oversaw the arrival and who might have been Teotihuacan's ruler. I referred to him then as "Spearthrower Owl," following an established nickname for one version of his distinctive hieroglyphic name (Figure 1).

Before the late 1990s, his hieroglyph had been seen as an impersonal reference, perhaps some sort of foreign title associated with Teotihuacan or perhaps the term for a military order from highland Mexico (Fialko 1988; Grube and Schele 1994; Proskouriakoff 1993; Schele and Freidel 1993:15, 156–157). Its function as a personal name was nevertheless clear to me from the patterns of its appearance in Tikal's inscriptions, as we will review shortly. As I proposed in my 2000 paper, Spearthrower Owl was the name of a powerful individual who acceded to power in 374 CE; he was also the father of the famous Tikal ruler named Yax Nun Ayiin, who was himself installed as a local king not long after that site's conquest. As we will explore later, a more accurate reading of Spearthrower Owl's personal name, based on phonetic and visual evidence, may have been something like "Eagle Striker." Here I will refer to him mostly by his older and more established nickname, as it is widely recognized in the literature and even in the popular press.

ix

Figure 1
Two principal name variants of Spearthrower Owl: a) Tikal, Stela 31, side caption; and b) Tikal, Marcador. Drawings by David Stuart.

My proposals from 2000 were controversial, and Spearthrower Owl's significance and role have remained debated topics over the last two decades. They have even emerged as a central point of discussion and debate in more recent literature focused on Teotihuacan's internal sociopolitical structure (Braswell 2003a; Carballo 2020; Headrick 2007:37–38; Nielsen 2014; Nielsen and Helmke 2008; Robb 2017:141, 209, 411; Sanders and Evans 2005). Speculations about his status have also appeared in debates on interactions between Teotihuacan and the Maya region and on whether we can consider those complex issues from a historical as well as an archaeological perspective. Some expressed skepticism about Spearthrower Owl's historical importance and connections to Teotihuacan, entertaining an alternative view that he may have been an "imaginary" figure in Maya written history, a Teotihuacan "abstraction" used for Tikal's own ideological messaging and glorification (Braswell 2003a:24). Geoffrey E. Braswell considered the possibility that he was the "ruler of a relatively minor Maya site" cited by a later Tikal king in order to bolster that ruler's own claim of succession (Braswell 2003a:26). Apparent references to raptorial birds and weaponry in Teotihuacan's own art span roughly two centuries or more, leading others to believe that such images are unlikely to be specific personal names but rather examples of a more generalized militaristic insignia, perhaps indicating a military order of some type (Carballo 2020). This view echoes much older interpretations that can be traced to their very first identification in the art of Teotihuacan (von Winning 1948, 1987), linking them also to the much later eagle warriors of Postclassic Central Mexico.

Here I revisit the topic of that 2000 paper, with the aim of offering a more complete presentation of the evidence in support of the idea that Spearthrower Owl was indeed a historical individual whose political legacy reverberated for generations among the lowland Classic Maya, and perhaps even among the people of Teotihuacan. Despite the widespread acceptance of this history among Mayanists, many of the epigraphic, iconographic, and historical particulars surrounding his life and influence will be presented here for the first time. The varied lines of evidence point to him being a powerful foreign individual in Maya history and an active participant in Maya dynastic politics, as well as "almost certainly the ruler of Teotihuacan" (Nielsen 2014:15).

Needless to say, staking out such a position quickly ushers us into long-standing debates about the nature of governance at Teotihuacan, much as it did when the idea was first proposed twenty years ago (Carballo 2020; Cowgill 2003). As scholarship on Teotihuacan grew rapidly throughout the 1970s and 1980s, divergent visions emerged on the nature of rulership, or even of its very existence in the political structures of Teotihuacan. For some, the lack of clear representations of dynastic rulers in Teotihuacan's art suggested a focus away from the sorts of individual kings or authority figures that we find in the Maya area. Others took a different view, noting Teotihuacan's emphasis on militarism and the clear sense of a controlled and rigidly designed urban community. As can be gleaned from the title of this work, I have come down more on the "singular authority" side of this debate, seeing a closer connection between the political cultures of Teotihuacan and the Maya Lowlands than is sometimes considered or described.

Teotihuacan's governmental arrangement has a conspicuous role in David Graeber and David Wengrow's best-selling book *The Dawn of Everything: A New History of Humanity* (2021), where it is presented as a strong case study of a "collective" system of authority, largely ignoring the alternative hypotheses and interpretations. Elsewhere, one of its authors asserts that "Teotihuacanos rejected dynastic personality cults" (Wengrow 2022). Many have welcomed this provocative book and its explicit linkage between the concerns of modern politics and models from prehistory, but it has also stirred some pushback within the field of political philosophy (Appiah 2021) and from social scientists and archaeologists with a firm grasp of Teotihuacan's complex archaeological record (Smith 2022). Here I can only restate my view that no obvious evidence exists of any "rejection" of centralized rule at Teotihuacan and that the nature of the city's visual culture may not be the clearest inroad into such questions. While I am sure this debate will continue, my intention with this study is to outline the evidence from Maya sources of at least one ruler who was prominent during one era of Teotihuacan's long history. Naturally, such evidence cannot address the nature of Teotihuacan's broader political structure over time and how it must have changed through the centuries.

The timing of Spearthrower Owl's life and reign appears to correspond to the Early Xolalpan phase of Teotihuacan's chronology, when that city's influence and economic power expanded in dramatic fashion throughout much of southern Mesoamerica. As we will explore in more detail, the historical records at Tikal note that Spearthrower Owl was probably one in a series of sequential rulers, offering a tantalizing hint at a broader "dynastic" arrangement that may have arisen at Teotihuacan during the years leading up to his rule beginning in 374 CE. It is tempting to connect this historical evidence with the significant changes that have long been perceived in the city's archaeological record around 250–350 CE, with marked indications of a major ideological shift and the arrival of a new political order. This is also a time when there is thought to have been a "substantial change in the nature of rulership" at the city (Murakami and García–Des Lauriers 2021:9). I should reiterate that even if we can assert the existence of a series of rulers at Teotihuacan, the precise nature of their office and the structure of their rule within Teotihuacan's larger sociopolitical system remain impossible to ascertain. Historical sources from the Classic Maya obviously cannot begin to tackle those broader issues involving Teotihuacan's long-term development as Mesoamerica's greatest urban area, and those debates and discussions will always be a constant element of Teotihuacan research. I argue here that we can now seriously engage some of these questions through the lens of written history—a transformative approach that was not really possible even when Spearthrower Owl's role began to come into focus two decades ago.

The interpretations put forward here must also be considered in light of new discoveries at Teotihuacan, including the many mural fragments recovered from the Plaza de las Columnas (Sugiyama et al. 2020). These paintings appear to have been done by Maya artisans in the very core of Teotihuacan's political and ceremonial space, and they are a clear testament to the importance of Maya elites in the fabric of that city, at least at a certain time. These have added a compelling new dimension to a wide array of other evidence, mostly from ceramics, that has long pointed to a significant number of Maya elites residing at Teotihuacan (Clayton 2005; Linné 1934). Interactions between Teotihuacan and the Maya area obviously went in both directions and, as we shall see, the history of Tikal's own dynasty may provide a useful historical framework for understanding the nature of this strong Maya presence at Teotihuacan. Spearthrower Owl's focus and interest in Tikal's political affairs soon after he took power cannot be random, and his efforts at conquest and overthrow must have been developed for particular political and maybe economic reasons. I suggest that some of the long-distance patterns of conflict were likely motivated by internal family dynamics and interpersonal relations, stemming from the close and probably long-lasting relationships between the Maya of the central Peten and Teotihuacan (Canuto, Auld-Thomas, and Aredondo 2020:386).

Recent archaeological investigations in the central Peten are now adding even more important archaeological dimensions to the monuments and historical information we are focused on here. For example, new excavations in Group 6C-XVI at Tikal are in the midst of revealing what may well be an "enclave" of Teotihuacan during the Early Classic period, near the area where the Marcador monument was discovered in the early 1980s (Houston et al. 2021). And the new discovery of extensive Early Classic fortifications and walls to the west of Tikal, near La Cuernavilla, may well date to the time of the Entrada, perhaps even earlier (Houston, Garrison, and Alcover Firpi 2019). Both history and archaeology can now show that the Entrada was far from the beginning of Teotihuacan's deep influence and presence in the Maya world. Rather, as I will discuss in detail, it was the singular flash point within a long era of mutual awareness and interaction.

Nor was the demise of the elderly Spearthrower Owl in 439 the end of such influence. As we will examine in some detail, Teotihuacan's decades-long political dominance in the central lowlands left an indelible mark on subsequent generations of Maya rulers as well as in the visual culture they channeled to represent their positions as inheritors of a foreign power structure. We have long known that the militaristic ideology of Early Classic highland Mexico exerted a very powerful message for later Maya elites and rulers, who incorporated the imagery of Teotihuacan into their own visual messaging, even after the collapse of the great highland city in the sixth century. What is new is that these influences came about through the history we can associate with Spearthrower Owl and his allies, and that they are often personal and historical in nature.

To set the stage for this detailed examination of Spearthrower Owl and his time, it is necessary to look more closely at the events of 378 and later, especially in the light of newer discoveries, epigraphic readings, and historical interpretations. The Entrada can now be rightly described as the single most important event of Early Classic Maya history, with long-lasting reverberations in the political and cultural world of the Maya Lowlands. Yet it was not an isolated event. The circumstances that led up to the "arrival of strangers" and the complex events that followed it can also be discerned in some detail within the written histories of Tikal and surrounding sites. Together with the latest archaeological investigations in both regions, we can begin to orient the pivotal year of 378 within the long-lasting relationship between the two regions. The historical framework offered here, even vague as it sometimes is, shows that the relationship between Teotihuacan and the Maya was never simple or straightforward but was as complex and nuanced as we would expect it to be.

NOTE

1 This date for the arrival event, January 16, 378 CE, is based on a slight revision to the Goodman-Martinez-Thompson correlation of the Maya and Christian calendars that was proposed by Martin and Skidmore (2012), with the correlation constant of 584286. Earlier statements placed it on January 13 (584283) or January 15 (584285). I prefer the Martin-Skidmore variant of the correlation based on its strong match with many contemporaneous lunar calendar records that reference the first visibility of the moon, after astronomical new moon, as its "arrival" (Stuart 2020). The Entrada to Tikal will, therefore, be identified here as having occurred on January 16, which, incidentally, corresponded with the darkening before first appearance of new moon.

1 THE ENTRADA OF 378 AND THE EARLY CLASSIC PETEN

THE EARLY CLASSIC HAS LONG BEEN A PROBLEMATIC AND POORLY KNOWN era within Maya archaeology and history. This was the case even before the debate surrounding the so-called Entrada episode of 378 CE, the pivotal flash point of Teotihuacan's presence in the Maya Lowlands that is the focus of this historical study. The situation is understandable when we consider that the Early Classic occupies those few centuries between the lengthy Late Preclassic (500 BCE–150 CE) and much more visible and complex Late Classic (550–850 CE), whose large constructions covered and obscured the underlying earlier remains. In one of the very few scholarly treatments of the Early Classic period, Willey and Mathews (1985:1) went so far as to say that "the Early Classic period has tended to be slighted in Maya archaeological research" due to the understandable focus on the more abundant Late Classic materials. The same can be said of approaches to political history, which of course emerged as a subfield of Maya studies in the 1980s and 1990s. Revealingly, one major synthesis of Maya political history from that time (Culbert 1991) ignored the Early Classic altogether and included no mention whatsoever of Teotihuacan's possible role in the region.

Maya field archaeology of the early and mid-twentieth century defined the Early Classic of the Peten region mostly through the material culture revealed in excavations at Uaxactun and Tikal, where Teotihuacan influence was detected in ceramics and sculptural styles of the later Tzakol period, corresponding roughly to the fifth century CE (at Tikal the corresponding ceramic phase was called Manik') (Black 1990; Ricketson and Ricketson 1937; Smith 1955). At Kaminaljuyu, in the highlands of Guatemala, intensive excavations also demonstrated a remarkable amount of Central Mexican presence in the parallel Esperanza phase (Kidder, Jennings, and Shook 1946). All of these projects, closely related in their respective vision and even in their key personnel, quickly gave rise to important research questions that have persisted up to the present day, focused on two related issues: basic chronology and interpretations of regional interaction (Arroyo et al. 2020; Braswell 2003b; Canuto, Auld-Thomas, and Aredondo 2020; Coggins 1975;

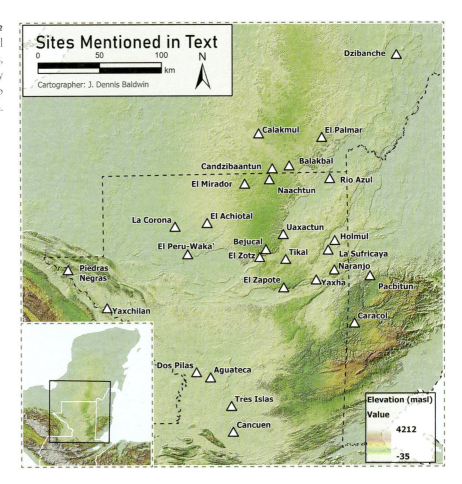

Figure 2
Map of the central Maya Lowlands, showing major Early Classic centers. Map by J. Dennis Baldwin.

Lincoln 1985; Sanders and Michels 1977; Willey and Mathews 1985). Another major question that emerged later, still often confronted, focused on the significance of the Early Classic within the larger trajectories of Maya cultural development, especially regarding its transition out of the Late Preclassic (Canuto, Auld-Thomas, and Aredondo 2020; Grube 1995; Traxler and Sharer 2016).

The evident collapses and abandonments of early centers such as El Mirador and Nakbe around 100 CE accentuate the importance of the Early Classic in our efforts to understand the broader issues of Maya history and cultural development. It was at that time that a new political culture emerged in the central lowlands, rooted in centuries of Preclassic development and complexity, yet reformulated in novel ways. We can now characterize this as the beginnings of Maya dynastic culture, something very difficult to trace any earlier than about 100 CE. Although many writers have seen the beginnings of the institution of Maya kingship deep within in the Middle or Late Preclassic (Freidel and Schele 1988a, 1988b; Saturno 2009; Sharer 1992), the "Classic" dynastic structure familiar from later times looks to be historically anchored to a later time frame, well after the collapses of El Mirador and related centers. I prefer to see the major centers of the Middle and Late Preclassic as qualitatively different from what emerged in the first

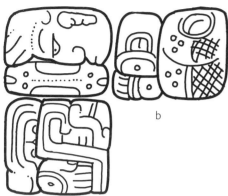

Figure 3
Selected names of early dynasts of the central Peten: a) Yax Ehb Xook of Tikal, from the "Deletaile tripod"; b) Naranjo founder, Naranjo, Stela 24; and c) Unohk'ab K'inich of Xultun, Xultun, Stela 18. Drawings by David Stuart.

two or three centuries CE, perhaps even in the sense of being "pre-dynastic" (Martin 2016:539). It was at this time that we see the emergence of the *k'uhul ajaw* title as a standardized office or position that was centrally placed within the political ideology.

By 200 CE, several important dynastic centers were established in the central lowlands, some of them emerging out of the earlier dominance of those large Preclassic cities (Figure 2). Tikal and its close neighbor Uaxactun appear to have been especially important, alongside a handful of other precocious centers in the eastern Peten region that would continue as major courtly centers well into the Late Classic, among them Naranjo, Xultun, and Dzibanche (ancient Kanul). Of course, the evidence for these places is highly skewed toward those sites that have been adequately investigated, though there were surely others.

Some years ago, I proposed that Tikal's dynastic founder was named Ehb Xook or Yax Ehb Xook, cited in several texts of the Classic period (Figure 3a). He likely lived in the second century CE, based on a rough calculation of reigns extending back in time (Martin 2003), but we lack contemporaneous sources from that period. He appears along with a handful of other primordial founders, including one who seems to have initiated the Naranjo (*Sa'al*[?]) dynasty, possibly from the same general time period (Schele 1986b, 1992) (Figure 3b). An even earlier individual may have ruled at Xultun as far back as the Late Preclassic, as suggested by a mention of a "37th Lord" who traced his origins back to a person named Unohk'ab K'inich ("Right-hand of the Sun") (Figure 3c). These are the first historical Maya dynasts known to us. The supposed time periods in which they lived, in the first and second centuries, provide us with a good estimate for

Figure 4
Names and images of "Foliated Ahau," an early Maya ruler of the second century CE: a) name glyph from Copan, Stela 1; and b) detail of carved shell from Dzibanche, excavated by Enrique Nalda. Drawings by David Stuart.

orienting the changes in political culture that took place at the start of the Early Classic (Martin 2020:120–121). And it is likely that these foundational rulers and the courts they ruled over were active at different times over the course of those one or two centuries, in what is sometimes called the "Proto-Classic" period.

One date stands out among the retrospective histories that hearken back to the murky beginnings of the Classic period. This is the *k'atun* ending 8.6.0.0.0 10 Ahau 13 Ch'en (December 20, 159 CE), cited in inscriptions at both Copan and Pusilha'. This is consistently associated with an ancient place-name possibly read as *Chihcha'* or *Chika'*, "Maguey Metate" (Stuart 2014), also known in the literature as the "Chi witz" place (Grube 2004; Stuart 2004b; Tokovinine 2013:119–120). It is also associated with a key historical name that I and others have called "Foliated Ahau" (Grube 2004; Martin 2016:531, 2020:120; Prager 2002:109–110; Stuart 2004b, 2012) (Figure 4). The place *Chihcha'* is difficult to locate geographically, but one example of its toponymic glyph occurs in an inscription fragment from Dzibanche, suggesting that it might be near that area, or in the central zone of the peninsula more generally, in the Peten or what is today southern Campeche. The text from Dzibanche is part of Fragment 7 and remains incomplete, but the *Chihcha'* glyph is well-preserved, as is that of another place-name below it, recognizable as *wi'te'naah* or *winte'naah* (Figure 5) (Tokovinine, personal communication, 2022). This second name is significant, for it has been identified as a likely place-name for Teotihuacan or one of its major structures (Fash, Tokovinine, and Fash 2009;

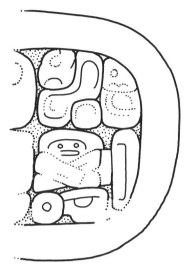

Figure 5
Inscribed stone fragment from Dzibanche, with early place-names *Chihcha'* and *winte'naah*. Drawing by David Stuart.

Stuart 2000). The Dzibanche text would, therefore, seem to point to connections between the elusive *Chihcha'* and Teotihuacan in the Early Classic.

A portrait of the early personage known as Foliated Ahau may be found on an elegant shell excavated from an Early Classic tomb at Dzibanche (Stuart 2004b) (Figure 4b). There we see a ruler seated upon a jaguar-skin cushion and cradling a two-headed serpent. His likely name glyph, in variant animate form, sits atop his head, attached via a paper-cloth strap. This name glyph is also what we sometimes refer to as the "Jester God," a quintessential symbol of Maya rulership as well as a specific mytho-historical character, perhaps even a prototypical king of the Classic Maya (Stuart 2012:140–141). Many carved shells from Classic Maya civilization bear portraits of distant ancestors, and the Dzibanche portrait seems to be a particularly elaborate example of the genre, representing a heroic individual of singular importance. Foliated Ahau may also be represented on the "codex-style" vase K2572, a Late Classic vessel likely produced within the Kanul court (Grube 2004). Realizing the later importance of Dzibanche in Maya history, as the base of the Kanul dynasty, and its evident significance also during the Late Preclassic and Proto-Classic, we may even entertain the thought that *Chihcha'* was in the same general area. Whatever the case, Foliated Ahau would emerge as a major historical actor memorialized by many different kingdoms, even those as distant as Copan and Palenque (Stuart 2013).

The inscriptions of Tikal, Uaxactun, and nearby central sites strongly suggest that these places played prominent roles in the initial developments of Classic dynasties in the region. The beginnings of Early Classic history seem to coalesce around these neighboring centers, whose monuments show the earliest Long Count dates known from anywhere in the Maya area (Mathews 1985; Willey 1985:15) (Figure 6). Cycle 8 monuments from these two sites alone account for about half of all that are known in the Maya area (Mathews 1985:33). Stela 29 of Tikal bears the date 8.12.14.8.15 13 Men 3 Zip (July 9, 292), and Stela 9 of Uaxactun recorded the possible date 8.14.5.12.16 9 Cib 14 Kayab (April 19, 323) (Figure 6a–b). Uaxactun's Stela 10 is probably even earlier, based on the style of its

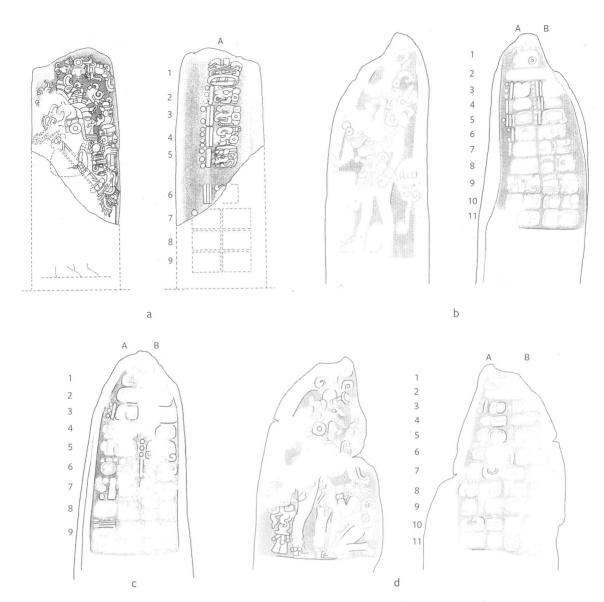

Figure 6 Selected early stelae from Uaxactun and Tikal: a) Tikal, Stela 29, front and back (after Jones and Satterthwaite 1982:fig. 49); b) Uaxactun, Stela 9, front and back (after Graham 1986:155, 157); c) Uaxactun, Stela 18, back (after Graham 1986:175); and d) Uaxactun, Stela 19, front and back (after Graham 1986:180). Drawings by William R. Coe (a) and Ian Graham (b–d).

eroded hieroglyphs. The early dates of Uaxactun were first noted by Sylvanus Morley (1937–1938:184–188), motivating the Carnegie Institution of Washington's program of excavation there in the 1920s and 1930s. The Tikal and Uaxactun stelae still remain the earliest dated monuments in the Maya Lowlands, even after extensive programs of investigation at a great many other Early Classic Maya sites. Although it may be tempting to see Uaxactun and Tikal as holding disproportionate roles in our interpretations of Early

Figure 7 Tikal, Stela 39, and its Uaxactun captive: a) Stela 39, front; b) detail of a captive; c) captive's name atop the head; and d) comparable name from Uaxactun, Stela 19. Photograph by David Stuart (a); drawing by Linda Schele © David Schele, courtesy Ancient Americas at LACMA (b); and drawings by David Stuart (c–d).

Classic Maya history and archaeology, their unique importance and central roles in early Maya history now seem inescapable. The two related centers were the most important players in lowland Maya history during the second through fourth centuries CE; they were places that saw the rapid emergence of a "new" elite culture focused on the ritual and dynastic concerns so familiar in later textual sources.[1]

It is frustrating that the very early inscriptions of Uaxactun are so poorly preserved and difficult to interpret. Stela 9's Long Count date has been interpreted in various ways, although, as just noted, it appears to date to 323 (8.14.5.12.16 9 Cib 14 Kayab), probably an accession date for a local ruler (Safronov et al. 2022). The inscriptions of Stelae 18 and 19 offer the earliest contemporaneous Period Ending dates known from Maya history, 8.16.0.0.0 3 Ahau 8 Kankin (February 3, 357), but the historical details are difficult to glean from their eroded hieroglyphs (Figure 6c–d). Using new photographs of these texts, Alexander Safronov and his colleagues have recently made a key observation, identifying a single historical name (**TZ'AK-bu**-VULTURE) on both monuments. They note its very strong resemblance to a named captive depicted on Tikal's Stela 39 (Safronov et al. 2022) (Figure 7). This latter monument dates to a later *k'atun*, at 8.17.0.0.0 1 Ahau 8 Ch'en (October 21, 376), and was dedicated by Tikal's early ruler Chak Tok Ich'aak I. If this identification is correct, we can reasonably conclude that Tikal and Uaxactun were at war with one another, with Tikal emerging victorious in the years leading up to 376, shortly before the Entrada events. It is important to point out that this war is not the Tikal-Uaxactun conflict proposed by Mathews (1985:44) and discussed in great detail by Schele and Freidel (1993:130–164). That reconstruction of events arose out of misinterpretations of the events surrounding the Entrada of 378, seeing the arrival episode instead as a local conquest of Tikal over Uaxactun. Still, we need not reject their views outright, for Stela 39 now points to a true war between these neighbors, coming slightly earlier.

Naachtun, to the north of Uaxactun, is a very large site that also was of great importance in the mid-fourth century. It has several Early Classic stelae, including Stela 23 with its Long Count date 8.16.4.10.1 6 Imix 4 Tzek (August 2, 361) (Nondédéo, Cases, and Lacadena 2019). This is given as the date for the erection of the stela, with no other historical context. We cannot know how the ruling family of Naachtun related to those of Tikal and Uaxactun at this time, but there does seem to be a closer connection forged after about 400, possibly through intermarriage. Naachtun played a role of some sort, still obscure, in the narratives of the Entrada of 378, pointing to its significance in regional politics during the first part of the Early Classic.

Tikal's own story during the second and third centuries is also murky, at least before the reign of Chak Tok Ich'aak, due to the lack of inscriptions from the time. This evidence, spotty as it is, has been discussed in detail by Martin (2003). Stela 29 comes earliest, perhaps recording an accession of a ruler in 292 CE (Figure 6a). The name of this ruler is not preserved in the text, but it does appear atop the head of the figure portrayed on the front of the monument. This bears a very close resemblance to some forms of the name Yax Nun Ayiin, which is used for two later kings in Tikal's history.[2] The same name is perhaps also included in the ancestral iconography on the right side of Tikal's Stela 1 (a monument that also mentions Spearthrower Owl in its main text) (Martin 2002:fig. 12b). The record continues to be opaque until we come upon the mention of another king who ruled sometime before 297, perhaps named Huun Bahlam ("Paper Jaguar"), otherwise known as "Foliated Jaguar." His name bears the same components we see in the name of Foliated Ahau, mentioned earlier, and the two may be related. A later female ruler, Ix Unen Bahlam, oversaw the *k'atun* ending 8.14.0.0.0 (September 1, 317), according to the same list of Period Endings on Stela 31 (Martin 2002; Stuart 2011).

Chak Tok Ich'aak was in power at Tikal at some point before 376, as we have seen, during an era that seems to have been especially unstable in the central Peten. The single most important source from his reign is Stela 39, discovered broken and cached within the E-group complex of the Mundo Perdido group (Ayala Falcón 1987) (Figure 7). This area was a major focus of ritual activity at Tikal from the Preclassic into the early centuries of the Early Classic up to the time of the Entrada. It was dedicated on 8.17.0.0.0 and was probably originally erected in the plaza of the Mundo Perdido. The text records the ruler's name alongside those of important ancestors, including his two parents. His father was Muwaan Jol (Martin 2003), likely a preceding king, and it is possible that his mother was the earlier queen Ix Unen Bahlam, named on Stela 39 in a slightly different form.[3]

Tikal's apparent victory over Uaxactun appears to have been a key historical event in Chak Tok Ich'aak's reign, and it may well prove to be important in contextualizing the circumstances leading up to the Entrada of 378. If nothing else, it sheds a small, incomplete light upon the fractious geopolitical landscape that existed in the central Peten in the fourth century. Warfare seems to have been common among the elites of the time, as also indicated by the many depictions of bound prisoners in other very early monuments of Uaxactun. What we know with more certainty is that a warrior named Sihyaj K'ahk' entered this fraught arena in 378 from the west, targeting Tikal and its ruler Chak Tok Ich'aak, evidently acting on behalf of his foreign overlord, Spearthrower Owl. We can presume that Sihyaj K'ahk' and Spearthrower Owl were aware of these internal Maya conflicts, and their arrival on the scene may indicate an intention to participate in them in some way. It is that complex turn of events we call the Entrada to which we now turn in detail, recorded in several different inscriptions.

A NEW LOOK AT THE ENTRADA

Many inscriptions of the central Peten recount the great arrival of 378, pointing to its transformative role in the history of the region. Archaeological finds in the two decades since my initial article have nearly doubled the number of its references, adding interesting new details and raising new questions. The Entrada event is highlighted on Tikal's Stela 31 and Marcador, as well as on Stelae 5 and 22 of Uaxactun (Stuart 2000). It is also mentioned in a painted text revealed on a palatial wall at the more distant site of La Sufricaya, near Holmul to the east (Estrada-Belli et al. 2009). Stela 15 of El Peru celebrated the important role of that center in the Entrada narrative, apparently as a stopping point on the eastward journey of the foreigners toward Tikal (Stuart 2000). This connection with El Peru has been dramatically accentuated with the very recent discovery of Stela 51, with its mentions of the arrival event at Tikal and of the prominent actors involved (Navarro-Farr et al. 2022). Here we will examine these references in the order of their complexity, gradually building up a sense of the details surrounding this pivotal episode in Maya history.

Several earlier discussions of the events of 378, including Proskouriakoff's initial interpretations, took much of their inspiration from Stela 5 of Uaxactun, with its unusual portrait of a striding Teotihuacan-style warrior (Schele and Freidel 1993:146) (Figure 8). Proskouriakoff (1993:8) described the figure as "dressed in a fashion foreign to the Maya of the period" and argued that he was "possibly conqueror of Tikal." She was the first to suggest that its inscribed Long Count date was 8.17.1.4.12 11 Eb 15 Mac, or January 16, 378, linking it to Stela 31 of Tikal and modifying an earlier reading proposed by Morley (1937–1938:1:184–188). It was the association with the warrior's portrait that led Proskouriakoff to posit this as the likely date for the "arrival of strangers"; she also noted the mention of the same date on the back of Tikal's Stela 31, with its portraits of other Teotihuacan-style figures. She was unable to read any of the names or the event glyph. The latter turned out to be a spelling of the verb *huliiy*, "he arrived" (**HUL-li-ya**),

Figure 8 The foreign warrior on Uaxactun, Stela 5, front and sides. Drawings by Ian Graham (after Graham 1986) © President and Fellows of Harvard College, Peabody Museum of Archaeology and Ethnology.

confirming Proskouriakoff's remarkable intuitive insight (Stuart 2000). The place-name that follows the verb is that of Tikal, *Mutul*, followed by the personal name of Sihyaj K'ahk'. Thus, *huliiy mutuul sihyaj k'ahk'*, "Sihyaj K'ahk' arrived to Mutul (Tikal)." Recent reevaluations of Stela 5 suggest a second Long Count date on its left side, perhaps referring to its later dedication by a local Uaxactun ruler known as "Sky Raiser" (Kováč and Barrois 2012; Kováč et al. 2019; Safronov and Beliaev 2017). The warrior on the front is now thought to be a lord named K'inich Mo', who was affiliated in some way with Sihyaj K'ahk' and the power structure he established. This name identification should remain tentative, however, as the glyphs near Stela 5's frontal figure seem to read differently. Nonetheless, he was clearly a foreigner, as Proskouriakoff surmised, and his prominence on the stela suggests that he was closely involved with Uaxactun affairs.

Figure 9 Name variants of Sihyaj K'ahk': a) Tikal, Stela 4; b) Tikal, Stela 31; c) Tikal, Marcador; and d) Tikal, Hombre de Tikal. Drawings by David Stuart.

Sihyaj K'ahk' appears in many Early Classic inscriptions in the Peten and even beyond (Figure 9). The name is based on the embedded verb *sihyaj*, "was born," with the noun *k'ahk'*, "fire," following. We can translate the full name in a couple of possible ways, one seeing *k'ahk'* as the simple subject: "Fire-is-Born." An alternative sees "fire" as a characterization of the action, as in "Born-in-Fire" (Houston, Garrison, and Alcover Firpi 2019). The latter analysis is attractive for its evocation of familiar mythic narratives of solar birth from Postclassic Central Mexico, such as the story of the deity Nanahuatzin casting himself in the ceremonial fire at Teotihuacan and becoming resurrected as the sun, Tonatiuh. Still, I prefer the first translation, "Fire-is-Born," due to the structural similarity with names we find in later Maya texts, where the verb *sihyaj* is followed by a deity's name, as in *Sihyaj K'awiil*, "K'awiil-is-Born," a name cited at Naranjo, and *Sihyaj K'in Chahk*, "Solar Chahk-is-Born."

As we will see, a prominent name from inscriptions about the Entrada is "*Sihyaj* 'Dart,'" also with close Teotihuacan associations. This is mentioned on a sculpture known as the Hombre de Tikal and on a stela at El Peru (see Figure 9d). The "dart" sign of this name is shown as a distinctively Teotihuacan-style weapon. It remains likely that this is an alternate name of Sihyaj K'ahk' (Stuart 2000), although Stephen D. Houston has recently proposed its possible distinction, naming a separate individual who also "arrives" to Tikal around the same time (see Houston, Garrison, and Alcover Firpi 2019). Whatever the case, both of these names appear to present a message of militarism, or even a new order of warfare: "Fire is Born" and "Dart(s) are Born." I suspect that these may have been contrived names that allude to the same person, and whose meaning(s) allude to the nature of Sihyaj K'ahk's role and Teotihuacan's intervention in Maya politics.

One point in favor of seeing these as a single name comes from El Peru, Stela 15 (Figure 10). As I presented in my original study on the Entrada history, Stela 15 contains a fascinating record of a day 3 Kan 7 Mac, or 8.17.1.4.4 (January 8, 378), coming only a few days before the arrival recorded at Tikal and Uaxactun (Stuart 2000). This important reference gives us a good indication as to the movement of Sihyaj K'ahk' from west-to-east, evidently using El Peru as a point of departure for the final push into Tikal. Sihyaj K'ahk's name appears in the Stela 15 passage along with another probable *huliiy* verb (Figure 10b). A few blocks later, we have the same event repeated, but now the "dart" sign is clear as the suffix, apparently as a replacement for *K'ahk'*. On

THE ENTRADA OF 378 AND THE EARLY CLASSIC PETEN | 11

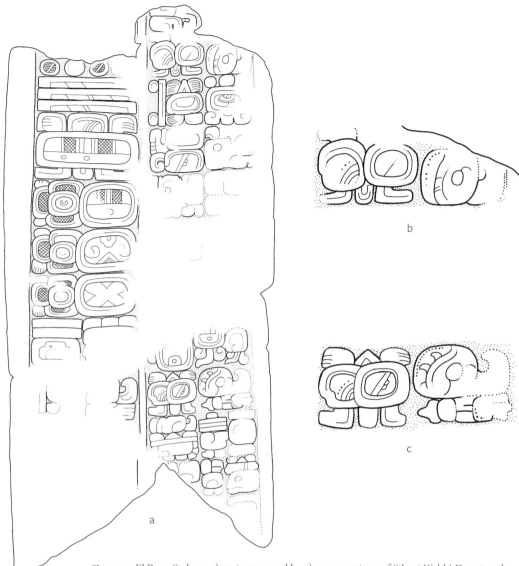

Figure 10 El Peru, Stela 15: a) main text; and b–c) two mentions of Sihyaj K'ahk'. Drawings by David Stuart, from photograph and field drawing by Ian Graham.

the recently discovered Stela 51 of El Peru, Sihyaj K'ahk's arrival to Tikal is highlighted, there giving his name again with the "fire" sign. It seems probable these are the same individual. Both names on Stela 15 are accompanied by the honorific title *kaloomte'*, which otherwise refers to powerful rulers who oversee more than one court or city-state (Martin 2020:77–83). This appears elsewhere with Sihyaj K'ahk', including on Stela 31, the Marcador of Tikal, as well as on Stela 5 of Uaxactun (Ková č and Barrois 2012). It is also frequently found with the name of Spearthrower Owl himself. The "dart" and "fire" substitution may hinge, in fact, on a parallelism we see in the hieroglyphic writing of Teotihuacan. There, the representation of darts is ubiquitous, yet on a painted bowl in the collection of the Art Institute of Chicago, we see an example of the common "shield

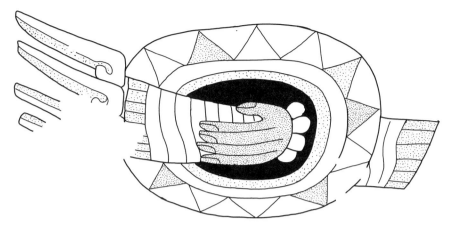

Figure 11
Glyphic form showing a replacement of "hand with darts" with "hand with torch," on a Teotihuacan-area vessel in the collection of the Art Institute of Chicago (inv. 1968.790). Drawing by David Stuart.

with darts" motif, where the projectile weapon is directly replaced by a hand holding a flaming bundle (Figure 11). Here, "fire" and "darts" occur as like-in-kind elements, and the shield would suggest the significance of fire as a weapon of war.

Just why a Teotihuacan dart would replace a logogram for "fire" is difficult to know, but it may pertain to the sense of the noun *k'ahk'* as also meaning "power" or "intensity" in some Mayan languages, in addition to its basic meaning of "fire." In colonial Yucatec, for example, we find the phrase *u k'ak'il k'atun*, "lo fuerte de la guerra" (Michelon 1976). In K'iche'an languages, *q'aq'* is a noun root in numerous terms having to do with authority, rule, and military prowess. Its abstracted form *q'aq'al* has a range of meanings that span "gleam, majesty, glory, fire, heat, fever" (Edmonson 1965:96). The name *Sihyaj K'awiil*, referring to a Late Classic individual cited in a text from Naranjo, would seem to be a similar sort of term for an abstracted notion of "power being born," given the semantic range of the term *k'awiil* that has emerged in recent years as having the sense of political power or authority (see Helmke and Awe 2016:14).[4]

The January 8 event cited on El Peru, Stela 15 (dedicated on 8.19.0.0.0) is best understood as Sihyaj K'ahk's entrance into that site, eight days before his transformative arrival to Tikal. There is no indication of it being a violent episode or war, unlike what we will see at Tikal. This key clue establishes Sihyaj K'ahk's eastward movement through the Peten, implying an origin somewhere even further to the west. As I and others have noted, this accords with his being described as an *ochk'in kaloomte'*, a western ruler. We also find on Stela 15 an example of the *wi'te'naah* or *winte'naah* glyph, mentioned earlier as a likely architectural name associated with Teotihuacan. The glyph's immediate context is unclear due to eroded segments of the inscription, but it may have served to specify Sihyaj K'ahk's point of origin, the beginning of the journey that, for the local scribe, culminated in his arrival at El Peru. The local ruler who dedicated Stela 15 was named K'inich Bahlam, an important Early Classic king who emphasizes his strong connections to Sihyaj K'ahk'. Much of the history remains unclear, but it is reasonable to suppose that K'inich Bahlam aided Sihyaj K'ahk' on his eastward journey, and that he may have been an enemy of Tikal's own king at the time, Chak Tok Ich'aak, whose days were very numbered.

Twenty years following Stela 15, we come to the dedication of El Peru, Stela 51, on the turn of the *bak'tun* at 9.0.0.0.0. This important monument was only recently unearthed, and it emerges as a key new source for understanding aspects of the Entrada narrative (Navarro-Farr et al. 2022). Its inscription specifically mentions Sihyaj K'ahk's arrival to Tikal in 378 (not to El Peru, unlike Stela 15's text). The front of the stela presents the striking image of a warrior in Teotihuacan-style dress, holding a rectangular shield and a spearthrower. He wears a helmet of a feline head, nearly identical to that worn by Yax Nun Ayiin on Tikal, Stela 4. I suspect it is a portrait of the local El Peru lord who took office after K'inich Bahlam, on November 28, 432 (8.19.16.16.12 5 Eb seating of Ceh), according to the incised hieroglyphs that appear around the subject's headdress. One remarkable feature of this stela is its clear mention of Spearthrower Owl, using the "atlatl-cauac" variant of the name we find on Stela 31 at Tikal. At the end of the phrase recording the local lord seating in office, we read that Spearthrower Owl "witnessed" the event, and that he was a *Mutul Ajaw*, a "Lord of Tikal." The use of this honorific title is extremely important, if not puzzling. We know that Tikal was ruled at this time by Sihyaj Chan K'awiil, the grandson of Spearthrower Owl and the son of Yax Nun Ayiin. It is, therefore, doubtful that we are to understand that Spearthrower Owl was the local dynastic lord of Tikal. Rather, given the complexities of the history we are exploring here, it seems most likely that the title indicates Spearthrower Owl's status as Tikal's overlord, centered at a place we know to have been the probable base of operations in the central Peten.[5] His witnessing of the vassal's accession is also curious, for it would at first seem to indicate that Spearthrower Owl was physically present at the seating. But this conforms to a pattern we see in other Maya texts, where rulers "see" and sanction the rituals of others, often in a hierarchical sense (Houston, Stuart, and Taube 2006:172–173). The word for "see" used here and elsewhere is *il* or *ila'*, which can also have the meaning of "to know." On Stela 51, the statement of Spearthrower Owl's witnessing may be one of a "knowing look," a sanctioning from afar. We might also entertain the possibility that the local El Peru lord, whose name is unknown, was crowned not at El Peru but in the highlands of Mexico, at Teotihuacan. This was the case, after all, with Copan's dynastic founder, K'inich Yax K'uk' Mo', who around this same time traveled to Teotihuacan to "receive authority" (*ch'am k'awiil*), returning to Copan months later.

Another record of the Entrada that comes from outside of Tikal and Uaxactun is from La Sufricaya's Mural 7 (Figure 12). Succinct and direct, much like the statement on Uaxactun's Stela 5, Mural 7 simply states "arrived to Tikal" (*huliiy*). The passage comes after the featured event of the painted text, commemorating the dedication of a building complex in 379, exactly one solar year after the Entrada event (Estrada-Belli et al. 2009). The inclusion of the toponym *Mutul*, for Tikal, is significant, for it describes the arrival as a nonlocal event, focused on distant Tikal and no other location. The subject here is not given as Sihyaj K'ahk', but simply as *k'awiil* (**K'AWIIL-la**). This is usually understood to be a deity name, the ancient name for the entity we know as God K, a supernatural being associated with royal power and lightning. *K'awiil* is what is "taken" or "grasped" upon the accession of some rulers, and it may physically refer to the God K scepters or effigies that are so common in Maya iconography. Recent epigraphic finds at Xunantunich have led us to consider a more subtle meaning surrounding the word, however. There, we see the records of an important moment in the political history of the Kanul dynasty, when one ruler appears to have overtaken another in a competition

Figure 12 La Sufricaya, Mural 7. Drawing by Heather Hurst, courtesy of the Proyecto Arqueológico Holmul.

for the throne (Helmke and Awe 2016). The defeat is recorded in a summary statement on Panel 4, as two juxtaposed events: *machaj k'awiil tahn ch'een Kanu'l, pahtaal k'awiil uxte'tuun*, "k'awiil is no more at the town of Kanul, (and) k'awiil is made (at) Uxte'tuun." This clearly describes the transfer of power from one court-center of the Kanul dynasty, Dzibanche (Kanul), to another at Calakmul (Uxte'tuun). We can entertain the possibility here that the word *k'awiil* conveyed a more abstracted sense of "power" or "authority," in addition to its more direct mythic and religious associations (see Helmke and Awe 2016:14). Such an interpretation provides an important spin on the recorded history of the Entrada, in describing the event not as Sihyaj K'ahk's arrival but as the arrival of "rule" or "authority" to Tikal. It could clearly imply an event of great political importance with widespread regional impact.

Stela 22 of Uaxactun goes a bit further in describing the nature of what occurred on January 16, 378 (Figure 13). In a retrospective account written many years later in 504 (9.3.10.0.0), the event is again "to arrive" but with the subject written simply as *ochk'in k'awiil*, "the western authority." We find no explicit mention to Sihyaj K'ahk' by name, only to the apparent nature of his presence at Tikal as a powerful foreigner. The directional reference agrees with his title *ochk'in kaloomte'*, and with others who we will see

THE ENTRADA OF 378 AND THE EARLY CLASSIC PETEN | 15

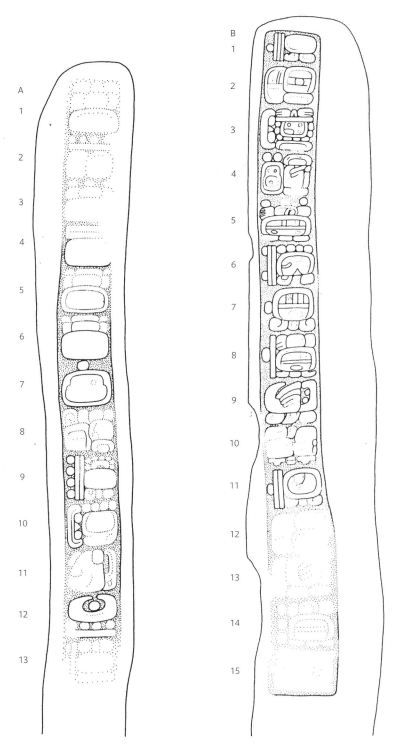

Figure 13 Uaxactun, Stela 22, left and right sides. Drawings by Ian Graham (after Graham 1986:191) © President and Fellows of Harvard College, Peabody Museum of Archaeology and Ethnology.

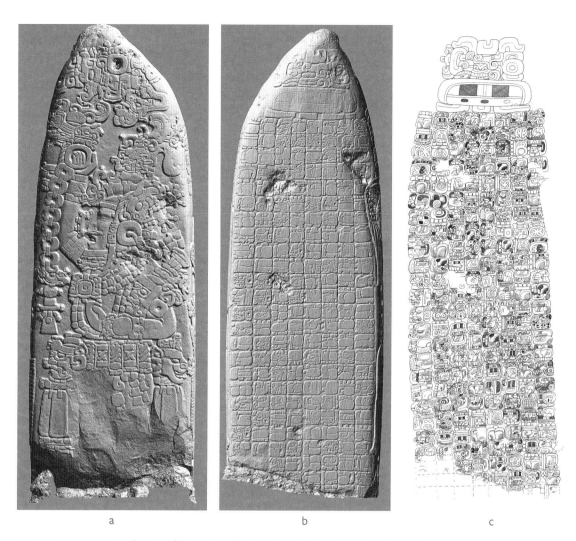

Figure 14 Tikal, Stela 31: a) front; b) back; and c) drawing of back. 3D scans and models by Alexandre Tokovinine, courtesy of the Corpus of Maya Hieroglyphic Inscriptions (CMHI), Peabody Museum of Archaeology and Ethnology (a–b); and drawing by William R. Coe, from Jones and Satterthwaite 1982:fig. 52b (c).

are associated with Teotihuacan-Maya history. In this inscription, the event of 378 was singled out as the one major historical event of the past, 116 years prior.[6]

Records of the Entrada become far richer and more detailed with key passages from the inscription on the rear of Tikal, Stela 31, dedicated in 445 CE (Figure 14). This contains the longest historical narrative from the Early Classic to come down to us. There, the description of the Entrada stands out as the first of several related historical events in Tikal's local dynastic history. In Columns C and D of that inscription, the Entrada account interrupts the steady flow of references to *k'atun*-ending celebrations up to 8.17.0.0.0, the same Period Ending recorded on Stela 39 (Figure 15). Chak Tok Ich'aak was its celebrant and is said to have raised a stone (*k'altuun*) at a place called *K'ante'el*.

THE ENTRADA OF 378 AND THE EARLY CLASSIC PETEN | 17 |

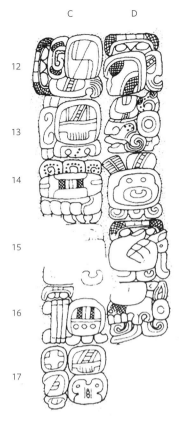

Figure 15

Passage from Stela 31 relating to the 8.17.0.0.0 *k'atun* ending of Chak Tok Ich'aak. Drawing by William R. Coe, from Jones and Satterthwaite 1982:fig. 52b.

It is possible that this refers to the erection of Stela 39 itself, with *K'ante'el* as the name of what we call the Mundo Perdido complex, or some part of it.

In the next passage, pertaining to the Entrada, a Distance Number of 1.4.12 leads from the *k'atun* ending to a very long passage, with the date 11 Eb highlighted with the deictic maker *ayal* (C19: **AY-ay-la**) (Figure 16). Many glyphs remain missing at the bottom of these columns, where the stela was broken away from its base (and never recovered in the excavations of Tikal's North Acropolis). The sole glyph for 11 Eb is a much-reduced statement for 8.17.1.4.12 11 Eb 15 Mac, and we can surmise that the use of the *tzolk'in* alone indicates the date's great historical significance, similar to the *k'atun* endings that precede it (indicated as 1 Ahau, 7 Ahau, and so on). The passage offers a far more detailed description of the nature of the 378 episode, with a sequence of three verbs and associated names and subjects.

First comes the somewhat enigmatic phrase, *tzutzuuy* (C20a: **TZUTZ-yi**) *yichnal* (C20b: **yi-chi-NAL**) *ook*...? (D20: **OOK-ki-tzi?**), "it ends in the presence of...?" The verb itself is clear, but the subject is less so—what exactly is "ending"? I read the hieroglyph that immediately follows the verb as *y-ichnal*, "in the presence of," but this seems to be an unusual and abrupt place for such a bridging phrase. Next comes the noun **OOK** with an infixed **ki**, above a sign that resembles the syllable **tzi**. I am not sure how to read this particular term, except that it seems to incorporate the noun *ook*, "foot, leg," apparently as the subject of the *tzutz* verb, perhaps with the fuller sense of

| 18 | SPEARTHROWER OWL

Figure 16
Passage from Stela 31 relating to the Entrada of 378 CE. Detail of 3D scan and model by Alexandre Tokovinine, courtesy of the Corpus of Maya Hieroglyphic Inscriptions (CMHI), Peabody Museum of Archaeology and Ethnology.

a "foot-ending," based in part on parallel expressions in other texts. If that is the correct understanding, we should remember that *ook* has extended meanings related to traveling and pathways. In Tseltal, the cognate form *ok* has in addition to its regular meanings of "foot, leg," the sense of a person's or animal's "trail, track, footstep" (*rastro, huella*) (Polian 2020:470), and in Ch'olan-Tseltalan languages, this idea of a pathway is reflected in the term *yokha'*, "ditch, channel," literally a "track of water" (note Ch'orti' *ok-ja'*, "ditch, brook, irrigation ditch" [Hull 2016:313]).[7] The Stela 31 event thus may refer to the "end of a trail," or a journey.

The extended phrase on Stela 31 continues with a verb reading **HUL-OOK-ja** (C21), also an unusual juxtaposition of terms. This may be a noun-incorporated verb, *hul-ook-aj*, "he (or it) 'leg-arrives,'" perhaps in the sense of "arrives by foot." Its subject is *ochk'in k'awiil*, "the west power" or the "west authority" (D21: **OCH-K'IN-K'AWIIL-la**). This is surely parallel to the phrase we encountered earlier on Stela 22 of Uaxactun, a simple statement of political takeover. But the subject on Stela 31 is specified even further with the personal name of Sihyaj K'ahk' (**SIH-K'AHK'**), at C22, followed by the title *kaloomte'* (D22). It is he whose journey has ended, having arrived to establish a new political arrangement.

The culmination of the Stela 31 passage comes at C23–C24, giving a third verb to describe the event. The first glyph is an adverb or relational noun that remains undeciphered (**ya** and **hi**[?] grouped with a kneeling human form), but we know from other

THE ENTRADA OF 378 AND THE EARLY CLASSIC PETEN

texts that it precedes a new verb within a passage, perhaps to highlight it rhetorically. What follows, as I pointed out in my earlier study, is a poetic expression for one's death, *ochha'aj* (D23: **OCH-HA'-ja**), "he water-entered" (see Fitzsimmons 2009:35). This same verb appears in Tomb 7 from Río Azul, recording the death of its occupant, and on an inscribed mask possibly from that site. It is also featured in mythological contexts where it records the death of the Maize God Juun Ixi'm, before his subsequent resurrection. On Stela 31, the subject is Chak Tok Ich'aak, the ruler of Tikal, conveyed only with his personal name glyph and no titles.[8]

This ends the lengthy passage regarding the Entrada, but we do find added onto these key events of history a supplemental statement in the next several glyphs, beginning with a Distance Number of 17.10.12. I suspect that this counts from an unstated accession date for Chak Tok Ich'aak up to the time of his death and burial. Here it is stated as *ochwitzaj*, "he was mountain-entered," apparently as reflection of his "water-entering." The burial place is named as *Chahke'l* ("Place of Chahk"), but it is impossible to know if this was a separate community or a sector within Tikal. When looked at overall, this section of Stela 31 presents a fairly detailed view of the events that occurred on 11 Eb—the ending of a journey, most likely, followed by the arrival of western authority with Sihyaj K'ahk', which then resulted in the death of the Tikal king Chak Tok Ich'aak.

⌣

Another major source for understanding the events surrounding the Entrada is the Marcador of Tikal, a small upright pillar found in 1982 in the deeply buried Group 6C-XVI, where it was erected in the center of a small patio or plaza (Fialko 1988). Its inscription includes multiple mentions of Spearthrower Owl, to whom the pillar was dedicated in the year 414. The text makes it clear that he was an even higher-ranking individual than Sihyaj K'ahk', who seems to have acted for or represented him in some capacity. As we will explore in much more detail in Chapter 3, the shaft of the monument bears two panels of hieroglyphs, as well as iconographic elements with clear allusions to Teotihuacan. In the opening section that pertains to the events of January 16, 378, we read of the arrival of Sihyaj K'ahk' to Tikal, then *och ch'een*, "he cave-enters" or "he town-enters," a well-established term for military conquest found in many other Maya texts (more on this in the following chapter). At the time of my earlier study, I had not recognized this one key hieroglyph, due to its highly ornate and creative form (see Stuart 2014). The *och ch'een* phrase describes defeat only in a very general way, and by enlisting the word "conquest" I do not mean to assert that a foreign army traveled unaided for eight hundred miles to invade the central Maya Lowlands. Rather, Tikal's overthrow presumably involved a number of Maya allies who aided Sihyaj K'ahk' and his forces, all of whom were willing participants in seeing the downfall of Tikal's ruler (Freidel, Escobedo, and Guenter 2007; Nondédéo, Cases, and Lacadena 2019). Identifying the *och ch'een* verb is important in confirming that the Entrada episode was a military victory over Tikal's ruler Chak Tok Ich'aak, establishing a new political arrangement with Sihyaj K'ahk', a major victor and protagonist. Spearthrower Owl's own role in this remains difficult to know, but he appears to be far less "present" than Sihyaj

Figure 17 Scene of traveling Teotihuacan warriors on a tripod vessel excavated in Problematical Deposit 50 at Tikal. Drawing by Virginia Greene, from Greene and Moholy-Nagy 1966.

K'ahk' in local Tikal affairs. He is the dominant player in many ways, fathering Tikal's king-to-be and celebrated as the main figure and "owner" of the Marcador monument. We will return to some of these historical points, but suffice it to say that there can be little doubt about the militaristic nature of the events of January 16, 378, and that Spearthrower Owl was the highest-ranking person among the principal agents of Chak Tok Ich'aak's downfall. The "arrival" was far from some benign diplomatic mission—it was a direct overthrow of the city's residing dynast, resulting in his death. It was, in the words of Stela 31, the arrival of a new "western authority."

We cannot address narrative aspects of the Entrada without mentioning the imagery on the remarkable cylinder tripod vessel recovered in 1959 from Problematical Deposit 50 at Tikal (Coggins 1975:177–182; Culbert 1993:fig. 58a; Greene and Moholy-Nagy 1966) (Figure 17). The unusually wide vessel shows figurative decoration similar to what we see on sherds recently excavated at Teotihuacan's Plaza de las Columnas. The complex scene has at least ten human figures and three architectural forms, apparently representing the directional movement of several people from one location to another. Four individuals wearing warrior gear and spearthrowers move leftward toward a radial structure, upon which stands a "Maya"-looking person bearing a quetzal feather bundle. Behind the four warriors are two other individuals wearing "tassel headdresses" and carrying lidded cylinder tripod vessels, possibly containers of cacao. Coggins (1975:181–182) considered that the imagery may "commemorate the arrival of Teotihuacanos to Kaminaljuyu, or at some other site" and characterized its narrative scene as a "milestone in the history of Maya art" for its depiction of multiple individuals. It may no longer stand out as a unique representation from the Early Classic, but the vase nonetheless has a singular importance as a narrative image. The specifics are sketchy, but we might now consider the likelihood that the image on the vessels pertains in a direct way to the events surrounding the Entrada of 378.

SIHYAJ K'AHK': HIS ROLE AND HISTORY

Given his role as protagonist during the Entrada, Sihyaj K'ahk' can rightly be described as one of the pivotal figures in the history of the Early Classic Peten. Despite this, many aspects of his persona and political authority remain elusive. Was he ethnically Maya? A Teotihuacano? And in either instance, what was his precise relationship to the higher-ranking power structures of Teotihuacan? These questions still remain difficult to resolve. Perhaps the best inroad into some of these problematic issues is to consider

Figure 18
Passage from Stela 31 relating to the accession of Yax Nun Ayiin, under the authority of Sihyaj K'ahk'. Detail of 3D scan and model by Alexandre Tokovinine, courtesy of the Corpus of Maya Hieroglyphic Inscriptions (CMHI), Peabody Museum of Archaeology and Ethnology.

the nature of political organization in the Peten in the decades after 378 and how Sihyaj K'ahk's role may have changed over time.

We must first ask what his official status might have been on the local scene, in the immediate wake of his arrival on a day accompanied by no small amount of drama and even violence. There is no accession date for Sihyaj K'ahk', nor did he ever claim to be a local *k'uhul ajaw* of the Mutul court, following in the footsteps of the defeated Chak Tok Ich'aak. That particular role would be filled within a couple of years by the installation of the young Yax Nun Ayiin, the son of Spearthrower Owl, under the aegis of Sihyaj K'ahk'. What emerges from the history of the subsequent two decades is a picture of Sihyaj K'ahk' as an "outsider" whose political influence in the Peten transcends the local institutions and geopolitics of the era. He appears on the scene and rules almost as a fait accompli, at least by virtue of his being the "west authority."

We can glean a few important details about Sihyaj K'ahk's role when we return to Stela 31 and the lengthy passage that immediately follows the record of the Entrada (Figure 18). This is the statement of Yax Nun Ayiin's accession in the following year, on 8.17.2.16.17 5 Caban 10 Yaxkin (September 13, 379) (the date is written in error as 10 Caban 10 Yaxkin, as Proskouriakoff first noted [see Jones and Satterthwaite 1982:15]).[9] The accession verb at E10 is abbreviated as **ti AJAW** and the name of Yax Nun Ayiin follows at F11. This is accompanied by two revealing subordinate clauses that describe the nature of the event in more detail. One starts with the verb *u ch'amaw*, "he takes it," and the object written as the number 28 with **PET**. I see this as a reduced spelling of the derived noun *peten*, "island, province," so "the 28 provinces." The sense of this, as I see it, is that Yax Nun Ayiin assumes the role as the ruler of Tikal, and perhaps also of a larger hegemony established in the wake of the Entrada the year before. A glyph at E13 may read **U-ku-chu-PAAT**, for *u kuchpaat* "it is his back-burden" or "cargo," referring to one's political duty and charge (note the colonial Yukatek meaning of *kuch*, "cargo, gobierno," also "asiento o estado de los principales, o el reinado" [Barrera Vásquez 1980:343]). These accession-related phrases are then followed by *u kabij sihyaj k'ahk'*, "it is the action of Sihyaj K'ahk'" (F13: **U-KAB-ji**; E14: **SIH-K'AHK'**). The statement makes clear that Sihyaj K'ahk' directly oversaw the installation of Yax Nun Ayiin as ruler, and, as we will discuss in more detail, there are good indications that Yax Nun Ayiin was little more than an infant at the time.

This hierarchical relationship between ruler and overseer is repeated on Stela 4 of Tikal, dedicated in 396 (8.18.0.0.0) (Figure 19). The principal event recorded in the back inscription is once more the accession of Yax Nun Ayiin eighteen years earlier. Here the young king is named as *yajaw kaloomte' sihyaj k'ahk'*, "the vassal of the kaloomte', Sihyaj K'ahk'," using a common phrase that establishes the superior rank of Sihyaj K'ahk' as an "overlord" (Houston 1993:139; Houston and Mathews 1985:fig. 12). A similar reference appears also on Tikal's Stela 18, dating the reign of Yax Nun Ayiin in the last two glyphs of the inscription (Figure 20). From these, it is apparent that Sihyaj K'ahk' was the "ruler of a ruler," at least at the time of the accession itself. At the very least, he appears to be the agent and representative of Spearthrower Owl, a higher authority, charged with overseeing much of the "new order" that was established in the central Peten up to 396 and beyond (Martin 2003:11–13; Stuart 2000, 2011).

Sihyaj K'ahk's role as an "overlord" went beyond Tikal, expanding in its geographic scope during subsequent years. We find direct textual evidence of this at a number of central Peten sites, including Uaxactun, El Zapote, Bejucal, and Río Azul, amplifying the pattern first pointed out in the murals of La Sufricaya, with its mention of the Entrada event. On Stela 4 of El Zapote, a very small center located twenty-two kilometers to the south-southeast of Tikal, we see the date 8.17.2.5.3 5 Akbal 1 Kankin (January 22, 379) opening a very poorly preserved inscription (Proskouriakoff 1993:14). The only discernable glyph in the entire text is the likely name of Sihyaj K'ahk'. Given the poor condition of Stela 4, it is impossible to interpret the Long Count date in any historical way, but it is significant that it falls just over a year after the arrival of Sihyaj K'ahk' and a

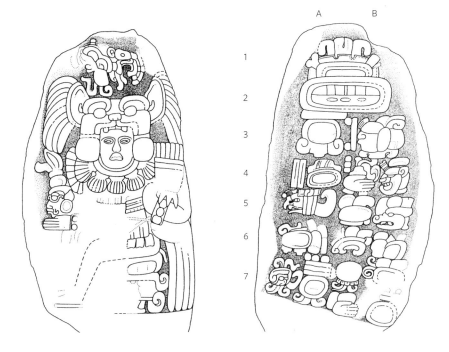

Figure 19
Tikal, Stela 4, front and back. Drawing by William R. Coe, from Jones and Satterthwaite 1982:fig. 5.

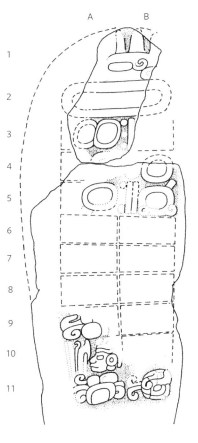

Figure 20
Tikal, Stela 18, back. Drawing by William R. Coe, from Jones and Satterthwaite 1982:fig. 26.

number of months before the accession of Yax Nun Ayiin. It may well refer to the installation of a local authority at El Zapote, or even to the founding of its small courtly center.

Sihyaj K'ahk's mention at El Zapote, while vaguely understood, provides circumstantial evidence of the site's participation in the new regional political order that he established, as do other indications from slightly later episodes recorded on its monuments. Stela 5 is an especially important source, dating to the later *bak'tun* ending at 9.0.0.0.0, in 435, probably sometime after Sihyaj K'ahk's demise (his last known mention comes in 406, on the monument known as the Hombre de Tikal, with an event twenty-eight years after the Entrada). Stela 5 was dedicated by the Tikal ruler Sihyaj Chan K'awiil (Spearthrower Owl's grandson), clearly indicating El Zapote's subservience to its great neighbor to the north. Sihyaj Chan K'awiil is, in fact, depicted on one of its sides, as indicated by the name in his elaborate headdress that displays the Principal Bird Deity. The stela's other side shows a woman who holds a squared element with a "Mexican year symbol," framing what appears to be the name glyph of Ix Unen Bahlam (Marcus 1976:39). This woman may well be the mother of Sihyaj Chan K'awiil, or perhaps another wife, and she is also featured on Stela 4 of El Zapote.[10] Stelae 1 and 5 from El Zapote appear to also name Spearthrower Owl, but in passages that are too damaged to read clearly (see Proskouriakoff 1993:14). Again, the importance of El Zapote in the new political arrangement after the Entrada seems clear, despite the lack of a firm understanding of the site's protagonists.

Bejucal, a small elite center near El Zotz, to the west of Tikal, likewise has a reference to Sihyaj K'ahk', in a clearer statement of political hierarchy (Carter, Gutiérrez Castillo, and Newman 2018; Garrison et al. 2016; Houston, Garrison, and Alcover Firpi 2019). Stela 2 bears the Long Count date 8.17.17.0.0 and cites the accession of an El Zotz ruler some twelve years prior, on 8.17.4.16.18 11 Etz'nab 1 Yaxkin (September 3, 381) (Figure 21). This is also close on the heels of the Entrada event of Yax Nun Ayiin's accession at Tikal. The local ruler (**CHAK-KAY**-ANIMAL.HEAD-**AHK)** who assumes office on this date is called the *yajaw* of the Kaloomte' Sihyaj K'ahk'. At this time, El Zotz and its king appear to have been influential players in Early Classic Peten politics and were perhaps engaged in military entanglements at the time (Houston, Garrison, and Alcover Firpi 2019). Stela 2's simple statement highlights Sihyaj K'ahk's regional influence, implying that he was directly responsible for the installation of Bejucal's ruler as king.

A recent discovery from the Proyecto Arqueológico Naachtun has revealed a monument that refers to the time of the Entrada and to Sihyaj K'ahk' (Nondédéo, Cases, and Lacadena 2019) (Figure 22). Stela 24 is incomplete, but it clearly exhibits an example of his name, juxtaposed with the *tzolk'in* date of 10 Chuen. This falls one day before 11 Eb, and so it is reasonable to suppose that it refers to the day before the Entrada, 8.17.1.4.11 10 Chuen 14 Mac. A local ruler is said to be the *yajawte'* of Sihyaj K'ahk', using a term that we know from other texts and that might refer to war captains (this should be carefully distinguished from the *y-ajaw* "vassal of" phrase). The implication may be that the local ruler of Naachtun was a Maya ally of Sihyaj K'ahk', not only a "vassal" who cooperated with the intruders from the west around the time of the Entrada. This would agree with a slightly later historical record at Tikal, on Stela 10, which suggests that Naachtun (**ma-su-la**, or *Masu'l*) was then an enemy of Tikal that was conquered.[11]

THE ENTRADA OF 378 AND THE EARLY CLASSIC PETEN

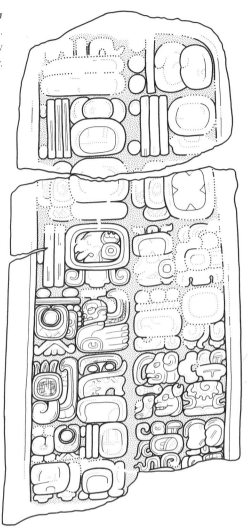

Figure 21
Bejucal, Stela 2.
Drawing by
Nicholas Carter.

Not far to the east of Naachtun is Río Azul, a major Early Classic center with its own strong ties to Teotihuacan in the Early Classic period (Adams 1999). Stela 1 records the Long Count 8.17.16.12.?, falling around late March or April 393, when the stela was evidently erected and dedicated. Near the bottom of the second column, after the name of the local ruler, we find an eroded glyph that strongly resembles Sihyaj K'ahk's personal name, possibly after the relational glyph *y-ajaw* (Beliaev 2017). If this is correct, it would express the same relationship he had over Yax Nun Ayiin of Tikal and the local ruler of Bejucal. Significantly, the Río Azul stela was dedicated over fifteen years after the Entrada episode.

Uaxactun's Stela 4 bears an important record of a ruler nicknamed "Sky Raiser" (*? K'in Chahk*), in power only a few years later at 8.18.0.0.0 12 Ahau 8 Zotz' (July 8, 396). He too is called a "vassal lord" (*y-ajaw*) of Sihyaj K'ahk', according to the recent reanalysis of that inscription by Safranov and Beliaev (2017) (Figure 23). "Sky Raiser" is also

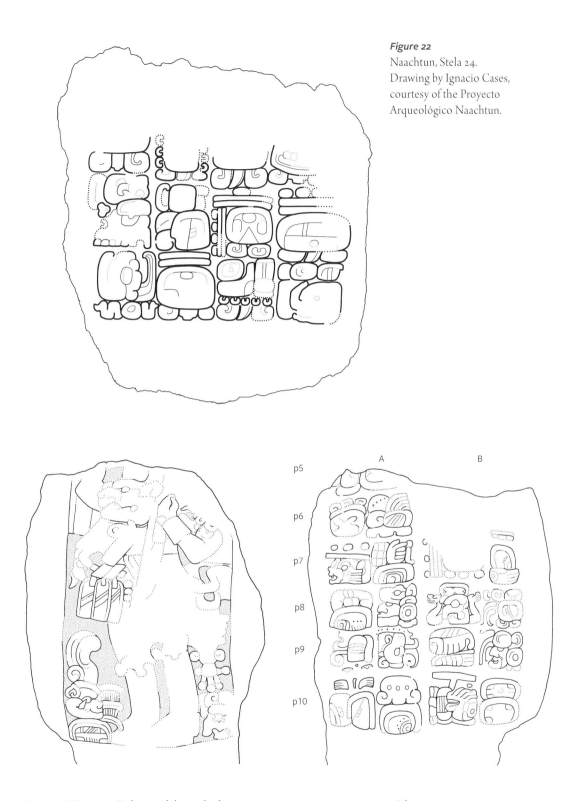

Figure 22
Naachtun, Stela 24. Drawing by Ignacio Cases, courtesy of the Proyecto Arqueológico Naachtun.

Figure 23 Uaxactun, Stela 4, with hieroglyph sequence on rear inscription naming Sihyaj K'ahk' and possibly Spearthrower Owl. Drawings by Alexander Safronov.

Figure 24
Name of Sihyaj K'ahk' on an unprovenanced shell object, current location unknown. Drawing by David Stuart, after a sketch by Stephen D. Houston.

featured on Stela 5, as we have seen, and he seems to have dedicated that monument as a remembrance of the Entrada. Stela 4's text continues with the mention of a second name after that of Sihyaj K'ahk', which begins with the honorific title **MAM**, "elder" or "grandfather" (Bp9b) as well as *kaloomte'* (Ap10a). The name itself, at Ap10, consists of a "blood" sign with a "cauac" element, and I suspect that this may be some variant of the Spearthrower Owl name we see on Stela 31 at Tikal and elsewhere, with "blood" replacing the sign for "strike" or "wound." As we will see, the same "blood" element is featured in what may be iconographic references to this ruler's name in Maya art. Whatever the case, Stela 4 establishes that Uaxactun was also likely under the authority of Sihyaj K'ahk' and Tikal at this time, an arrangement that had already been in place for nearly twenty years.

One other enigmatic mention of Sihyaj K'ahk' comes from a unprovenanced shell object, the current location of which is now unknown (Figure 24). The elaborate object, inlaid with jade and spondylus shell, was viewed by Stephen Houston around 1983 in the office of Gordon Ekholm, then a curator at the American Museum of Natural History (Stuart and Houston 2018). It was evidently in private hands at the time. Houston sketched several of the glyphs on the shell, which included the sequence of three glyphs reading **ya-AJAW SIH-ja** [**K'AHK'**], *yajaw sihyaj k'ahk'*, "(he is) the vassal of Sihyaj K'ahk'." Without further context or documentation, it is impossible to know what further details this enigmatic object might be able to tell us of Sihyaj K'ahk' and his connections with the political organization of the Peten.

A likely sculpted portrait of Sihyaj K'ahk' comes from El Peru's Stela 16, a fragmented stela that shows a Teotihuacan warrior, bearing the distinctive nose ornament, tassel headdress, and shell collar and wielding an atlatl in his right hand (Freidel, Escobedo, and Guenter 2007:199–200; Guenter 2014) (Figure 25). The vertical bands of glyphs to either side of the portrait record at least two dates and their associated events. At left, one of the few preserved glyphs is a month record of 3 Tzec, perhaps corresponding to the Period Ending 9.1.10.0.0 5 Ahau 3 Tzec (465). The right column records another date,

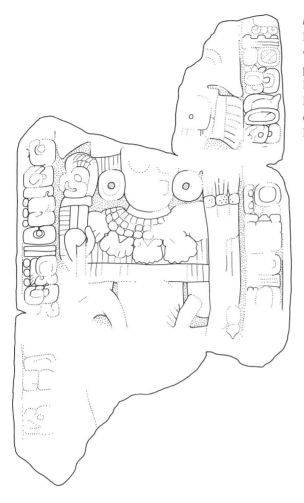

Figure 25
El Peru, Stela 16, with a possible portrait of Sihyaj K'ahk'. Drawing by David Stuart, based on photographs by Ian Graham.

too incomplete to read, with an event of dedication using the verb *tz'ahpaj (u) lakam-tuun* (**tz'a-pa-ja LAKAM-TUUN**), "(his) stela was erected," followed by the probable name of Sihyaj K'ahk', here using the same "dart" element as found on Stela 15. The phrase is apparently under-spelled, omitting the possessive pronoun on *lakamtuun* that would normally link the object to Sihyaj K'ahk's personal name, but the sense is clear: "the stela of Sihyaj K'ahk'." This phrase points to the stela being Sihyaj K'ahk's portrait and does not indicate him being present or alive as late as the Period Ending in 465 (an impossibility, most likely, given his central involvement in the events of 378, and assuming the 465 date is that of El Peru's Stela 16). This seems best interpreted as a retrospective portrait of the earlier "conqueror" who we know had an important role to play in El Peru's own Early Classic history. We lack any direct textual reference to Sihyaj K'ahk's death, but he does seem to still be alive in 406, as indicated by his mention on the Hombre de Tikal sculpture.

One surprising portrait of Sihyaj K'ahk' comes from a Late Classic vessel now in the collections of the Museo VICAL in the Hotel Casa Santo Domingo in Antigua, Guatemala (Beliaev, Stuart, and Luin 2017) (Figure 26). This unusual vessel has two

Figure 26
Late Classic vessel depicting Sihyaj K'ahk' and a warrior named Kupoom Yohl Ayiin (not pictured), Museo VICAL, Antigua, Guatemala. Photograph by Dmitri Beliaev.

standing warriors, each named with an adjacent caption. One is named as Sihyaj K'ahk', the other as Kupoom Yohl Ayiin ("Cut-out Is the Heart of the Alligator"), probably a Maya subordinate, but from an unknown site (Beliaev and Houston 2019). It is uncertain which caption refers to which portrait, with Bassie-Sweet (2019) suggesting that the captions go in front of the respective figures. I agree, and it is interesting that Sihyaj K'ahk' would, in this case, be the less elaborately dressed of the two. Kupoom Yohl Ayiin wears the mosaic helmet and holds a large War Serpent staff, whereas Sihyaj K'ahk' wields a spear. Another Late Classic vase in the collection of the Montreal Museum of Fine Arts, just recently reported, also bears a named portrait of Sihyaj K'ahk' with clear Teotihuacan attributes (Matteo and Gillot 2022). He is one of two seated warrior figures who wear feathered back devices with "year signs." Each holds a spearthrower accompanied by a large glyph-like element featuring a single circular eye surrounded by blood and feathered tufts—all elements we will see again in our consideration of emblematic name glyphs in Chapter 4 (to anticipate, I suspect that these are emblematic personal names in reference to Spearthrower Owl). The name of Sihyaj K'ahk' appears with the title *ch'ajoom*, commonly used among Maya elites throughout the Classic period and perhaps related to the casting of incense.

Figure 27
Detail of a Late Classic vessel (K3092), depicting a Teotihuacan-style warrior. Photograph by Justin Kerr.

It is significant that the Antigua and Montreal vessels must have been made at least a couple of centuries after the Entrada (both clearly date to after 600 CE). Their appearance strongly resembles warriors depicted on later Classic polychrome vessels, also with Teotihuacan styles and attributes, such as vase K9317 (Matteo and Gillot 2022:51), as well as others (K3092 and K4680 stand out as other important examples) (Figure 27). These vessels do not always label the portraits with name captions, but it stands to reason that they may have served a similar purpose as visual remembrances of an earlier era, commemorating heroic warriors and Teotihuacan patrons of the Early Classic. Those who accompany Sihyaj K'ahk' on the Antigua and Montreal vases may have been local vassal lords, similar to the individuals we find mentioned at Tikal's subordinate sites in the late fourth century.

YAX NUN AYIIN: THE POSSIBLE BOY-KING OF TIKAL

Yax Nun Ayiin, son of Spearthrower Owl, requires a bit of fleshing out at this point as a prominent if short-lived actor in the stage of Tikal's politics. As a ruler installed at Tikal shortly after the arrival of 378, he seems to have been Sihyaj K'ahk's principal charge.

Figure 28
Portraits of Yax Nun Ayiin with accompanying text captions, left and right sides of Tikal, Stela 31. 3D scans and model by Alexandre Tokovinine, courtesy of the Corpus of Maya Hieroglyphic Inscriptions (CMHI), Peabody Museum of Archaeology and Ethnology.

Three of his portraits are found on the sides and front of Stela 31, which was dedicated by his son Sihyaj Chan K'awiil in 445 (9.0.10.0.0 7 Ahau 3 Yax). Two images on the left and right sides of the monument correspond to views of the same individual from two respective sides, lending the monument a remarkable three-dimensional affect (Figure 28). Yax Nun Ayiin appears to be standing behind the portrait of his son on the front. Text panels above his two portraits identify him and present some details about his role and family relations, including two separate statements that he was the son of Spearthrower Owl. On the front of the stela, above his portrait, we see him as deceased,

Figure 29
Iconographic depiction of Yax Nun Ayiin as solar ancestor atop the front of Stela 31. Note his name glyph (b) as the deity's headdress. Drawing by William R. Coe, from Jones and Satterthwaite 1982:fig. 51c.

as the ancestral solar god looking down upon his son. His name hieroglyph is integrated into the physical form of the deity, along with solar-related titles (Figure 29).

Yax Nun Ayiin's ethnicity has long been a key question. His image as a "Teotihuacan warrior" on Tikal's monuments spurred many early discussions of the issue (Coggins 1975; Proskouriakoff 1993). Coggins also identified his likely tomb, Burial 10 in Tikal's North Acropolis, based on the many Teotihuacan-inspired ceramics, as well as a crocodile jade that bears a striking resemblance to the reptilian element of his name glyph, found within it. Moreover, she inferred from various lines of evidence that "Curl Nose," as she called him, was "probably of combined Mexican and Kaminaljuyu heritage" (Coggins 1975:145). This was a prescient observation, given that she did not know at that time of the all-important parentage statement from Stela 31, stating his filial relationship to Spearthrower Owl. One of those relationship glyphs between their names is explicit as a kinship term reading *y-une(n)*, "the son of (the man)."

The more recent study of his likely physical remains has complicated this story. In an important work, Wright (2005) conducted a strontium isotope analysis of the osteological remains from Burial 10, concluding that the principal individual from the tomb spent his youth at Tikal or in the central Maya Lowlands, not in highland Guatemala or

Mexico. She notes that "the best available candidate for Yax Nun Ayiin's remains shows a strontium isotope ratio consistent with those of a local Tikal child" (Wright 2005:97). She analyzed a single adult canine tooth that she identified as likely being from the tomb's principal skeleton, presumed to be Yax Nun Ayiin. Several other skeletons in the tomb were of sacrificed children. She notes that poor preservation and problems in documentation presented significant challenges for her study, but she confidently concludes that no occupant of Burial 10 spent their childhood years in the highlands of Central Mexico at Teotihuacan. The implication is that Yax Nun Ayiin could not have been an invader from afar.

The historical record may actually agree with Wright's insights, as we have touched upon above only briefly. Sources for the history of his reign include Stelae 4, 18, and 31, which, when taken together, strongly point to the possibility that Yax Nun Ayiin was installed as a king of Tikal as a young child. One piece of evidence is his "title of age," written twice on Stela 31 as "the (one) k'atun *ajaw*," which suggests that he was younger than twenty years old (see blocks F19 and I2–J2). One such title appears in association with the 8.18.0.0.0 Period Ending in 396, the principal ceremonial event of his reign, which was commemorated both on Stela 4 and on the heavily damaged Stela 18 (see Figures 19–20). Given his accession date in 379, Yax Nun Ayiin may not have been more than three years old when he was established as Tikal's king. A more explicit statement of his young age may occur in the inscription on the back of Stela 4, where the final passage (A7b, B7a) appears to say that the same 8.18.0.0.0 *k'atun* ending was "18 years after he was born(?)" (see Figure 19). The identification of the birth verb of Stela 4 (at B7a) remains very tentative, based on the shape of the hieroglyph as **SIH-ji-ya**, but if correct it would show that Yax Nun Ayiin assumed the crown at Tikal as an infant or very small child of just one year of age, a historical scenario that is consistent with the strontium data presented by Wright. We know of similar instances of small children assuming kingship elsewhere in Maya history, such as the Late Classic ruler of Tonina, who was two years old when crowned, and K'ahk' Tiliw Chan Chahk, a powerful ruler of Naranjo who was only six years of age when he became *ajaw* (Martin and Grube 2000).

While the scenario of Yax Nun Ayiin as a foreign child-king might agree with Wright's strontium analysis, it also raises significant questions. Who was the mother? And how did the child, whatever his age, come to arrive at Tikal if his father ruled elsewhere? We lack clear records of the mother's identity, although given the place of Spearthrower Owl in Tikal's own family history, we might speculate that she was a local Maya woman connected in some way to Tikal's royal family. She may have traveled to Spearthrower Owl in Teotihuacan, where the son was born (Wright 2005:90). Did he return to Tikal as an infant with his mother or in his mother's womb?

Such points cannot be readily answered. One possible mention of his mother comes from Tikal's Stela 1, in an incomplete text that is still difficult to understand in many of its details (Figure 30). One of its hieroglyphs (A25) is surely the name of Spearthrower Owl, displaying the prominent "atlatl" sign and also the phonetic complement **ja-** (one of the important clues to the **JATZ'** reading of the atlatl itself, as we will see). Two blocks before this, at A24, we find what could be **ya-AT-na**, for *y-atan*, "wife of . . ." (Lounsbury

Figure 30 Tikal, Stela 1. Drawing by William R. Coe, from Jones and Satterthwaite 1982:fig. 1b.

1984; Stuart 1997). Some inner details are difficult to see and not given in the drawing, but this seems to be a reasonable identification (Martin 2003). Interceding between these two glyphs is Yajawte' K'inich (Bz4: **ya-AJAW-TE'-K'INICH**), which serves as a personal name in many inscriptions outside of Tikal; its role here is uncertain, but it may be in reference to Spearthrower Owl, the "possessor" of the *y-atan* term. The name of the wife is difficult to identify here. One of the of the preceding glyphs is a known title or ancestral name reading *Unahb'al K'inich* (Bz3: **U-NAHB-la-K'INICH**), but this is never known elsewhere to be used with women's names. An earlier "baby" sign (**UNEN**) in combination with other elements may be part of a personal name (Martin 2002), along with **K'AWIIL**, but there are too many unknowns here to be certain. Whatever the case, Stela 1 may at least provide an indirect mention of Spearthrower Owl's spouse, the mother of Yax Nun Ayiin. The presence of such a reference in a Tikal text in association with other known local names or titles could serve as support for the view that she was a member of Tikal's extended royal family.

Other potentially important sources of information about this time period are the glyphs on several inscribed bones from Burial 116, the resting place of the important Late Classic ruler Jasaw Chan K'awiil (Figure 31). A few of these delicate objects bear short texts that possibly pertain to the history leading up to the 378 conquest. One such bone, Miscellaneous Text (MT) 34, bears the name of Sihyaj K'ahk', with the title *ochk'in kaloomte'*, in association with the Calendar Round 9 Manik' 10 Xul (Figure 31a). Given the presence of his name, we can perhaps best place this at 8.17.0.15.7, or August 27, 377, just five months before his arrival in Tikal in January 378. The verb of the text is best interpreted as *ehmiiy* (**EHM-yi**) "he descended." The same verb is featured on two other inscribed bones from the set (MT 31 and 35), one of which precedes the name of Yax Nun Ayiin, along with the important and suggestive architectural name **WIIN?-TE'-NAAH**. Thus "Yax Nun Ayiin descended from the *wiinte'naah*," and in association with the date 4 Cib 14 Ceh (Figure 31b). If we seek to place this date within Yax Nun Ayiin's lifetime, we only have the option of 8.17.2.3.16, or December 26, 378, a year after the conquest of Tikal and nearly nine months before Yax Nun Ayiin's own accession there under the auspices of Sihyaj K'ahk'. What is "descent" referring to in these two texts, exactly? As we have seen, *wiinte'naah* (still a tentative reading of the glyph) names certain architectural monuments (*naah*, "house") associated with dynastic foundation and with Teotihuacan (Stuart 2000) (Figure 32). Fash, Tokovinine, and Fash (2009) suggest it may have referred directly to the Temple of the Sun at Teotihuacan, a place associated with ritual fire. It also seems clear that there were Maya "versions" of this type of structure associated with the religious practices and ideologies of Teotihuacan. Whatever the case, the association of the name with Teotihuacan and its ceremonial spaces is well-established.[12]

Given their historical timing, these terse statements on the Burial 116 bones are perhaps best interpreted as departure dates for the protagonists concerned, with Sihyaj K'ahk' "descending" in the late summer of 377 on his way to conquest, and Yax Nun Ayiin leaving for his destination and eventual crowning at Tikal in late 378.[13] We might also entertain the possibility that the infant Yax Nun Ayiin "descended" from a pyramid in some ritual context, in preparation for his new role as the ruler of a distant polity. This would echo the indications of a similar foundational event in Copan's history, when K'inich Yax K'uk' Mo' "took *k'awiil*," or "received authority," at the same *wiinte'naah*. If so, the passage on MT 35 may allow us to physically place Yax Nun Ayiin at Teotihuacan while he was an infant, before his installation as child-king at Tikal. Such biographical details of father and son are still opaque, but we can at least be certain that Yax Nun Ayiin was consistently portrayed as a "Teotihuacano" even if he spent most of his life at Tikal, and that Spearthrower Owl played a significant role as his father and distant king.

The portrait of Yax Nun Ayiin on the face of Stela 4 is unusual in several respects (see Figure 19). He is shown frontally and appears to be seated upon an iconographic throne of some sort—a highly unusual pose and presentation found only on Tikal's Stela 18, also dating to the same year (8.18.0.0.0) (see Figure 20). On Stela 4, he wears the feline headdress and spondylus shell collar similar to those we see in his portrait on the left side of

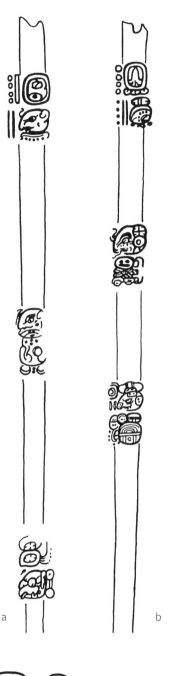

Figure 31
Tikal, Miscellaneous Texts 34 (a) and 35 (b), with mentions of the "descents" of Sihyaj K'ahk' and Yax Nun Ayiin (after Moholy-Nagy 2008:fig. 195d–e).

Figure 32
Three variants of the *wiinte'naah* glyph, a Teotihuacan-inspired place or structure name. Drawings by David Stuart.

THE ENTRADA OF 378 AND THE EARLY CLASSIC PETEN | 37

Figure 33
The "Fire Mountain" (*k'ahk' witz*) place-name associated with 8.18.0.0.0: a) base of Stela 18, front; and b) hieroglyph on Stela 31 passage. Drawing by William R. Coe, from Jones and Satterthwaite 1982:fig. 18a (a); and drawing by David Stuart (b).

Stela 31. In one hand, he holds the head of a Maya deity, the Jaguar God of the Underworld, and in the other, a possible "Tlaloc" or Storm God head. A comparable visual reference to a Teotihuacan deity may appear in his portrait on Stela 18, where a small tassel headdress is just visible, resting upon his lap. The "throne" on Stela 18 is, in fact, a mountain or *witz* head, with an apparent "fire" glyph attached to its front. This is surely the same **K'AHK'-WITZ** place-name referred to in the inscription of Stela 31 (Block F17), cited as the locale of his celebration of the 8.18.0.0.0 Period Ending (Figure 33). This may be an important reference to the Guatemalan Highlands, for *k'ahk' witz* describes a "fire mountain," a volcano (note the historic place-name *Q'aq'a Vitz* translated by Edmonson [1965:96] as "volcanic peak").[14] It remains possible that Yax Nun Ayiin's most important ceremonial act on the *k'atun* ending took place not at Tikal but at or near some distant volcano. Might this have been conforming to some Teotihuacan type of ceremonial practice, rooted in the highlands? Although comparisons of these two portraits are difficult due to poor preservation, it seems likely that they served as a pair of monuments dedicated on the same day, with representations of Yax Nun Ayiin as a Teotihuacan warrior (Stela 4) and in a possibly more Maya fashion (Stela 18).

Stela 31's inscription suggests that Yax Nun Ayiin's reign was fairly short, lasting only a little more than twenty-five years, until his possible death on 8.18.8.1.12 2 Ik 10 Zip

Figure 34
Stela 31 passage (F16–F19), recording the possible death of Yax Nun Ayiin. Drawing by William R. Coe, after Jones and Satterthwaite 1982:fig. 52b.

(June 18, 404). The time span is probably conveyed by the Distance Number 1.5.2.5 that follows the record of the 8.18.0.0.0 *k'atun* ending, written at F20 and E21 and parallel in structure to the one written earlier for the reign of Chak Tok Ich'aak (D24 and C25) (Figure 34). The verb at E22 (**i-KAM**) is a variant of the intransitive verb *I kam(i)*, "then he dies." If he were inaugurated as a young child or an infant, he could not have been much older than twenty-five years at the time of his passing. No descriptions or circumstances of his death appear anywhere at Tikal, but he would have left a very young son to succeed him, later known as Sihyaj Chan K'awiil.

Yax Nun Ayiin's wife, the mother of his son and the future ruler Sihyaj Chan K'awiil, is cited in the latter's parentage statement of Stela 31. She also appears as a hieroglyphic "belt head" with the son's portrait on the stela's front (Figure 35). Her name appears to be the head of a jaguar solar god, without the customary feminine name prefix **IX**-, indicating perhaps her fusion with that deity after death. Her emblem glyph is a combination of elements that resemble **i-ka**, recently identified as an emblem glyph local to the site of Itzimte, located to the west of Lake Peten Itza (Beliaev and Verpetskii 2018). She was a woman of the Peten, evidently, but likely not an original member of Tikal's own ruling line.

THE ENTRADA OF 378 AND THE EARLY CLASSIC PETEN

Figure 35
Names of the spouse of Yax Nun Ayiin, from Stela 31's text (a) and from belt device worn by her son Sihyaj Chan K'awiil (b). Drawings by William R. Coe (a) and David Stuart (b).

The latest mentions of Sihyaj K'ahk' and Yax Nun Ayiin come from the Hombre de Tikal, an unusual three-dimensional sculpture of a seated man with an incised hieroglyphic text on the back (Fahsen 1988) (Figure 36). This was excavated in Structure 3D-43 in the North Group (Laporte and Herman 2003:375–378). The inscription is still opaque in many places, but what we can tease out of it makes it an important historical source for the later years of Teotihuacan influence and involvement in Tikal's affairs. The opening date is given as 1 Eb 10 Yax (8.18.10.8.2, or November 6, 406), probably corresponding more or less to the dedication of the sculpture. The verb (C1) is missing completely, but the protagonist or subject is given as Yax Nun Ayiin (C4), perhaps already dead for over two years at this point, if our tentative reading of Stela 31 above is correct. The glyphs that precede his name give us a so-called impersonation phrase (Houston and Stuart 1996), indicating the ruler's supernatural identity. This deity's name or title is **TAJ-AL-la CHAN-na-K'IN-ni**, a variation on a title Yax Nun Ayiin holds on Stela 31 (B22), where he is cited as the father of Sihyaj Chan K'awiil. It is also the designation Yax Nun Ayiin takes in iconographic form on the front of the stela, looming above Sihyaj Chan K'awiil as a celestial ancestor (see Figure 29). There, he is the sun god (**K'IN**) with "sky" indicated by a hand as its jaw (a diagnostic of **CHAN**). He grasps a snake from whose mouth emerges the hieroglyphic name of a very remote Tikal ancestor, "White Owl Jaguar." The deceased Yax Nun Ayiin thus conjures or gives birth to an even more distant ancestor, which may relate to the **AL** "child of woman" sign in the titular phrase. Whatever the case, the main point here is that the 406 date on

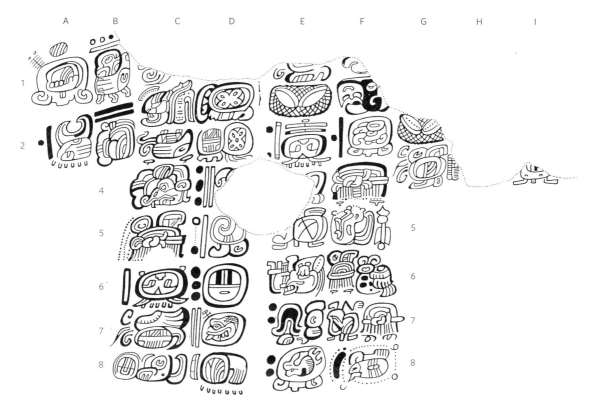

Figure 36 Inscription of the Hombre de Tikal sculpture. Drawing by Rene Ozaeta, after Fahsen 1988:fig. 1.

the Hombre de Tikal is likely a posthumous reference to Yax Nun Ayiin, using the same deified identity he has on Stela 31. It is possible that the 1 Eb date records his formal apotheosis as a celestial ancestor, a named aspect of K'inich Ajaw. The next passage of the Hombre de Tikal is very difficult to tease apart, but we can say that it reckons back to an earlier date, 10 Chicchan (18 Tzec, 8.18.7.3.5, or August 6, 403), when some unknown event happened, not far in time from the possible death of Yax Nun Ayiin. The 1 Eb 10 Yax episode is then restated as a "seating" (of Yax Nun Ayiin?) under the authority of someone whose name is missing.

The next columns of the text relate an event of great importance, possibly a *second* arrival of Sihyaj K'ahk' on June 4, 406, twenty-eight years after the initial Entrada. The verb at E4 is largely missing, but it can be reasonably reconstructed as a form of the verb **HUL-li**, with the **MUT-la** (Tikal) place-name in the following block. The subject is the *kaloomte'* (F5: **KAL-ma-TE'**) named Sihyaj K'ahk', using the form of the name attested at El Peru, with the Teotihuacan dart in place of the customary **K'AHK'**. (There remains a possibility that the two names are distinct, but the use of the "dart variant" on Stela 15 of El Peru strongly points to their equivalence.) The interpretation of this event as a reappearance of Sihyaj K'ahk' is supported by the verb at F7, **2-HUL?-li**, possibly another variant of **HUL** with the adverb *cha'* or "two" or "again." The subject is

THE ENTRADA OF 378 AND THE EARLY CLASSIC PETEN | 41

restated as the *kaloomte'*, with Tikal specified as the place of the arrival ("the kaloomte' again arrives to Tikal"). Beliaev and colleagues (2013:148) were the first to recognize this second arrival event in the Hombre de Tikal's inscription and reasonably suggest that the event was motivated by the death of Yax Nun Ayiin in 404. Sihyaj K'ahk' appears to have had left Tikal for a time (returning to highland Mexico?), but was drawn back due to the political complications brought on by the young Tikal king's unexpected demise.

The status of Tikal's rulership in the ensuing two decades is difficult to characterize, given our significant gap in the historical records from the time. The death of Yax Nun Ayiin seems to have involved the "succession" (Stela 31, E23: **u-TZAK-bu-ji**) of someone named Sihyaj Chan K'inich, who we might be able to equate with the son otherwise known as Sihyaj Chan K'awiil. He would have been quite young at the time of his father's death, however, and an apparent accession record at the bottom of Columns E and F on Stela 31, now missing, may well have involved some other individual on 8.18.15.11.0 3 Ahau 13 Zac, or November 27, 411. We can be sure that Sihyaj Chan K'awiil was on Tikal's throne by the time of the Period Ending of 426 (8.19.10.0.0) and when he dedicated Stela 31 in 445. Whatever turmoil or uncertainty had led to the crowning and short-lived reign of his father many years earlier, Sihyaj Chan K'awiil seems to have governed over a relatively stable period of Tikal's early history. And it was during his reign that Spearthrower Owl himself, Yax Nun Ayiin's grandfather, passed away on June 11, 439, having reigned on his own distant throne for sixty-five long years. It is to him that we can now turn, to examine where he may have ruled, and how he relates to the protagonists discussed so far.

NOTES

1 One good indication of Tikal's importance as a foundational center in the Peten region comes from a historical mention of the first dynast Ehb Xook on an Early Classic vessel known informally as the "Deletaile tripod," published by Hellmuth (1988). There we read that its owner was a lord of Ucanal (K'anwitznal), yet he possibly cites Ehb Xook as his distant ancestor. At the very least, the inscription highlights Ehb Xook's recognition as an important historical founder on a more regional scale.

2 The identification of the name on Stela 29 of Tikal as Yax Nun Ayiin is tentative, but the alligator (**AYIIN**) and element of the name was clear on inspection of the original monument at Tikal in March 2022. The knot-like element tied onto the reptile's head certainly could correspond to a known form of the supposed **NUN** logogram (an alternative reading of this sign seems highly likely, in my opinion). If indeed the same, it would establish three Tikal rulers sharing this name, two in the Early Classic and one in the Late Classic. If this is the case, it would confirm that the better-known Yax Nun Ayiin, installed as ruler in 379 under the auspices of Sihyaj K'ahk', used a name that was already local to the Tikal ruling family. This can be taken as a good indication of his family ties to the older Tikal lineage, as has been suggested (Coggins 1975:220; Martin 2002).

3 The name of the mother who is cited on Stela 39 consists of **IX** followed by a distinctive "chin-strap head" sign, then **BAHLAM**. The "head" sign remains undeciphered, although I have considered the possibility that it is an alternate head variant for **UNEN** ("infant") given the presence of the name Ix Unen Bahlam in Early Classic Tikal history (Martin 2002). This finds some slight support, perhaps, in the depiction of a sacrificed infant or small child on Stela 13 of Yaxha, who seems to wear a similar chinstrap. This odd facial feature also appears on one of the children being born from the bursting gourd depicted on the north wall of the San Bartolo murals. If the mother's name is Ix Unen Bahlam, it would indicate that both of Chak Tok Ich'aak's parents had served as Tikal rulers, with the mother on the throne as early as 317. This may be excessively early. Without further evidence, or a better idea of Chak Tok Ich'aak's own accession date, I hesitate to push this interpretation much further.

4 This brings up an interesting question regarding a possible connection between the personal name of *Sihyaj K'ahk'*, "Fire (Power[?]) is Born," and his direct role in establishing a new political order in the Peten. The name, while clearly a personal reference, may yet have a descriptive function, referring to the creation of a new authority in the region.

5 The newly identified "Lord of Tikal" title for Spearthrower Owl deserves more comment, of course, but it has only very recently been revealed by the excavation of the Proyecto Arqueológico Waka', just in time to be mentioned here. One important aspect of the title is how it probably related to mention of the 378 Entrada on the stela's main text, physically adjacent to the Spearthrower Owl name, where it is said that Sihyaj K'ahk' "had arrived to Mutul." The stela seems to draw a connection between the arrival and the title, with Spearthrower Owl labeled as the lord who oversees events, either literally or figuratively. No doubt much more will be said on Stela 51 when it is fully published and analyzed by Olivia Navarro-Farr and her colleagues in the near future.

6 On Stela 22, the Distance Number that accompanies the Period Ending 9.3.10.0.0 presents a mathematical problem and seems to involve a revealing error. As written, it is 6.1.4.12, as Morley (1937–1938:1:193–196) was first to recognize. The day sign that follows, corresponding to the starting point of the calculation, is 11 Eb, also as Morley noted. However, if we subtract this interval from the Period Ending, we reach back to 8.17.8.3.8 3 Lamat 11 Uo, obviously not in agreement with what we see written on the stela. Morley opted to see it instead as a forward count, resulting in an error in the resulting *tzolk'in* position (requiring 13 Eb instead of 11 Eb). However, the historical statement that accompanies the 11 Eb day (*huliiy ochk'in k'awiil*, "[when] the west authority had arrived") makes it reasonably certain that this refers to 8.17.1.4.12 11 Eb 15 Mac. Revealingly, the written Distance Number 6.1.4.12 incorporates the last three numbers of this Long Count for the Entrada event. I suspect that the mistake in the Distance Number arose

from the scribe looking at the wrong sequence of numbers as he copied them, probably from a book page where 8.17.1.4.12 was adjacent to 6.8.13.8. The scribe began correctly with a "6" but then transcribed the wrong series in the last three numbers.

7   The phrasing of the Stela 31 passage, or parts of it, are known from other Maya texts, including a recurring phrase that occurs in the Dresden Codex, where **OOK** usually takes a **K'UH** sign prefix, in the combination **K'UH-OOK-tzi?**. This would be comparable to the **OOK-ki-tzi?** term at D20 on Stela 31. On Lintel 1 of Tikal's Temple IV, a sequence of glyphs related to the record of a war against El Peru shows an even stronger resemblance to Stela 31's phrase, with the verb *tzutzuy* followed by the possessed noun *y-ook* (**yo-OOK-ki**) (see Temple IV, Lintel 1, Block C7). The patron deity of El Peru was captured in this war, and it is significant that *tzutzuy y-ook* occurs with events that happened a day later, when it goes on to say *i huli mutuul*, "then he arrived at Tikal." I suspect that *tzutzuy y-ook* both here and on Stela 31 must relate to the idea of travel, or to the end of a journey. The sense in both texts may be "his foot(steps) ended."

8   The significance of *och ha'*, "to water-enter," as a term for death in historical contexts probably derives from the specific mythological cycle of the Maize God's death and resurrection, and the significance of water in that narrative (Quenon and Le Fort 1997; Scherer 2015:62). On the "Berlin Vase," we see the Maize God in death, in direct association with the more common death term *och bih*, "road enter" (see Grube and Gaida 2006:117–131). However, the iconography on this remakable vase emphasizes the deity's presence in water, alongside several weeping women. This parallels the depiction of the Maize God's "water-entering" on Late Classic ceramics, establishing a good functional overlap between the two phrases.

9   The writing of 10 Caban in place of the required 5 Caban is a surprising error, but it is perhaps explained by the isolated *tzolk'in* station 8 Men recorded just beforehand, at E7. 10 Caban is only two days after 8 Men, so it may have been the result of a scribe's erroneous assumption that the dates were in close temporal sequence. I suspect that the 8 Men date instead corresponds to its first occurrence prior to the 5 Caban 10 Yaxkin accession, or 8.17.2.13.15 8 Men 8 Zotz' (July 30, 379). This may be the date associated with the **T'AB-yi wi-TE'-NAAH** verbal statement at the very top of Columns E and F, which may be more concerned about Yax Nun Ayiin's pre-accession preparations, "ascending to the Winte'naah." Whether this took place at Teotihuacan, Tikal, or elsewhere is impossible to know.

10 The known principal wife of Sihyaj Chan K'awiil was named Ix Ayiin K'uk', portrayed on Tikal's Stela 40 with her spouse and son, as well as named on Stela 13 and an unprovenanced cache vessel now in the Ruta Maya Foundation collections in Guatemala City. The role and status of the El Zapote woman is open to question, but her prominence there, at what amounts to a small elite residential center away from central Tikal, raises a number of interesting questions. The site was mapped by Ian Graham but is still in need of close archaeological investigation.

11 The mention of Naachtun on Tikal, Stela 10, is based on the toponym **ma-su-la**, which Nikolai Grube has suggested refers to Naachtun (Martin and Grube 2000:46). This identification remains somewhat tentative, however.

12 In previous studies, I identified the glyph as a possible Teotihuacan place-name (Stuart 2000) and posited that it might read as *wi'te'naah*, "tree-root house." This analysis is now unlikely given the more recent clues that have emerged that a core noun in the term is *win* or *wiin*, a noun still of unknown meaning (Estrada-Belli and Tokovinine 2016).

13 Seven or eight inscribed bones comprise this particular set from Burial 116 (Moholy-Nagy 2008:61–62; Trik 1963). All are similar in format, bearing six hieroglyphs arranged as three pairs, with a date and simple verbal statement. In addition to the "descent" references, we have two records of ceremonial "conjuring" (*tzak*) of the deity Waxaklajuun Ubaah Chan, the Mayan name of the Teotihuacan War Serpent, on 13 Chuen 9 Xul, possibly 8.17.5.16.11, or August 22, 382 (MT 33 and 36). This is said to have occurred at a place named **NIK-TE'-WITZ**, *Nikte' Witz*, or "Flower Mountain," which has its own strong Teotihuacan connections (Taube 2004b). Another bone (MT 37) is incomplete, but bears the name of Kupoom Yohl Ayiin, the same individual who appears with Sihyaj K'ahk' on the vase discussed earlier from the Museo VICAL

in Antigua, Guatemala. His repeated associations with the main protagonist of the Entrada suggests that Kupoom Yohl Ayiin played an important role in that history, as yet undetermined.

14 The name Q'aq'a Vitz or Q'aq'awitz appears in several ethnohistorical sources from the Maya Highlands as a personal name in creation and migration accounts, or as a place-name (Carmack and Mondloch 1983; Cojti Ren 2021; Maxwell and Hill 2006:2). As Judith M. Maxwell and Robert M. Hill note (see also Frauke Sachse, personal communication, 2022), this name is not analyzable in K'iche' or Kaqchikel, where *juyu'* is the word for "mountain," from proto-K'iche'an **juyub*. It, therefore, must be a borrowing from a non-K'iche'an language, where *witz*, "hill," is ubiquitous.

2 INTERPRETING SPEARTHROWER OWL

OUR OVERVIEW OF THE ENTRADA OF 378 AND ITS RAMIFICATIONS IN local Peten politics raises many new questions about the power dynamics of the Early Classic period, not the least of which is the nature of Sihyaj K'ahk's own authority and rule. As the apparent regent at Tikal's court as well as a regional leader, he appears to have ruled over a geopolitical structure that incorporated at least a dozen Peten courts and kingdoms. And as we have seen, many of these "vassal" (*y-ajaw*) relationships may have arisen as mutually advantageous alliances; it was not simply a case of a distant enemy strong-arming his way into local affairs. What emerges from the sources at Tikal is that Sihyaj K'ahk' was acting as an agent or representative of an even higher political authority who is named by the "Spearthrower Owl" hieroglyph.

To review some key points, my initial proposal that this man was a ruler of Teotihuacan (Stuart 2000) resulted from a detailed consideration of Tikal's inscriptions, using several lines of evidence:

1. The "Spearthrower Owl" or "Atlatl Cauac" hieroglyph identified by Proskouriakoff and others stands for a personal name for a ruler, not as a title or more general designation, as others had earlier supposed (Coggins 1975:143; Proskouriakoff 1993:11–13; Schele and Freidel 1993). As noted and as we will discuss at some length, "Eagle Striker" may be a preferable analysis of his personal name.

2. This name refers to a key historical actor associated with the Entrada on January 16, 378, which saw the arrival at Tikal of Sihyaj K'ahk' and the apparent overthrow and death of the Tikal ruler Chak Tok Ich'aak. Spearthrower Owl wielded considerable influence in establishing this new order and seems to have been of higher rank than Sihyaj K'ahk'. This episode corresponds to a time of intense influence and interaction between Teotihuacan and the Maya region, as long discerned in the archaeological records of both areas.

3. Spearthrower Owl's status as a ruler is indicated by a record of his accession date, May 5, 374 (8.16.17.9.0 11 Ahau 3 Uayeb), when he is explicitly installed as *ajaw* ("lord"). It is also indicated by his paternal relationship to Yax Nun Ayiin, who came to be installed as Tikal's king within a year of the Entrada itself. In his three known

| 47 |

portraits at Tikal, Yax Nun Ayiin is depicted as a "Teotihuacan" warrior; he was, in turn, the father of the ruler Sihyaj Chan K'awiil, who returned Tikal to a more "Maya" presentation of royal ritual in the early fifth century (Proskouriakoff 1993:11–15).

4. Spearthrower Owl's extraordinary reign of sixty-five years fits nowhere within the local dynastic history of Tikal, despite his clear family connections to Tikal's ruling line. His son's accession to Tikal's throne in 379, therefore, represented a significant break in that city's dynastic succession and existed independently of Spearthrower Owl's own place of rule.

5. A recurring motif in the art of Teotihuacan, the "owl and weapons" (*lechuza y armas*) design (von Winning 1948, 1987:1:85–91) is a variant of Spearthrower Owl's personal name using the emblematic mode of writing prevalent at Teotihuacan (Taube 2000, 2002). These appearances are consistent with the presentation of personal names and, therefore, could serve as references to a local ruler.

This final point was, at the time, the most speculative of all, while the others remain generally agreed upon by those who have studied the inscriptions of Tikal and its environs (Beliaev et al. 2013; Martin 2003; Martin and Grube 2000). Taken together, the evidence strongly indicates that Spearthrower Owl was a foreign leader who wielded great influence in the central Maya area during a very long reign. As such, he stands as a revealing source for ongoing debates and discussions of Teotihuacan's political structure and the role of highland Mexico in Maya history.

NAMES AND VARIANTS

The variants of Spearthrower Owl's name are presented in Figure 37. The first hieroglyph that we today identify as Spearthrower Owl's name was noticed in the 1960s, with its true function refined over the course of the ensuing decades. It is likely that Proskouriakoff first noted its distinctive form on Stela 31 at Tikal soon after the monument's discovery in 1962, later discussing it in her posthumous book on Maya history (Proskouriakoff 1993:11–13). She described it as the "cauac shield" with an atlatl prefix (see Figure 37a). She noted its strong evocation of Teotihuacan weaponry and warfare, as well as its repeated appearance in the text panels directly above the portraits of "Mexican warriors" on the sides of the monument. This prompted Proskouriakoff to suggest that the glyph was a foreign reference, possibly describing a foreign army associated with the ruler "Curl Snout" (Yax Nun Ayiin being the more accurate, though still imperfect, reading of the name we use today). For her, the glyph was not a personal name but rather a title or collective term of some sort. As Coggins (1975:143) stated: "Proskouriakoff has suggested that the name of these foreigners whom we call Teotihuacanos, after the presumed city of their ultimate origin, was the 'Tlaloc shield-spearthrower' people for the Maya who described them by their national (?), or clan (?) regalia: the Tlaloc shield and spearthrower (which should probably be considered more emblematic than militaristic)." As we will see, Coggins's general view remains influential, especially outside of Maya studies.

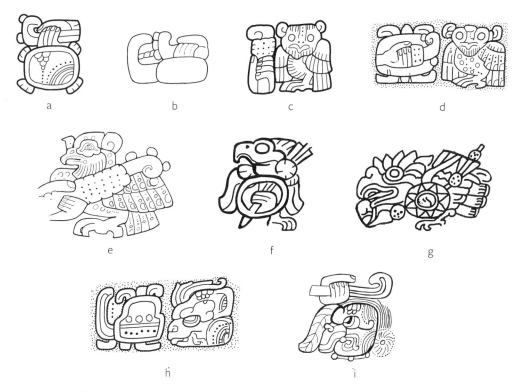

Figure 37 Variants of the name for Spearthrower Owl. Drawings by David Stuart.

This interpretation was taken up some years later by Schele and others (Grube and Schele 1994; Schele 1986a; Schele and Freidel 1993), who expressed general agreement with Proskouriakoff, seeing the atlatl-shield combination as a "conqueror title" (Schele 1986a). Schele also identified more variant forms of the glyph on the Tikal Marcador monument, discovered shortly before in the early 1980s (and the subject of the next chapter). These versions show the "atlatl" sign before a front-facing bird resembling an owl (substituting for the "cauac shield"), prompting the nickname "Spearthrower Owl" (see Schele and Freidel 1993:156–157) (Figure 37c–d). Schele's characterization of the glyph as a general reference or title was partially due to the striking "foreign" appearance of the glyph, a form very different from any other personal name known in Maya inscriptions. This exotic aspect of the name glyph is a basic point we should keep in mind as we examine its complex history and patterns of use.

Beginning in the 1980s, I posited a different interpretation of the "Spearthrower Owl" glyphs not as militaristic titles but as variants of one personal name (Stuart 1985, 2000), an interpretation accepted by Schele (Schele and Freidel 1993:156). This was based on several clues, one being the glyph's appearance in a parentage statement for Yax Nun Ayiin on Stela 31, in the same text where Proskouriakoff had earlier noted the direct association of the glyph with the Mexican-style warriors. Parentage statements were first identified by Jones (1977) and later greatly expanded by Schele, Mathews, and Lounsbury (n.d.). Jones had correctly identified a glyph for "child of father" in Late

INTERPRETING SPEARTHROWER OWL | 49

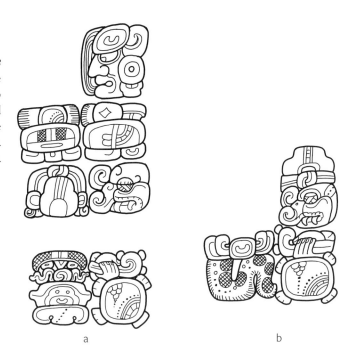

Figure 38
Parallel statements of the child-father relationship between Yax Nun Ayiin and Spearthrower Owl, from the side captions of Tikal, Stela 31. Drawings by David Stuart.

a   b

Classic Tikal inscriptions, where it linked the names of sons and fathers. And although he did not mention it in his study, this same relationship glyph precedes the "atlatl-cauac" glyph on Stela 31, in a lengthy phrase naming Yax Nun Ayiin, establishing beyond any doubt that "Spearthrower Owl" must be a personal name (Figure 38). This was no doubt the basis for Jones and Satterthwaite's (1982:65) brief but prescient description of the glyph on Stela 31 as the "cauac shield name." In my own proposal of a variant child-father relationship glyph in Stela 31's text, I again highlighted its function as a name glyph for a person (Stuart 1985), providing the foundation for my later historical reading of it as a possible Teotihuacan ruler.

Given the complex history and ongoing debates, it is important to point out other textual environments that confirm that these variant glyphs are all a personal name, not a general title or reference. Our later examination of Tikal's Marcador will show that the "Spearthrower Owl" glyph refers to the specific owner of the monument, in what amounts to a fairly rigid setting where only personal names are known to occur. Also, on the Marcador and on Stela 31, variants of the "Spearthrower Owl" glyph follow **yi-ta-ji**, a common "conjunction" term (*y-ita-ij* or *y-et-ej*) regularly found in connection with personal names (so strong is this association that I once erroneously considered **yi-ta-ji** to be a kinship term as well [see Stuart 1993:347]). However, the most direct indicator of its personal scope of reference comes from its association with the title *kaloomte'* or *ochk'in* (west) *kaloomte'*, indicating someone of great importance and authority (Martin 2003, 2020) (Figure 39). We have already seen how Sihyaj K'ahk' assumed the same *kaloomte'* title in a number of texts at the same time. Its literal meaning remains somewhat obscure, but I suspect that it is an agentive noun based on the Ch'olti' verb root *kal*, "to make, do," in combination with an embedded object *te'*, "tree,

Figure 39 The title *ochk'in* (west) *kaloomte'* with the name of Spearthrower Owl, on an inscribed earspool from the Río Azul area. Note the Teotihuacan style of the name with dart and shield. Drawing by David Stuart.

plant," thus *kal-oom te'* "tree-maker" or "plant-maker." As a glyph, the root *kal* is often represented with a logogram depicting the storm god Chahk holding a hafted axe, perhaps a fitting reference to this etymology, referring to the deity who engenders the floral world. "Plant-maker" may be based on a mythic reference to the creation of maize and to related primordial events of dynastic foundation. Its presence with particular rulers may well indicate their importance in establishing and overseeing newly conceived political arrangements and alliance networks, perhaps with an underlying agricultural or cosmological metaphor.

Spearthrower Owl's title "west *kaloomte'*" fits within the title's larger conceptual basis in four-directional cosmology, as discussed most recently by Martin (2020). For example, a ruler at Ek Balam is named as a "north *kaloomte'*"; at Lamanai, Belize, we have an "east *kaloomte'*"; and a "south *kaloomte'*" is cited at Copan, Honduras. Otherwise, we find "west *kaloomte'*" used almost exclusively with Late Classic rulers in the western lowlands, such as K'inich Janab Pakal at Palenque and Shield Jaguar II at Yaxchilan, anchoring its distribution in the western Maya region. "West *kaloomte'*" is also well known as an honorific title for K'inich Yax K'uk' Mo', the Early Classic dynastic founder of Copan, probably a reflection of his close historical ties to Teotihuacan. We can posit that Spearthrower Owl's use of *ochk'in kaloomte'* likewise reflects his orientation in that direction, within a frame of reference grounded in the Maya landscape.

Texts from outside of Tikal, including one bearing the "west *kaloomte'*" title just discussed, also elaborate on Spearthrower Owl's hierarchical relationships with other Maya rulers of the Peten. The key relationship in these cases is given with the term *y-ajaw*, "the lord of," used to express a hierarchical relationship between junior and senior rulers within the Maya political landscape (Houston and Mathews 1985; Martin 2003, 2020:240–241). This is the same term of relationship we have seen used to link various subsidiary local lords to Sihyaj K'ahk', as on Stela 4 at Tikal and at Bejucal. We also encountered the same *y-ajaw* phrase on Uaxactun, Stela 4, where the local ruler "Sky Raiser" was called the "lord" (*y-ajaw*) of Sihyaj K'ahk' as well as, possibly, Spearthrower Owl. The latter name appears more clearly in the example shown in Figure 40, from a vase from the Naranjo region, where Spearthrower Owl is named again as a *kaloomte'*. Here we see that an unknown individual, presumably a local lord or nobleman of the Naranjo or Río Azul region, is "the lord of" Spearthrower Owl. Another example (not illustrated) from an inscribed earspool names a Maya ruler of Río Azul in a similar way. He bears a "*chatan winik*" title that we can associate with sites in the very northern Peten, at Nakbe, Calakmul, and Achiotal (Canuto, Auld-Thomas, and Aredondo 2020; Vázquez López et al. 2016). These are short statements on objects without secure

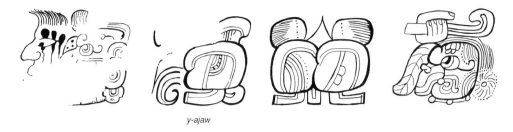

y-ajaw

Figure 40 Statements of hierarchy between a Maya ruler and Spearthrower Owl, from a tripod vessel perhaps from the Naranjo region (K7528). Drawing by David Stuart.

Figure 41 Spearthrower Owl as a "maize name" on Stela 31, with comparable examples: a) Tikal, Stela 31, front headdress; b) "Chak Tok Ich'aak" name from unprovenanced cache vessel, Tikal area; c) "Sihyaj Chan K'awiil" name from Tikal, Stela 31, front; d) "Naatz Chan Ahk" name from Naranjo, Stela 45; and e) "Lady K'atun" name from Piedras Negras, Stela 3. Drawings by David Stuart.

provenience, yet they are important indications that the new political order that was established in the Peten region in and around 378 by Sihyaj K'ahk' (and possibly others) involved Spearthrower Owl as the ultimate authority.

Returning to Tikal, we find a version of Spearthrower Owl's name, very Teotihuacan in appearance, in the detached headdress that Sihyaj Chan K'awiil holds aloft on the front of Tikal's Stela 31 (Figure 41a; see also Figure 14a). This particular context, embedded in iconography, is especially revealing and important, for it leaves no choice but to interpret the "Spearthrower Owl" hieroglyph as a personal name. The bird appears in

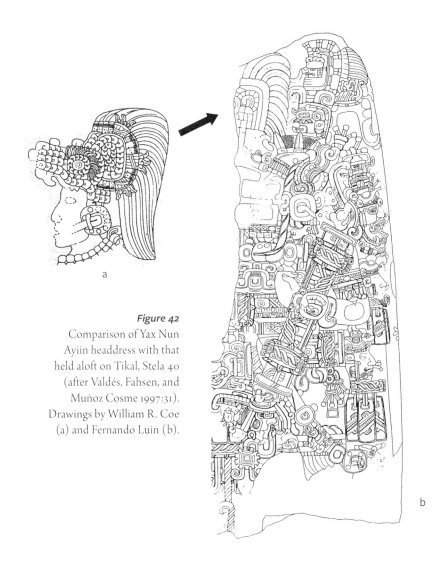

Figure 42
Comparison of Yax Nun Ayiin headdress with that held aloft on Tikal, Stela 40 (after Valdés, Fahsen, and Muñoz Cosme 1997:31). Drawings by William R. Coe (a) and Fernando Luin (b).

the basal cartouche element within an elaborate representation of maize foliation, in a pattern we see in Early Classic portraiture as a means of labeling figures by their personal names (Figure 41b–e). Parallel examples usually show a circular cartouche enclosing a name glyph, with a maize plant or sprout emerging above, or directly from the glyphic form (Figure 42). In one Late Classic example of such a "maize name" device, the headdress of "Lady K'atun" on Stela 3 of Piedras Negras shows a *k'atun* (*winikhaab*?) sign in her headdress as part of the same ornate maize plant, now highly abstracted (Figure 41e). Such maize names are clearly based on the iconographic representation of the foliated maize cob, *nal*, and they liken the personal name of an individual to the maize cob itself. While outside the scope of this study, these consistent forms raise interesting questions about the familiar associations of maize with personhood and personal identity in Maya worldview.

In sum, these visual patterns leave no doubt that "Spearthrower Owl" and its equivalents are hieroglyphs for a personal name from Maya history, not some "military

INTERPRETING SPEARTHROWER OWL | 53 |

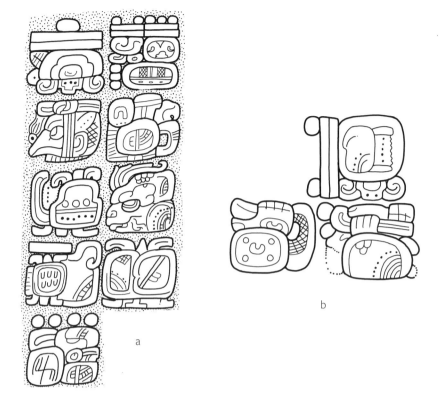

Figure 43
Two biographical events of Spearthrower Owl: a) accession from the Marcador; and b) death on Stela 31. Drawings by David Stuart.

emblem" or title as once supposed. The image on the front of Stela 31 can be interpreted as the Tikal ruler Sihyaj Chan K'awiil holding aloft a headdress specifically identified with or attributed to his recently deceased grandfather, Spearthrower Owl, whose death date is featured near the end of the stela's main text. Here we can draw a parallel to the similar scene that appears on Tikal, Stela 40, where K'an Chitam, the son of Sihyaj Chan K'awiil, holds aloft a Teotihuacan-style mosaic helmet in the form of a feline head, probably in reference to his own grandfather, Yax Nun Ayiin, and the helmet he wears on the sides of Stela 31 (Valdés, Fahsen, and Muñoz Cosme 1997) (Figure 42).

As we will examine in more detail in the next chapter, the Tikal Marcador records that Spearthrower Owl assumed rulership (*joy-aj ti ajaw*) on May 5, 374 (8.16.17.9.0 11 Ahau 3 Uayeb) (Figure 43a). The record of his death (*ochbih*) appears on Tikal's Stela 31 and possibly also on El Zapote, Stela 5, corresponding to June 11, 439 (9.0.3.9.18 12 Etz'nab 11 Zip) (Figure 43b). This gives Spearthrower Owl an extremely long reign of over sixty-five years, implying that he must have been of a fairly young age upon assuming the throne. We have no record of his birth. Needless to say, he must have been mature enough to have fathered Yax Nun Ayiin at some point before the son's own accession at Tikal in 379, even if the child were an infant at the time of his crowning (Stuart 2000). If he were a young adult of eighteen years of age in that year, Spearthrower Owl would have been born around the year 360. This would put his minimum age at death at roughly age seventy-nine. If Yax Nun Ayiin was much older on his accession—say eighteen or so—then we can place Spearthrower Owl's age at his death around his

Figure 44 Tikal, Stela 32. Drawing by William R. Coe, after Jones and Satterthwaite 1982:fig. 55a.

mid-nineties. In either scenario, he was a long-lived king, and he far outlived his own son by several decades.

The timing of Spearthrower Owl's eventual death in 439 helps to explain his importance to the historical narrative presented on Stela 31, the monument that bridges Tikal's post-Entrada history with its deeper dynastic past (Stuart 2011). The stela was dedicated by Sihyaj Chan K'awiil on the Period Ending 9.0.10.0.0, or October 19, 445, only six years after Spearthrower Owl's demise. Yax Nun Ayiin, shown on the stela's sides, was long deceased by this time (having died in 404, possibly at the age of twenty-six), and his reign was already a fairly distant memory. The mention of Spearthrower Owl's death comes near the end of the stela's very long inscription, almost as a culminating event, and his name is again featured in the parentage statements in each of the two text panels above the portraits of Yax Nun Ayiin, linking three generations with explicit iconographic and textual references.

The famous image of a Teotihuacan warrior on Tikal's Stela 32 may be a portrait of Spearthrower Owl wearing the "tassel headdress" (Figure 44). Unfortunately, we have no date for this important sculpture. We can just make out the head of a raptorial bird, possibly an eagle, used as a pectoral or emblematic device just over the chest of the front-facing warrior. Virginia Fields was the first to associate this bird with the "owl and weapons" motif in Teotihuacan art (cited in Schele and Freidel 1993:449–450), and indeed the bird's head strongly resembles that in the name from the Stela 31 headdress. If this is the same, it may point to the only known contemporary portrait of Spearthrower Owl from a Maya context. In this light, it is important to recall Clara Millon's (1973, 1988) key identification of the tassel headdress as a possible insignia of Teotihuacan rulership, or at least of very high status.

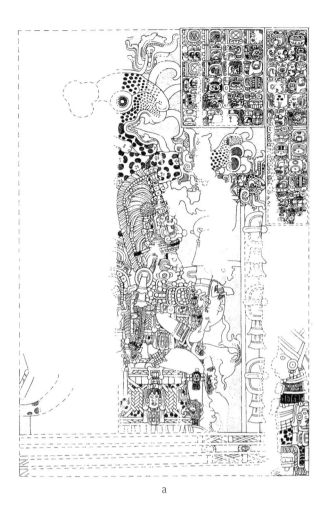

Figure 45 Lintels 3 and 2 of Tikal, Temple I. Drawings by William R. Coe, after Jones and Satterthwaite 1982:figs. 70 and 69.

Spearthrower Owl's memory persisted for centuries in the art of Tikal and other centers. As discussed elsewhere (Stuart 2000), the thirteenth *k'atun* anniversary of his death was cited on Lintel 3 of Temple I, a Late Classic sculpture that recounts Tikal's defeat of the Kanul ruler Yuknoom Yich'aak K'ahk' in 695 (Figure 45a). Forty days afterward, the Tikal ruler Jasaw Chan K'awiil "returned in the Great Jaguar Place" (*sut-aj t-u-nuk bahlam nal*), referring to the captured palanquin of the Kanul ruler (Martin 1993). This may refer to his "return" from the war campaign, or more likely to a ceremonial circuit or procession in commemoration of the victory. This occurred on 9.13.3.9.18 12 Etz'nab 11 Zac (September 15, 695), exactly thirteen *k'atuns* after Spearthrower Owl's death on 9.0.3.9.8, sharing with it the same position in the *tzolk'in* calendar, 12 Etz'nab. This long-term connection was first noted by Schele (Schele and Freidel 1993:158, 208–209); it might even seem coincidental, were it not for the scene on the immediately adjacent Lintel 2, showing Jasaw Chan K'awiil dressed in an elaborate Teotihuacan warrior's

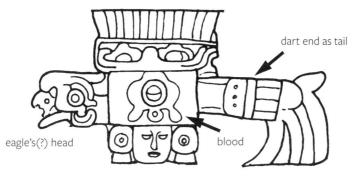

Figure 46
Facade sculpture from Tikal, Structure 5D-57, with detail of headdress. Drawing by Linda Schele © David Schele, courtesy Ancient Americas at LACMA.

attire, including repeating symbols of the Teotihuacan War Serpent (Figure 45b). In the accompanying caption, the ruler is labeled as being in the guise of Waxaklajuun Ubaah Chan, the Mayan name for this militaristic deity.

This explicit neo-Teotihuacan imagery accompanies the narrative of Calakmul's defeat in order to present a case of historical parallelism, likening Tikal's victory in war to Spearthrower Owl's military accomplishments in the Maya region over two centuries earlier. It would seem that the events of 378 represented the "epitome of conquest" in Tikal's eyes and still resonated in the memory of Tikal's royal family. Upon entering the inner chambers of Temple I, a viewer would first have seen Lintel 2 with its portrait of Jasaw Chan K'awiil as a Teotihuacan warrior, followed by Lintel 3, with the king's image as contemporary victor over Kanul. Timing the victorious procession or "return" to the 260-year anniversary of Spearthrower Owl's death gave even greater meaning to the occasion, linking one victor to another.

A related image from Tikal's Structure 5D-57 confirms this explicit ancestral reference. There, we see another portrait of a victorious warrior, presumably Jasaw Chan K'awiil, dressed in Teotihuacan war regalia and now holding a bound captive (Figure 46). The accompanying inscription states that this prisoner display came thirteen days after the Kanul defeat recorded in Temple I (Schele and Freidel 1993:205, 208). In the portrait, the ruler wears an elaborate headdress composed of the full body of a raptorial bird, with its tail feathers shown as the end of a dart. In the center of the bird's body is a trilobed Teotihuacan "blood" or "heart" symbol (Langley 1986:296) indicating a chest wound. As we will discuss in more detail in Chapter 4, the combined elements of a weapon, heart or blood, and a raptorial bird closely replicate the components of Spearthrower Owl's name. That is, the headdress may well be a name glyph, collapsing the identities of Jasaw Chan K'awiil with that of his long-deceased foreign ancestor, thus continuing the themes featured in Temple I. In addition to being a foreign authority, Spearthrower Owl may have become a symbol of military prowess and conquest two and a half centuries after his demise, as commemorated by Tikal's later kings. His mutual status as an outside conqueror and celebrated ancestor may reflect some of the internal family tensions that set the stage for the Entrada of the late fourth century, when Spearthrower Owl was instrumental in replacing one Tikal ruler by his own son.

⌒

We have so far touched on only a few of the principal variants of Spearthrower Owl's hieroglyphic name as they appear in Maya texts and iconography (see the full array of examples presented in Figure 37). These have all been recognized as identical forms since the early 1990s (Nielsen and Helmke 2008; Schele and Freidel 1993:156, 449; Stuart 2000:481). In all, we see at least two conspicuous elements: an atlatl or other weapon, and a raptorial bird, long identified as an owl but possibly an eagle. These two features form the essential logographic ingredients of the name, with added elements and substitutions providing possible clues to their phonetic values.[1]

It is important to point out that this name exists not only in the Maya hieroglyphic spellings noted so far but also in more iconographic environments that are Teotihuacan in style and inspiration. The clearest of these is the name we saw in the headdress held aloft on Stela 31, showing the bird with a feathery crest in full-figure with a "dart-and-shield" element over its body. A similar version of the name also occurs on an Early Classic jade earspool possibly from Río Azul (see Figure 37f). These are variants of what von Winning (1948) originally identified as the *lechuza y armas* ("owl and weapons") motif in Teotihuacan art, although these telling examples from the Maya world were unknown to him at the time. Clara Millon (1988:129) and René Millon (1988a:147) refer to this same Tikal example as a "war emblem." The components are the same as what we see at Teotihuacan—a weapon combined with a raptorial bird—and their different appearance and arrangement can perhaps be explained by the Maya scribe's desire to replicate specific signs of the Teotihuacan writing system.

The identification of the bird as an owl arose from a few intersecting lines of evidence, especially in the wake of the discovery of the Marcador monument at Tikal, with its prominent display of the bird as both an emblematic sign and a hieroglyphic element. The owl identification was no doubt influenced by the frontal presentation of the bird in the two examples of the name from the text of the Tikal Marcador (the text where the "Spearthrower Owl" name was first applied) showing prominent circular eyes and feathery "ears" on the heads or a crest. Frontality for human, animals, and birds is a common trope in Teotihuacan art (Klein 1976; Kubler 1967). A broader comparison of birds in other glyphic and iconographic variants of the name suggested are decidedly less owl-like. We see feathery crests, elongated and slightly hooked beaks, and large spotted and mottled feathers. In profile representations, an eagle or a hawk (both being from the order *Accipitriformes*, unlike owls) identification appears to be a stronger match, as Karl Taube (personal communication, 2018) has pointed out to me (Figure 47). There seems

Figure 47
Eagle consuming human hearts, from Chichen Itza and Tula. Note the resemblance to the raptorial birds in Figures 37 and 49–55. Drawings by David Stuart.

to be considerable resemblance among them, and they raise the strong likelihood that the bird featured in the royal name under discussion is, in fact, an eagle. All share distinctive features, with "blood," "heart," or "gore" motifs at the tips of their beaks. The circular eyes, echoing the familiar "goggles" of Teotihuacan art, are a regular feature of these raptorial birds (see Figure 37f–g) and a visual allusion their distinctive piercing gaze.

The suggestion of an owl derived from a few other epigraphic clues that now seem unlikely in retrospect. Mathews (cited in Schele and Freidel 1993) has suggested that the "cauac" sign of the "atlatl cauac" variant reads as the syllable **ku**, pointing to a possible connection to the word *ku* or *kuy* in Yukatek, meaning *lechuza agorera* (Grube and Schele 1994). This is a cognate of the word *kuj* in Ch'olan and Tseltalan languages (Kettunen 2017; Schele and Freidel 1993:450). However, it would be strange to see a syllable used in such a way, paired with a preceding logogram. Its distinctive form at Tikal and El Zapote, with small nubbin-like elements in the corners, also hints strongly that it is distinct from **ku**, presumably a logogram substituting for the bird. Schele identified the "owl" as equivalent to the bird's head hieroglyph we read as **ki**, once erroneously thought to also be read as **ku** or **KUN**, "seat" (Schele and Looper 2005:345–346). However, those logographic forms are head variants of **CH'EEN**, "cave; town, community." This leaves little if any epigraphic evidence in support of the *kuh* or *kuy* reading for the Marcador bird and its relatives, at least on the basis of hieroglyphic sign substitutions and patterns. That said, the word *kuy* meaning "owl" is well-attested in other contexts, spelled in a more transparent fashion as **ku-yu,** as also noted by Grube and Schele (1994). This includes a spelling cited on Lintel 46 of Yaxchilan as **K'AHK'-TI' ku-yu**, for *K'ahk' Uti' Kuy*, "Fire is the Mouth of the Owl," naming a ruler of the Namaan court, based at the ruins of La Florida, Peten. The spelling **ku-yu** also appears in the name of a supernatural bird, *uxlajuun chan winkil kuy*, "the 13-sky-person-owl" (Kettunen 2017). The avian depicted with the *kuy* term is a mottled raptorial bird of some sort, but it seems to be distinct from the owls or eagles we see with the spearthrower or darts. Significantly, the syllabic combination **ku-yu** never once appears in any of the known variants of the "Spearthrower Owl"

INTERPRETING SPEARTHROWER OWL | 59

glyph, hinting at some important distinction among terms and avian species. For now, I prefer to see these birds as eagles rather than as owls, recognizing that "Spearthrower Owl" is by now a well-established nickname for Tikal's overlord.

How the "cauac shield" element is equivalent to the bird remains a mystery. This question is partly due to the uncertainty as to what the "shield" truly represents. The four tuft-like elements along its outer edge give it a vague resemblance to similar features on circular shields in Maya art. Yet the "cauac" markings could indicate a stony quality to whatever the sign actually represents. On the Tikal Marcador, this element assumes an even more complex look as a cauac head in profile, resembling an animated stone that serves otherwise as the logogram **TUUN** or the syllable **ku** (see Figures 37h and 43a). In another example from a looted Tzakol III tripod vessel (K7528), the name appears with the same "cauac" head but slightly elaborated with floral-like elements (see Figure 37i). These head variants cannot logically be **TUUN** given their pattern of alternation with the "owl" or "bird" elements, so their reading remains difficult to pin down. Distilling a pattern from these examples, we have a single logogram that can be shown as a full-figure bird, alternating with a "stony" sign that is also a logogram, presumably with the same lexical value.

Moving on to the prefixed element of the name—the representation of a hand holding a club or spearthrower—there is solid evidence for reading this as a logogram for **JATZ'**, a widespread Mayan verb root meaning "to strike, to beat." This comes from important phonetic clues that appear in several Early Classic texts. To begin, Tikal's Stela 1 displays the name with the prefix **ja-** attached to the front (see Figure 37b), as well as fuller sequences of syllables that appear on the Marcador (E3 and F3) and on Stela 5 from El Zapote (see Figure 37h). On these, we see the "hand-with-club" element replaced by the grouping of syllabic elements **ja-tz'o-ma**. These fuller spellings go beyond the simple verb root to indicate a derived form *jatz'-oom* where *-oom* is an agentive noun ending, "striker" or "hitter." (Boot [2010] attributes the **ja-tz'o-ma** analysis to Albert Davletshin, although it was considered independently by the author and other epigraphers since the late 1990s.) Derivational endings such as *-oom* can often be omitted in reduced or truncated spellings of personal names, especially when scribes preferred to use logograms, but they seem clearly indicated in these more phonetically transparent variants.

We have already seen that the hand-with-club **JATZ'** sign alternates with a hand holding a dart or spear. This latter variant form has strong visual ties to Teotihuacan writing and iconography (Figure 48). All are nonetheless variants of a single underlying logogram that depicts hands bearing "striking" weapons of war. Whereas Maya versions of the name show this weapon above or to the left of the glyphic compound, the dart-and-shield "overlaps" with the bird, still functioning as an independent sign, as we see in the writing system of Teotihuacan. The visual distinctions among these weapon-with-bird combinations stem from an occasional scribal desire to evoke a Teotihuacan "look and feel," adopting foreign conventions for a foreigner's name. Another possible variant of **JATZ'** that appears in Late Classic Maya texts has been identified and discussed by Zender (2004) and may be a more generic representation of "striking," showing a hand grasping a stone (Figure 48g). It remains possible, however, that the "stone-in-hand" sign has another reading altogether, as an alternate form of the syllable **tz'o**.[2]

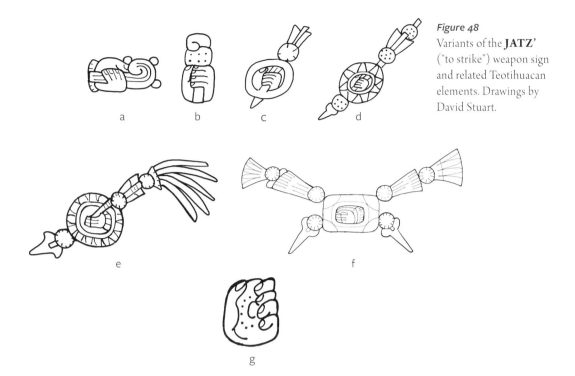

Figure 48
Variants of the **JATZ'** ("to strike") weapon sign and related Teotihuacan elements. Drawings by David Stuart.

In early Mayan vocabularies, the word *jatz'* exhibits a number of interesting associations with warfare, and even with the weaponry we associate with Central Mexico. It is attested in Ch'ol as well as throughout Yukatekan languages with the meanings "to hit, strike, fight." In Yukatek, we find *u hats' hats'ab* is glossed as *cuchillada, golpe de cuchillo o de espada* (a stab, jab from a knife or sword) (Barrera Vásquez 1980:183). It is significant also that *hats'ab*, the instrumental noun form, is glossed in colonial Yukatek as *macana o espada de los antiguos nativos; consistía en una vara de tres palmos de largo y tres dedos de ancho, sus extremos contenien afilados hojas de pedernal* (sword of the ancient Indians consisting of a shaft three handspans long and three fingers wide, its end fixed with flint blades) (Barrera Vásquez 1980:184). This describes a weapon similar to the Central Mexican–style "sword" or *macuahuitl*, like that shown held by the striding figure on Uaxactun's Stela 5, who also wields an atlatl. In the glyphic name under consideration, the visual "weapon complex" used for writing the word *jatz'* features either an atlatl or a dart, which are often paired or juxtaposed in the portraits of Teotihuacan warriors in both Maya and Central Mexican art. They would seem to be logically associated elements in militaristic iconography, whose connection was extended into the writing system and to the rendering of the name, at least in the Early Classic period.

In earlier studies, I and other epigraphers preferred to analyze the full name as something along the lines of *Jatz'oom Kuy* or *Jatz'oom Kuuj*, often translated as "Striker Owl" (Boot 2010; Kettunen 2017; Lacadena and Wichmann 2004; Nielsen and Helmke 2008). This Mayan name is at times even applied to his name glyph as it appears in Teotihuacan imagery (Robb 2017). "Striker Owl" would describe an aggressive, weapon-wielding bird. Nielsen and Helmke (2008) prefer to translate it more specifically as *Jatz'oom Kuy*,

"Owl-will-strike," but there may be reason to look at it slightly differently; the -*oom* is most likely not a future verb ending, but rather an agentive noun derivation followed by its direct object (these two functions of this suffix are probably related). This would agree with parallel titles and expressions known from the hieroglyphs, such as *kaloom-te'*, "plant-maker(?)," or *joch'oom-k'ahk'*, "fire-driller." Assuming the name *jatz'oom*-BIRD is parallel, it would indicate that the owl or eagle is the direct object or recipient of the "striking" action, not the agent. Thus, a "striker of eagles." As we will see, there is ample visual evidence in iconographic examples of the ruler's name that conform to this semantic analysis, showing the raptorial bird wounded and bloodied.

Perhaps it is significant that the more Teotihuacan-style variants of the **JATZ'** sign are careful to show the weapon in the grasp of a *human* hand. This would seem to indicate its fundamental separateness and detachment from the bird's body, with which it is usually grouped. This is especially clear in the example from the large rosette atop the Tikal Marcador, which visually alludes to the idea of hitting or striking the bird (see Figure 37e). In other cases, we also see a small circular element or shield over the middle of the owl's body, encompassing the grasping hand that is not really held by the bird, as we might at first assume, but rather by the striker or hitter. In the parallel examples from Teotihuacan art and writing, this same juxtaposition of a weapon and a raptorial bird shows that they are separate and overlaid elements in what is also a combination of hieroglyphic signs.

One final point needs to be addressed regarding the full form of Spearthrower Owl's name, as we can best understand it at present. The word *jatz'oom* is, of course, a Mayan expression, spelled phonetically in two inscriptions, as well as a vividly descriptive phrase like many other royal names we find in Mesoamerican languages (Colas 2004). Would we not expect a non-Maya individual, a ruler of Teotihuacan, to be named with glyphic spellings that include phonetic indications of a foreign language, say Totonacan or Nahuatl (Boot 2010; Whittaker 1986)? Possibly, but the name spellings we have examined clearly prioritize lexical and semantic clarity over the phonetic representation (and, of course, we are still unsure of what language was spoken at Teotihuacan). There is ample precedent for the translation of proper names in Mesoamerican history, as in the deity names K'uk'ulkan or Quq'umatz, two localized Mayan translations of the Nahuatl Quetzalcoatl, "Feathered Snake." Spearthrower Owl's political agent in the Peten, Sihyaj K'ahk', might present a similar case of a Mayan name for an individual who in the historical sources seems to be a foreigner, although his precise background and place of origin remain unresolved questions.

SPEARTHROWER OWL IN THE WRITING OF TEOTIHUACAN

Images of raptorial birds with weapons appear with some frequency in the art and writing of Teotihuacan; many of these images might also be interpreted as name hieroglyphs (Stuart 2000; Taube 2000). This is the same *lechuza y armas* ("owl and weapons") motif mentioned before, widely interpreted as "heraldic insignia for the class of warriors belonging to the highest level of the military hierarchy" (von Winning 1987:1:85–91) (Figures 49–50). Grube and Schele (1994) originally noted their visual equivalence to

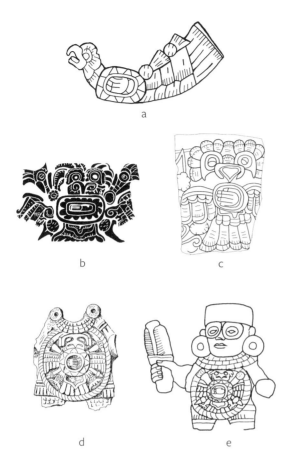

Figure 49 Selected examples of the "owl and weapons" glyph in the art and writing of Teotihuacan. Drawings by David Stuart (a and c), Hasso von Winning (b), Laurette Séjourné (d), and Linda Schele (e); drawings b and d from von Winning 1987:1:figs. VII6c, VII9c.

Figure 50 Hieroglyphic name on shield, from a ceramic disc from Teotihuacan. Drawing by David Stuart.

the "Spearthrower Owl" glyphs at Tikal, yet resisted the idea that such images might be personal names. However, with our newly refined knowledge of the Teotihuacan writing system, I argue that the "owl and weapons" motif can be analyzed as a written element that is more or less equal in function to the names we have discussed so far and that conform to the established logographic conventions of Teotihuacan's hieroglyphs (Helmke and Nielsen 2021; Taube 2000). It is important to note that elements of Teotihuacan writing assume both "simple" forms, as we see on the famous Tetitla floor paintings, as well as larger "emblematic" forms that may be visual elaborations on the same elements. Much as we see in other traditions of Mesoamerican writing, Teotihuacan's system, at least in its more complex iteration, exhibits a good deal of overlap between categories of glyphs and what we usually take to be iconography (Nielsen and Helmke 2014). Maya examples of Spearthrower Owl's name show a similar range of forms that cross over into iconographic presentation, some of which, as others have shown, exhibit a clear connection to the "owl and weapons" glyphs at Teotihuacan. As with Maya examples, the raptorial bird in Teotihuacan examples can appear both in frontal and profile views. The hieroglyphic nature of the composition is indicated by the darts with circular shield that overlays the bird's body, never truly "held" by the bird in a way that suggests it is armed. As noted, the hand within the circle is always that of a human, parallel in every way to the hand that wields the atlatl, club, or stone in Maya **JATZ'** signs. In the "owl and weapons" motif, it seems we have two separate and super-imposed signs.

At Teotihuacan, this "owl and weapons" motif is most frequent on cylinder tripod ceramics and on molded and modeled figurines from the Xolalpan and Metepec phases. It is well-known as a circular medallion on the chests of warrior figurines, where the owl appears frontally with a central "shield" and two crossed darts over the bird's body (Figure 49e). Identical examples of such figurines have been found at Teotihuacan, Azcapotzalco, and Chapultepec, on the western shore of Lake Texcoco (Garcia Cháves 2002; von Winning 1948). The placement of the "owl and weapons" motif on the chests of the warriors is highly reminiscent of the possible name shown on the Teotihuacan warrior depicted on Stela 32 from Tikal, which may represent a Maya version of the same visual presentation (we will examine other cases in Chapter 4).

We also see it on a large Teotihuacan-style ceramic figure recovered from Lake Amatitlan, Guatemala, that displays the very same sign with a goggled warrior who stands upon a box-like platform (Berlo 1984:149–150). The object is considered purely Teotihuacan in style, although the unusual form seems restricted to this and other objects recovered by Stephan Borhegyi at the lacustrine site of Lavaderos. The bird and the crossed darts appear on the front of the object's base, probably as a glyphic label for the figure. The most complex and detailed example of this very same "owl and weap-ons" design appears on a ceramic disc from Teotihuacan (Figure 50), possibly a vessel lid or a mirror back, but without an accompanying figure (Robb 2017:209). This is a late work dating to the Metepec phase and, therefore, perhaps a retrospective mention of the important Teotihuacan ruler.

The same frontal bird motif appears on a fragment of a cylinder tripod illustrated by Seler (1998:6:236), where the bird wears the "tassel headdress" associated with author-ity (Millon 1973, 1988) (Figure 51a). A circular element resembling a shield with two crossed darts appears across its front.[3] This is clearly related to images on other cylinder vessels where the same bird is in profile, often in combination with a human figure. One example excavated by Linné (1934:60) at Teotihuacan bears several repeating represen-tations of the "owl and weapons" motif with a goggled warrior, and a nearly identical vase was illustrated by Caso (1972:fig. 39b) (Figure 51b). Hellmuth later identified a few "provincial" examples of the same design on cylinder tripods from the Tequisate region of Guatemala (Hellmuth 1975:12–13) (Figure 51c).

Significantly, these profile representations are identical to "iconographic" versions of Spearthrower Owl's name at Tikal, as seen in the headdress on Stela 31 and on the ves-sel lids from Group 6C-XVI (Figure 52). Their strong resemblance and other glyphic versions of the name shown in Figure 37 should leave little doubt as to their visual equiv-alence, as has long been acknowledged. Logically, this fundamental sameness leads me

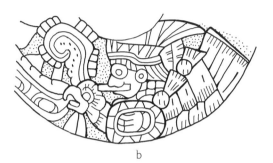

Figure 51
Spearthrower Owl names on cylinder tripods: a) Teotihuacan ceramic fragment (Seler 1998:6:fig. 166b); b) Teotihuacan tripod excavated by Sigvald Linné (Caso 1972:fig. 39b); and c) cylinder tripod from Tequisate region of Guatemala (Hellmuth 1975:pl. 4c).

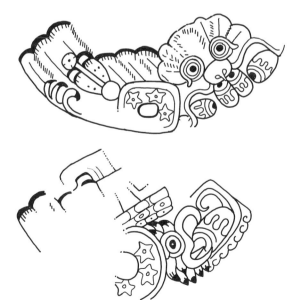

Figure 52
Eagle-and-dart (Spearthrower Owl) hieroglyphs from lids of cylinder tripods excavated at Group 6C-XVI, Tikal. Note the possible "tassel headdress" on the lower example. Drawings by David Stuart.

Figure 53
Bird with "shield-and-darts" sign, from Techinantitla murals, Teotihuacan. Drawing by David Stuart.

to interpret the "owl and weapons" motif at Teotihuacan not only as some general "heraldic" sign or a symbol of a military order but also as a personal name hieroglyph, often in association with depictions of human figures. I take these to be portraits of Spearthrower Owl or Eagle Striker, not unlike other named figures in Teotihuacan-style art.

Other well-known representations of raptorial birds with darts and shields appear in the mural paintings from the Techinantitla area of Teotihuacan, related to the images we have discussed (Berrin 1988:169–183; Robb 2017:411) (Figure 53). These exist in fragmented form; their broader visual contexts are far from clear, but we nonetheless see several standing birds in profile, with a separate "shield and hand-grasping-dart" sign superimposed over the bird's chest. I doubt that these birds are "armed," but rather are best seen as full-figure bird hieroglyphs combined with the separate "arms" sign. Nor do the birds at Techinantitla always resemble eagles or owls, as they often look more like quetzals and are generally painted green with red and blue details (Berrin 1988:164). Here we are reminded of some of the same ambiguities in identifying raptorial birds and other avian species in Mesoamerican art and writing, where categories often appear to overlap. It is hard to know whether these Techinantitla paintings are examples of the "owl and weapons" hieroglyph or not, but they certainly include the same "weapons" sign, and internal variations among the birds suggest they could involve still other hieroglyphic forms or personal names (Berrin 1988:pl. 19).

Nielsen and Helmke (2008) discuss the presence of a variant of the "Spearthrower Owl" glyph in the murals of Atetelco, in combination with a toponymic reference to hills or mountains (Figure 54). This is not the familiar owl with the central shield and crossed darts, but a simpler arrangement showing a frontal owl with an atlatl. Note that the "atlatl" element is placed directly over the center of the owl's body, reminiscent of what we find in some Maya variants. Nielsen and Helmke accept the view that Spearthrower Owl is a personal name in Tikal's historical record, yet they see the role of these glyphs at Teotihuacan as somewhat distinct, more likely to be a deity reference that was later adopted by one or more individuals as a personal name. As they point out, nowhere in Mesoamerican art does a personal name ever serve as a toponym (the Nahuatl place name Huitzilopochco, "Place of Huitzilopochtli," may be an exception).

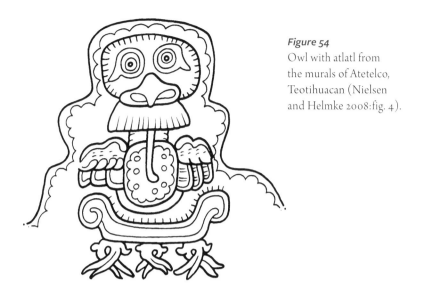

Figure 54
Owl with atlatl from the murals of Atetelco, Teotihuacan (Nielsen and Helmke 2008:fig. 4).

They instead offer a functional parallel between the imagery of Spearthrower Owl at Teotihuacan and that of the Mexica deity Huitzilopochtli, depicted in some colonial sources as an armed bird and thus bearing a vague resemblance to the "Spearthrower Owl" motif. They suggest that the "Spearthrower Owl" motif referred to a similar ancient deity associated with militarism, represented at Atetelco as presiding over a mountainous local landscape.

The presence of the name among mountains and other elements in the Atetelco mural raises interesting questions, not the least of which centers on the nature of glyphic imagery at Teotihuacan, and the difficulties in parsing writing from iconography and from other visual representation. However, I do not follow Nielsen and Helmke's preference for interpreting the form as a deity name, as opposed to a more personal or historical reference, in that setting. There is considerable room for alternate interpretations, especially given how little we know about the conventions of Teotihuacan art and text-image relationships. Perhaps personal name glyphs could appear within a variety of unexpected settings—a lesson similar to that which we have learned from insights into the nature of Teotihuacan script (Helmke and Nielsen 2021; Taube 2000, 2002). Some of these questions were anticipated long ago by George Kubler, who saw Teotihuacan artisans as "less interested in recording appearances than in combining and compounding associative meanings in a quest for viable forms of writing" (Kubler 1967:5). Could Atetelco's design show the personal name of the ruler, visually expressing his domain over the landscape? The overarching point here, acknowledged by Nielsen and Helmke, is that the "Spearthrower Owl" name at Atetelco is indeed the same as what we find at Tikal and elsewhere at Teotihuacan. The question that remains concerns the scope of its reference. I see the direct association of the "owl and weapons" motif with representations of people, in figurines and on ceramics, as strongly pointing to its role as a personal name, and its integration within complex mural programs, such as what we find at Atetelco, may not be too surprising given the appearance of probable name glyphs in other murals at the site.

Figure 55
Design on a rectangular shield on a column at the Palace of Quetzalpapalotl, Teotihuacan. Drawing by David Stuart.

Another example of Spearthrower Owl's name may be identifiable on carved support piers on the western side of the so-called Palace of Quetzalpapalotl (Figure 55). There, we find repeating avian representations within rectangular frames, perhaps meant to replicate war shields (we will soon discuss similar shields in the monuments of Piedras Negras, with their frontal presentations of raptorial birds). Over the upper chest, we see two symmetrical curved elements, conflated with wings, below which is an attached "heart" sign, placed centrally over the heart of the bird. The curved wings recall the forms of clubs or spearthrowers (or obsidian blades), as we see in the various **JATZ'** signs in Maya spellings. With the "heart" element emphasized, it seems beyond coincidence that what we may have here are the principal components of the Mayan name *Jatz'oom*-BIRD, emphasizing the imagery of striking or wounding. This identification should remain very tentative given the later Metepec date of the Quetzalpapalotl complex. However, it may be significant that the rectangular war shields shown on monuments at Piedras Negras are also later in date, wielded by warrior-kings who lived centuries after Spearthrower Owl's death, evoking Teotihuacan militarism and a past history (García–Des Lauriers 2017; Stone 1989) (see Figure 70). Therefore, I hold out the possibility that those eagle-like birds in the Palace of Quetzalpapalotl might also have served as emblematic references to the glorified Teotihuacan ruler, functioning much like those costume elements and shields in Maya art, seemingly personal mentions that came centuries after Spearthrower Owl's lifetime.

The earliest example of a shield bearing the name glyph of Spearthrower Owl comes from Tikal, where we will now return. This is featured prominently atop the so-called Marcador, the most important historical source for understanding the Entrada as well as other aspects of Spearthrower Owl's own status and role in Peten history.

NOTES

1 In my original compilation of Spearthrower Owl name variants, I mistakenly included one variant that now can be shown to be distinct (Stuart 2000:fig. 15.14g). This comes from Tikal's MT 32, a bone from Burial 116. The original drawing of the bone's text showed what appeared to be an owl-like bird after a handheld weapon. However, Dmitri Beliaev recently shared photographs of the bone showing that the head is clearly an **AYIIN** logogram, proving it to be instead the name Kupoom Yohl Ayiin, who still seems to have played some part in the greater Entrada narrative. Despite earlier assertions and speculations, no examples of Spearthrower Owl's name seem to include *(y)ohl*, "heart." I thank Dmitri for sharing his images and his important observations on the name on Tikal MT 32.

2 The possible syllabic function for the "stone-in-hand" sign discussed by Zender was first pointed out to me by Stephen Houston (personal communication, 2010).

3 The eagle with shield and a tassel headdress recalls the image on one of the cylinder tripods excavated at the Mundo Perdido at Tikal (see Figure 52). The tassel headdress is damaged, but the feathers and "year sign" elements are visible. Given the headdress's well-known association with rulership, I suggest that these images help support the interpretation of such bird images as personal preferences (that is, hieroglyphic forms) naming the ruler.

3 THE TIKAL MARCADOR
A Monument of Conquest

THE TIKAL MARCADOR WAS DISCOVERED IN 1982 BY THE PROYECTO Nacional Tikal during tunneling in Group 6C-XVI, a small elite residential group to the south of the Mundo Perdido complex (Laporte and Fialko 1990) (Figure 56). It was found broken and cached within a small platform designated as Structure Sub-4B, which was constructed in the center of a patio (Laporte 1987). Deposited with it within the platform was a fragment of a large stucco sculpture, a human face that was presumably once a part of some imposing architectural decoration nearby. Juan Pedro Laporte and Vilma Fialko believed that the Marcador was erected atop the Sub-4B platform, as reflected in the published architectural renderings from their project. The entire complex of 6C-XVI was subsequently buried under deep fill around 425 CE, and the reason for its relative invisibility on the surface of the archaeological site today remains an important question.

The overall form of the Marcador is unique in the Maya region, although a few stones of similar shape and presentation have been attested at Teotihuacan and elsewhere in highland Mexico. It can best be described as a cylindrical shaft supporting a sphere with a flaring element below, all topped by a flattened, disc-like array of feathers framing a central glyph or image. The shaft bears two rectangular panels of hieroglyphs, and the circular upper element is also two-sided, giving the Marcador a clear front and back. The inscription bearing the Initial Series date allows us to identify its side as the "front" of the monument (see Figure 60a).

The Marcador has proven difficult to classify as a sculptural type. Upon its discovery, its similarity to a composite "stela" excavated in 1963 at La Ventilla, Teotihuacan, was immediately recognized (Aveleyra Arroyo de Anda 1963a). This important sculpture was found without firm archaeological context near the surface of a field of a local ranch, but subsequent excavations seem to have established its original position atop a bench or platform in the center of a small patio "flanked on four sides by houses" (Aveleyra Arroyo de Anda 1963b:235). It is apparently of Classic date but is said to have been moved from an earlier setting and reused in a later construction dating to the Coyotlatelco period (650–800 CE). One aspect of the La Ventilla stela that has gone largely unanalyzed is its ornate decoration, especially the many interlaced designs that are clearly in the style of the Gulf Coast or Veracruz region. This is especially interesting

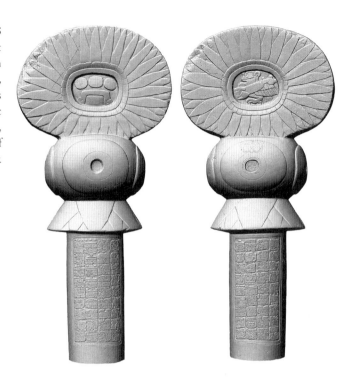

Figure 56
The Tikal Marcador, front and rear views. Optical scan by Alexandre Tokovinine, courtesy of the Corpus of Maya Hieroglyphic Inscriptions (CMHI), Peabody Museum of Archaeology and Ethnology.

given that its archaeological context in the Coyotlatelco phase reflected the presence of "people of mixed ethnocultural affiliations" (Aveleyra Arroyo de Anda 1963b:237). The design may anticipate some of the distinctive designs of later "Huastec" art of the Late Classic period, as seen at El Tajin. The La Ventilla stela also was quickly likened to two images of similar upright pillars in the paintings of Tepantitla, on either side of an apparent ballgame where numerous individuals are shown playing and holding clubs. For this reason, the La Ventilla sculpture was quickly identified as a "stela-marker" or as a "ballgame marker" (Aveleyra Arroyo de Anda 1963b:236), and this label has been applied to the Marcador as well ever since its discovery. Other column-like sculptures have been recently discussed from Cerro de los Monos, Guerrero (Nielsen and Helmke 2020).

Schele and Freidel (1993:299–301) interpreted the form of the Marcador as replicating a battle standard. In a somewhat related vein, I concur with Bassie-Sweet (2019:171–176) that the monument instead represents an upright weapon—a spear, a dart, or a mace—combined with a circular shield attached to its top, much like emblems of war we have already seen in Teotihuacan visual culture. The Marcador's columnar shaft would be the upright weapon, with the small spherical element above perhaps representing the down feathery tuft of a dart. It may also be a mace-head, similar to the *quauhololli* weapon used in Late Postclassic Central Mexico.[1] As Taube (1992a:192) notes, "Teotihuacan shields are frequently round with a raised rim surrounded by feathers," which is a perfect description of the circular rosette atop the sculpture. This identification is supported by the large "Storm God" icon that appears in its center on the Marcador's front side. This familiar element has been discussed by many scholars, including Langley (1992:249–253), who points out that one of its most common

Figure 57 Examples of war shields with central hieroglyphic names or personal references: a) "U Nahb K'inich" ancestral name or title on shield held by Bahlaj Chan K'awiil, Dos Pilas, Stela 9, detail (drawing by David Stuart); and b) K'inich Yax K'uk' Mo' full figure on rectangular Teotihuacan-style shield, from west side mosaic sculpture Structure 10L-16 at Copan (Fash 2011:65).

contexts is as a decorative motif on circular war shields, an association that may well have lasted until the Late Postclassic period on Aztec-era *chimalli* shields that emulated the Teotihuacan form (Langley 1992:251–259).

As a representation of a combined weapon and shield, the Marcador can be thought of as a three-dimensional image of a familiar pairing of signs found throughout Mesoamerican art and writing (Helmke 2013:4). This appears in Central Mexico as the *mitl chimalli*, "arrow-and-shield," hieroglyph for war found in the annal pages of the Codex Mendoza, for example. Among the Classic Maya, we find the paired words *took'*, "flint knife," and *pakal*, "shield," also used as a common term for war and as a frequent iconographic element signifying the sacred duties of warfare, as on Palenque's Tablet of the Sun or Tablet of the Slaves (see Figure 75a). Its Teotihuacan equivalent, at least visually, would be the shield-dart combination we see in some versions of Spearthrower Owl's personal name, functionally equivalent not only to *took' pakal* but perhaps more specifically to the action described by the Mayan term *jatz'*, "to strike, attack."

As to what amounts to a three-dimensional hieroglyph, a dart thrust into the ground, the Marcador's central placement in a plaza or patio may well have served as an overt symbol of conquest, far more direct in its messaging than its interpretation of a "battle standard." In the pictorial histories of Oaxaca, a spear or dart that pierces the earth or a specific place-name was a widespread symbol for military conquest (Smith 1973:33). Here it is perhaps significant that the Marcador's text and imagery make it clear that the Marcador sculpture was "of" Spearthrower Owl, owned by him. The prominence of his name glyph within the rosette of the circular shield is an explicit statement of attribution, and the inscription again names him in direct connection with the object. Other examples of war shields, either circular or rectangular, show that they could be used similarly as frames for name glyphs, emblematic or otherwise, even with feather arrays that resemble the form of the Marcador (Figure 57). If it was a symbol of warfare erected in the plaza of Group 6C-XVI, it was perhaps conceived as the "marker" of Spearthrower Owl's own role in the conquest of Tikal. Interpreting the Marcador monument in such a way resonates well with the narrative that is given in the inscription, which highlights the arrival of foreigners and the defeat of Tikal in 378, as well as the monument's own dedication late in the reign of Spearthrower Owl a number of years later.[2]

SIDES AND NARRATIVE STRUCTURE

The two faces of the Marcador are carefully designed to emphasize their own integrated message of iconography and text. It is very much a "sided" monument, meaning that its design and imagery were carefully composed to be seen and read in order as separate parts, one before the other, before being considered as a narrative whole. The front displays the abstracted "Storm God" motif within the shield, with the date of the Entrada episode featured below, featuring Sihyaj K'ahk' as the protagonist. The rear displays the name of Spearthrower Owl on the opposite side of the shield, with his biographical details forming the beginning of the text panel directly below. The back text also focuses on the dedication of the stone some thirty-six years after the Entrada, linking it directly to a similar sort of event that had happened around that time, perhaps an earlier Marcador of some sort as yet undiscovered. This presents a broader historical context for the events of 378, framing the Entrada temporally with a prior event (the inauguration) and a later contemporaneous point of focus (the dedication). A front-to-back reading, therefore, juxtaposes the narrative elements in important ways, providing the reader with different protagonists, local and distant toponymic references, and differently named deities. Sihyaj K'ahk' seems to be the protagonist on the front, while his overseer Spearthrower Owl is the focus of the back. The curious twin faces incised on the spherical form of the Marcador's back, just below the ruler's large name, might even be interpreted as a representation of this dual focus (Figure 58). It is significant that not one known dynastic ruler of Tikal is mentioned anywhere in the two Marcador inscriptions.

The glyphs featured on the two opposite sides of the circular shield—the "Storm God" element and Spearthrower Owl's personal name—also appear together in the second of the text panels at Blocks E8–F9 (Figure 59). These make up the subject of the verb *tz'ahpaj*, "was erected," bound as a grammatical unit in the dedication phase that is the highlight of the entire narrative. Together, the two sides of the shield repeat the subject, providing an even more specific label for the Marcador as the object of Spearthrower Owl. The possessed noun and its possessor, the essence of the monument, thus exist as the two large hieroglyphs on the front and back of the monument.

Turning to the particulars of the inscription (Figure 60), we find four events recorded in the entire narrative, with one highlighted and featured on each side or segment, as shown in boldface below:

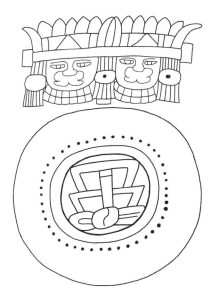

Figure 58
Detail of a carving on spherical portion of the Marcador's rear. Drawing by David Stuart.

Figure 59
The ownership phrase from the rear text panel of the Marcador (Blocks E8–F9). Drawing by David Stuart.

FRONT:

| **8.17.1.4.12 11 Eb 15 Mac** | **January 16, 378** | **Sihyaj K'ahk' arrives at Tikal; conquest** |

BACK:

8.16.17.9.0 11 Ahau 3 Uayeb	May 5, 374	Spearthrower Owl's accession
8.18.17.14.9 12 Muluc 12 Kankin	**January 24, 414**	**Dedication of Marcador**
8.19.0.0.0 10 Ahau 13 Kayab	March 25, 416	Period Ending

The two featured events are the Entrada and the dedication of the Marcador thirty-six years later (both events fell in late January of their respective years). These are "fronted" in terms of the larger historical narrative. The remaining two dates, both on the back, note the accession of Spearthrower Owl in 374 CE and an anticipated *k'atun* ending in

THE TIKAL MARCADOR | 75

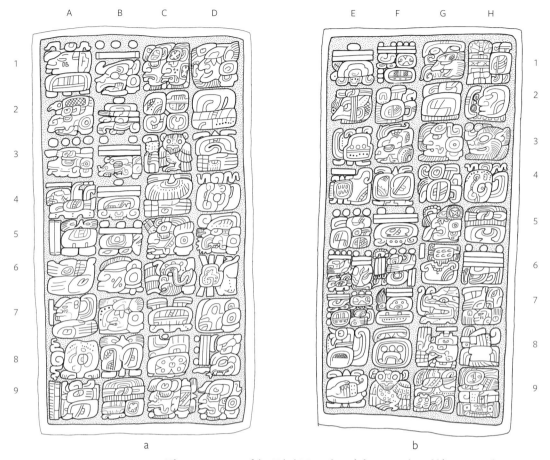

Figure 60 The inscriptions of the Tikal Marcador: a) front panel; and b) rear panel. Drawings by David Stuart.

416, soon after the marker's dedication. It is interesting to see that one of these backgrounded dates exists in the more distant historical past while the other exists in the near future, yet to occur. This provides an early example of what might be called "narrative centering," a common rhetorical structure of Maya texts wherein the time frame of historical evidence reflects a Maya desire to "centralize" one or more featured episodes by orienting them around symmetrical references to the past and the future. In the Marcador's inscription, the past and future bracket and highlight the most significant and contemporaneous event of all—the dedication of the stone itself in 414. From this, we see that the Marcador's account of the Entrada is a retrospective one, removed by over three decades from the event.

THE FRONT TEXT: ARRIVAL AND CONQUEST

The Marcador's front text opens with a familiar date: 8.17.1.4.12 11 Eb 15 Mac, or January 16, 378, the arrival day of Sihyaj K'ahk' (A1–B9). Two aspects of the date as written are unusual. First, unlike the other components of the Long Count, the *k'atun* position at

A2 does not include a bar-and-dot number, as only a head sign occupies its glyph block. At first, it seems as if the required number 17 was simply omitted by the scribe for some unknown reason. However, on closer inspection, it seems that the head itself may hold more than it might seem, for it is not simply a head variant for the *k'atun* but also may include an animated number 17, possibly in visual combination with the period glyph. The second unusual aspect of the opening date is the month glyph, which is clearly written in error as 10 Mac where 15 Mac would be required.

The record of the moon age (B5–A7) notes that the moon was twenty-eight days old (B5), thus in a period of approaching full darkness. This accords well with the invisibility of the moon on January 16, 378. What comes next in Blocks A6 and B6 is difficult to analyze, falling outside of the normal conventions of moon age records in Maya texts. A6 displays two distinct "hand" signs combined into a single block. One with its thumb upturned looks to be the logogram **AL**, usually used to spell the root *'al*, "woman's child." The smaller hand displaying a beaded wristlet is otherwise known to be **K'AB**, "hand, arm." It is tempting to link the combination of **AL** and **K'AB** to the term *(y)alk'ab*, found in lowland Mayan languages as the word for "finger" (literally "child of the hand"). There is no way of confirming this reading, beyond the simple association of two signs that otherwise have these respective values. The single head sign at Block B6 also presents a challenge. It shows a "death marking" on its cheek, but otherwise is difficult to relate to other known signs.[3] Given its position before Glyph C at A7, it is possible that it is an elaborate head variant of the pronoun **U-**. A7 itself can be analyzed with the nominalized verb root *k'al* (the hand sign) meaning "raise, appear," its subject being the "first Maize God moon" within the hand's palm (**NAAH-IXI'M?-UH**). This refers to the first month within the lunar semester of six lunations named for the Maize God.

The calendric information in the opening passage ends with Glyph A7, after which we come to the main verb and subject. The verb is **HUL-ye**, *huley*, "he arrives," recording the same description for the Entrada that we find in other texts (B7). This particular variant of the arrival verb went unrecognized until shortly after my original 2000 essay and, therefore, was not included in that analysis. The glyph's form is complex, utilizing the profile head variant of the syllable **ye** and a prefix that is a much-reduced version of the "footprint" sign that forms the basis of one of the main logograms for **HUL** ("arrive"). This spelling is unusual in giving us the suffix *-ey*, an archaic form of the far more common *-iy* or *-iiy* "past-time" suffix we find on intransitive verbs. It is equivalent to the form *huliiy*, "he arrived," that we have seen at Uaxactun, La Sufricaya, and elsewhere. The subject is the familiar name of Sihyaj K'ahk' (A8), who bears the *kaloomte'* title directly afterward (B8). A second title for Sihyaj K'ahk' appears in A9, prefixed by **AJ-** and ending in **-TE'**. The intervening signs are difficult to identify, except for the apparent **NAL** superfix above. This glyph ("he of *? te' nal* ?") remains difficult to analyze. Finally, at B9 we find **MUT-CHAN-na-CH'EEN**, for *mutuul chan ch'een*, "(at) Mutul, the sky-and-cave," a clear reference to Tikal itself using the place or court name of the Classic period. The pairing of *chan* and *ch'een* is a common ritual expression of location, probably used to name the local ceremonial centers, central plazas, and other nodes of political and religious authority.

The last two columns of the front text (C and D) expand on the "arrival" episode with further explanation and details. Rather than seeing it as a simple continuation,

Figure 61
Side views of an inscribed sculpture fragment in the Tikal bodega (after Beliaev et al. 2013:149). Drawing by David Stuart, after Philip Galeev.

however, there is reason to think that the scribe has partitioned the text at this point, with Columns A and B comprising one event statement—the arrival itself—and C and D comprising another rhetorical or compositional unit of text. The parsing and design of texts using columns as units of composition is an important aspect of formal inscriptions, although still poorly studied.

Glyph C1 shows two profile heads, one for **AK'AB** and another for **K'IN**. We can analyze this in one of a couple of ways. At first, it may seem to be related to similar pairings of opposed nouns, as in the combination of signs for "day" and "night" to represent the concept of **TZ'AK**, "complete, be whole." However, here it might also be seen as a temporal adverb, marking the elapsed time from the transition of night to day, in the sense of "next day." It is followed by a repetition of the verb *huley* (**HUL-ye**) and then a new place-name at C2, spelled **ku-pu-?-CH'EEN**. The parallel with B7–B9 is clear, with a new arrival at a new place, perhaps the day after the initial appearance at Tikal (*mutu'l chan ch'een*). This same place appears on a small Early Classic stone fragment from Tikal, stored in the site bodega, reported by Beliaev et al. (2013:149) (Figure 61). This may have been recovered by the Proyecto Nacional Tikal from the same area where the Marcador was found, but its exact archaeological context remains unknown. While speculative, the possibility arises that the **ku-pu-?** place refers to a specific area or space within greater Tikal, where Sihyaj K'ahk' established himself immediately after the arrival on 11 Eb. The area of Group 6C-XVI or the nearby "Cuidadela" quickly spring to mind (Houston et al. 2021).

The first mention of Spearthrower Owl comes in Block C3, immediately after the "conjunction" term spelled **yi-ta-ji**. This glyph, so common as a linkage between names and pre-posed before verbs, is usually taken to be a term meaning "with" or "and." It clearly incorporates the third person pronoun *y-* before a root or stem *it* or *ita*. Later spellings of this as **ye-ta-ji** may suggest a connection to the proto-Mayan root **ety*, "fellow, companion" but there remain a number of questions about how to best analyze the hieroglyphic term. Here, it might at first suggest that Spearthrower Owl was in the company of Sihyaj K'ahk' upon his arrival, but I highly doubt this was the case. We know that *et* and its various cognate derivations can refer to a broad array of associations, of acting and doing things in coordination and conjunction. *Eta* in Yukatek is "friend" (*etail*, "amigo," *etailil*, "amistad") (Barrera Vásquez 1980:158), pointing to a more general sense of a close connection between individuals.

The connections between the two major players may be noted in more detail through a poetic couplet we find at D3 and C4 on the Marcador, **NOH-K'AB** and **TZ'EH-K'AB**, respectively, for "the right hand, the left hand" (Stuart 2002). Directly after comes the name of Sihyaj K'ahk' (D4: **SIH-AJ-K'AHK'**). Here we confront a complex question of syntax, for we have a second protagonist named quickly on the heels of another, and a verb above (*huley*) without a clear subject indicated in the glyphs that immediately follow it, only a place-name. Given that Sihyaj K'ahk' is the only named subject of the first arrival verb (B7–A8), there can be little doubt that he is also the subject of the repeated *huley* expression at D1. Sihyaj K'ahk' is eventually named in the passage, but not before the scribe has placed a key piece of information beforehand—that Sihyaj K'ahk' is the "ally" or "friend" of Spearthrower Owl (D2, C3). This may well be an example of a "disrupted" syntactical order, used to highlight a new and essential piece of information that establishes Sihyaj K'ahk's essential role as a representative of a higher-ranking ruler, in association with a place (**ku-pu-?**) where the Marcador would eventually be erected. My tentative interpretation here is that Sihyaj K'ahk' arrived "with" Spearthrower Owl, in the sense that he was his representative and operative, his "right and left hands."

Another couplet appears at C5 and D5, two profile heads each fronted by the preposition sign **ta-** (*ta*, "in, at, by means of"). These are the two small elements that project diagonally from the noses, following a common Early Classic convention. The first head is the animate variant of **TE'**, for *te'*, "tree, plant, staff," while the second at D5 is more difficult to identify. It seems a "stone"-like head with a crenellated edge along its nose. I suspect this may be an early variant of the head sign for **TOOK'**, "knife, flint." The couplet construction would be *ta te' ta took'*, "with staffs (and) with knives." This agrees with other pairings of these terms that we sometimes find in Maya texts, as in the term *te' took' baah*, a glyph sometimes found in records related to war, as well as the specific titles *baah te'* and *baah took'*, associated also with captive taking and warfare (Houston 2008). The couplet on the Marcador further characterizes the nature of the "arrival" as something far from benign, and it may relate rhetorically to the paired "hands" mentioned just a few blocks earlier. Upon arrival, Sihyaj K'ahk' was at the ready "with staffs and with knives."

The description of the arrival and its consequences culminates in C6 with the verb spelled **OCH-CH'EEN**, *och ch'een*, "he cave-enters," or "he town-enters" (Figure 62). This is now well-established from many other examples as a term for conquest and military defeat (Helmke and Brady 2014; Martin 2020:213–215; Stuart 2014). This particular form on the Marcador was not included in my original study of the Entrada narratives

THE TIKAL MARCADOR | 79 |

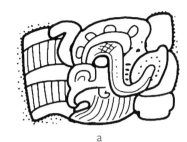
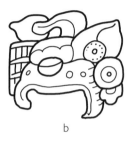

Figure 62
Examples of the **OCH-CH'EEN** ("cave entering") hieroglyph for conquest: a) Marcador, Block C6; b) Naranjo, Stela 45, front, detail; and c) Yaxchilan, Stela 18. Drawings by David Stuart.

but was later recognized with its creative visual combination of the **OCH** and **CH'EEN** elements, showing the snake tail "entering" the eye of the bird. The important implications of this hieroglyph could not be any clearer in terms of written history, describing the event of January 16, 378, as a conquest of Tikal at the hands of Sihyaj K'ahk', probably acting on behalf of (the "right and left hands" of) Spearthrower Owl.

The remaining glyphs of the front panel are difficult to understand in full, but we see at least two references to prominent deities, as well as the sign **K'UH**, "god, holy thing" (D7). I suspect we, therefore, have a closing section that focuses on the religious dimensions of Tikal's conquest and on the gods who sanctioned it. The first clearly identifiable name is that of the so-called Teotihuacan War Serpent (Taube 1992b, 2012), who, as we have noted before, is named in the Maya inscriptions as *Waxaklajuun Ubaah Chan*, "Eighteen are the Heads of the Snake" (D8: **18-na-u-BAAH-CHAN**). Here it is specifically described as "western" (C8: **OCH-K'IN**). In Maya iconography, the War Serpent is depicted as a Teotihuacan deity, closely associated with warfare and militarism. In its origin, it is perhaps an animate weapon of war, related to the Xiuhcoatl of late Postclassic Central Mexico. The name is reminiscent, too, of the warrior title *holkan*, "snake head," from colonial Yukatek sources. Finally, in the last glyphs at C9 and D9, we find a paring of **K'IN(ICH)** and **AK'AB(?)**, representing the solar god in both his day and night aspects. These could be the names of deities, but it is also possible they give closure to the text by replicating the paired heads in C1 (**AK'AB-K'IN**) at the very beginning of this second passage. Their intent is unclear, but one possibility is that they describe the violent events of the Entrada as lasting "a day and a night."

THE BACK TEXT: DEDICATION AND REMEMBRANCE

The inscription of the rear panel opens with a date record that shifts the time frame away from the Entrada episode that was highlighted on the front panel. The first glyph (E1)

Figure 63
The "Five ? Mountains" place-name on the Marcador, Blocks E4, G6. Drawings by David Stuart.

is simply 11 Ahau (**11-ta-AJAW**, *buluch ta ajaw*, "Eleven at Ajaw"), written alone with no corresponding month record. At first glance, this is highly ambiguous as a chronological statement, no more than a simple *tzolk'in* record. But the Distance Number in the following block (F1) immediately serves to clarify the relationship of 11 Ahau to the date recorded on the front panel (establishing beyond any doubt that one panel precedes the other). The interval is 3.13.12, which when subtracted from 8.17.1.14.12, reaches 8.16.17.9.0 11 Ahau 3 Uayeb. The arrangement here—a day followed by a temporal modifier in the form of a Distance Number—is highly unusual, but it is indicative of the idiosyncrasies we sometimes see in Early Classic inscriptions. The scribe opens Panel II with a simple date record, but quickly orients it to the history recounted this far on the other side, almost as a parenthetical statement ("Eleven at Ahau, [which] is 12 days, 13 score days and three years before . . ."). The event phrase that accompanies the 11 Ahau date comes at E2 and F2, reading **JOY-ti AJAW-wa**, for *joy(-aj) ti ajaw*, "he was encircled(?) in the rulership." The date of this accession is interesting for several reasons. First, it falls on 11 Ahau 3 Uayeb, within the five-day "month" at the end of the 365-day vague year. This would have been meaningful to any Mesoamerican day-keeper, and one can only presume that it was timed to coincide with the beginning of the new year only two days later, falling (if we represent it in Maya terms) on 8.16.17.9.2 13 Ik seating of Pop.

The name of Spearthrower Owl at E3 and F3 is partly phonetic: **ja-tz'o-ma**, discussed above, followed by an animate cauac head that must somehow stand for the bird. This is then followed by very revealing titles for the new ruler. One reads **5-?-WITZ**, "Five ? Mountains," repeated also slightly later in the text (Figure 63). The middle element of the place glyph, before **WITZ**, bears a strong resemblance to a sign known from later inscriptions as the syllable **no**, each showing small aligned U-shapes as a distinctive feature. Several writers (Fash, Tokovinine, and Fash 2009:218; Whittaker 2012) have interpreted this place name title as **HO'-NO(J)-WITZ**, "Five Great Mountains." Nielsen and Helmke (2008:474) offer a different view of the middle sign as **HO'-NOOM-WITZ**, "Five Small-bird Mountain." Both of these readings are unlikely in my view. As noted, the middle sign is attested as the syllable **no** in several environments, but its presence in the Marcador's place-name, between two clear logograms, strongly indicates that it ought to be a logogram as well (the supposed **-ma** is integral to the sign). This is what prompted their seeing the **no** syllabic sign as *NOJ, but this value is otherwise never attested in Maya script. It is likely significant that the **no** syllable is derived from a representation of cotton cloth, shown throughout Mesoamerican art as a white surface with small U-shaped elements regularly spaced (Stuart and Houston

Figure 64 Representations of cotton cloth and snow in highland Mexico: a) logogram **ICHKA-**, "cotton" in Nahuatl writing; b) logogram **MALAKA-**, "spindle whorl"; c) cotton spinner in the Codex Mendoza; and d) snow-capped mountains in the Codex Zouche-Nuttall. Drawings by David Stuart.

2018). We find such markings in depictions of cotton blossoms (*ichcatl*) and on white cloth or cotton spindle whorls (*malacatl*) in early colonial art and writing, and in the Postclassic codices from Central Mexico and Oaxaca (Figure 64a–c). In Mixtec codices, we find it atop mountains as a representation of snow, a substance evidently likened to bright white cloth (Caso 1984:1:pl. 20; Williams 2013:67) (Figure 64d). Such U-shaped elements are also attested in the Maya region as a marker for cotton, as seen on a large cloth bundle on a small panel fragment excavated from Temple XVII at Palenque (see Stuart 1998b:fig. 31). This same visual form is probably the motivation for the **no** syllable itself, given that the word for "cotton cloth" throughout lowland Maya languages is *nok'*. This is cognate to Common Mayan *nooq', "cotton (cloth or thread)." Elsewhere I and others have suggested "cotton cloth" as the visual origin of the **no** syllable, based on this noun root (Houston, Robertson, and Stuart 2000:328). The most logical possibility for a reading of the sign in the Marcador toponym could, therefore, be as a logogram (for that is what it must be) reading **NOK'**, "cotton cloth." The tentative result is **HO'-NOK'-WITZ**, "Five Cotton-cloth Mountains." I suspect that this name verbally describes snow-capped mountains, as we see depicted in later codices. "Snow" is hardly a common word in the languages of the lowland Maya, and it is reasonable to consider that Mayan speakers and scribes may have participated in this attested visual (and linguistic?) metaphor (Stuart and Houston 2018). If this is the case, the place-name can only refer to the central highlands of Mexico, where we find several snow-capped peaks (among them Orizaba, Popocatepetl, Itzaccihuatl, Nevado de Toluca, Cerro La Negra, and La Malinche).

Figure 65
Spearthrower Owl's title as "the fourth sequential ruler" (**4-TZ'AK-bu-AJAW**), from Tikal, Marcador, Block E5. Drawing by David Stuart.

The second of the titles for Spearthrower Owl, at E5, reads **4-TZAK-bu-AJAW**, or *(u) chan tz'akaab ajaw*, "the fourth sequential ruler" (Figure 65). This is a familiar "successor" title identical to what we see in many other Maya inscriptions, based on the derived form *tz'ak-Vb* (Riese 1984; Schele 1992; Stuart 2003). Its meaning here could not be any clearer: Spearthrower Owl, whoever he was and wherever he ruled, was the fourth of a set of rulers or kings.

The Marcador text panel continues on to its main point: its own erection and dedication many years later, on 8.18.17.14.9 12 Muluc 12 Kankin, or January 24, 414 CE. This date is recorded at F5–F6, with numerous calendrical elements: Glyphs G9 (E6a) and F (E6b), as well as a record of the moon age at fifteen days (F6a) within the third lunation of the "night jaguar" moon (F6b). The supplemental information continues with a Distance Number of 2.3.11 (F7), which expresses the interval of time between 12 Muluc and the upcoming *k'atun* ending 8.19.0.0.0 10 Ahau 13 Kayab. This appears at the end of F7 (**K'AL-ja-TUUN**, *k'ahlaj tuun*, "the stone was raised") and at G7 (**ti-10-AJAW**, *ti lajuun ajaw*, "on 10 Ajaw"). All of these calendrical "anchors" to the moon and to the looming *k'atun* ending serve to highlight the importance of the dedication date. The main point of the Marcador text, like many other monuments, is to mark its own creation and placement.

The verb is **tz'a-pa-ja**, *tz'ahpaj*, "it was erected" (Grube 1990) but the subject is not the standard one we would expect, *u lakamtuun*, "his/her stela." In its place we have a logogram that must in some manner refer to the Marcador itself. The hieroglyph is the very same "Storm God" insignia that we see in the frontal medallion or rosette at the top of the Marcador, clearly as some sort of self-reference, accounting for its use as a hieroglyph here. As mentioned, the motif appears in numerous contexts in Teotihuacan iconography, as Langley (1986) and von Winning (1987) show, but its nature is not clear from those occurrences. An abstracted visual connection to the Teotihuacan Storm God seems clear enough, but it is unclear if this association has much bearing on the significance of the sign as a logogram within a Maya text. What would be its actual reading, or at least its semantic frame of reference in relation to the Marcador? In this context, its significance as a "Tlaloc" image may not be so important. The prominent display of this very same image on circular shields in Teotihuacan art is probably more relevant in this context, given that the form of the Marcador may correspond to a dart or a spear with a shield that has been symbolically thrust into the earth as a sign of conquest. If this is correct, the "Storm God" hieroglyph might represent the same type of shield, and more generally the weaponry associated with its owner, Spearthrower Owl. This interpretation remains highly tentative, although more likely than the previous interpretations of the stone as a "war banner" or "ball court marker."

The owner of the Marcador, as we have seen, is Spearthrower Owl, written in two glyph blocks at the base of Columns E and F with the logographic forms: **JATZ'** and the full-figure raptorial bird. Here, **JATZ'** is also combined with the syllable **ma**, indicating the suffix we see in the more phonetically transparent version of the name up above at E3 and F3. **JATZ'-ma** here is an alternate spelling of **ja-tz'o-ma**, for the agentive noun *jatz'oom*, "striker." The bird now replaces the "cauac" head used in the previous mention of Spearthrower Owl and is identical to the bird we find in the two examples of the name on the front text panel.

As on the front, the final two columns of the rear text present several difficulties in interpretation. Much of this has to do with the ornate Early Classic paleography, as well as with the complex array of information evidently being conveyed. Within the structure of Columns G and H, we can identify several names, some historical and at least one other in reference to a supernatural being associated with Teotihuacan and its military ideology. Parsing the elements of this passage, while challenging, may provide a bit more historical context to the events of the Entrada and to the nature of Tikal's complex politics at the time the Marcador was erected.

The hieroglyph at G1 reads **U-KAB-ji-ya**, using a head variant of **ji** within which is infixed the sign **KAB**. The phrase is *u kab(i)jiiy*, familiar from many Maya inscriptions as a statement of oversight or responsibility, meaning "(the event is) the work of" or "(the event is) the responsibility of." It typically follows statements of ritual action, here the erection of Spearthrower Owl's monument. Normally we would expect a name to immediately follow, and at H1 we do seem to have some sort of personal reference or title, anchored to the title *ajaw* (**AJAW-wa**), "lord, noble." The first half of the block shows a very complex combination of elements, vaguely resembling some architectural form. All we can say with assurance is that the glyph remains undeciphered, and that it is a title of whoever oversaw the act of the Marcador's erection, probably not a personal name.

The pair of glyphs at G2 and H2 provide a key phrase **TZ'AK-bu U-KAB-ji**, repeating part of the *u kabij* phrase we just saw (the *-iiy* deictic suffix is now omitted). The combination introduces a new verbal phrase based on the derived form *tz'akbu* or *tz'akab*, "follows" or "continues" (Stuart 2011), and *u kabij* is its frequent subject. The sense of the fuller phrase *(u) tz'akbu u kabij* here is "(he) continues the work of . . . ," then specifying the name of a predecessor or ancestor. A number of parallel forms of the same expression appear in the inscription of Stela 31, as I have discussed in a previous study (Stuart 2011). Here we also find a third component of the phrase, at G3, read as **MAM**, the word for "grandfather, grandson," or more generically for "ancestor," which, in turn, precedes a personal name at H3. The sequence given in G2–G3 now can be seen as an example of the even more complete phrase reading *(u) tz'akbu u kabij (u) mam*, "he continues the work of his grandfather (or ancestor)." In other examples from Maya texts, this same statement is designed to link a contemporaneous event or ritual with a similar illustrious act of the past, overseen by "grandfathers." It is one rhetorical way of establishing a like-in-kind repetition of history, and here the clear implication is that the erection of the Marcador sculpture was a repetition or a "follow up" to a similar event in the historical past.

The predecessor's name at H3 is otherwise unknown in Tikal history. The main sign looks to be a canine head with a small mane, perhaps a fox-like animal, with a small glyphic prefix on its forehead resembling the syllable for **ch'a**. Without further examples of the name, it remains impossible to decipher, but a reading based on **CH'AMAK**, "gray fox," seems to be a good possibility (Davletshin and Houston 2021; Prager 2021). Here I will refer to him here as "Fox," only as a convenient term of reference. The **MAM** sign at G3 that precedes his name may indicate that Fox was the grandfather of the contemporaneous actor (given at H1) who oversaw the Marcador's placement, so it is reasonable to argue that he must have been a local person of authority at some point prior to 414. What follows at G4 and G5 supports such an interpretation, providing a revealing description of Fox as the *y-ajaw* (G4: **ya-AJAW-wa**) or "vassal of" Sihyaj K'ahk' (H4). It describes the same "vassal" relationship seen in other Early Classic inscriptions of the central Peten, where local Maya lords are said to be under the authority of Sihyaj K'ahk' or of Spearthrower Owl himself. The statement strongly suggests the Fox was a local Tikal lord who has gone unrecognized before now and who lived at a time before the time of the Marcador's dedication. I suggest that he played a significant role in Tikal's political scene for a short period around the time of Sihyaj K'ahk's arrival, for the glyph following the name of the foreigner is again the verb *huley* (G5: **HUL-ye**) followed by the place-name of Tikal, surely a repetition of the opening 378 event from the front text panel. This now is a subordinate clause, in the sense that Fox was "the vassal of Sihyaj K'ahk' (when) he had arrived at Tikal . . ." Such an interpretation fits the chronology implied by the *mam* reference, pertaining to a nobleman who lived in 378 and who was a grandfather of another person who oversaw the Marcador's erection thirty-six years later in 414. The implication here is that the arrival of Sihyaj K'ahk' saw the placement of a similar monument of conquest, overseen by Fox. It is plausible that the later lord even replicated an earlier action or ceremony through the dedication and erection of the Marcador itself.

The individual I call "Fox" may have been a local ruler of Tikal, an early ally of Sihyaj K'ahk', but he will remain an enigmatic figure without further information coming to light. It is probably significant that Spearthrower Owl's son, Yax Nun Ayiin, was also called a *y-ajaw* or vassal of Sihyaj K'ahk', as mentioned on Stelae 4 and 18. This occurred late in the year 379, when the likely infant-king was crowned under Sihyaj K'ahk', who then seems to have served as the regent on the Tikal throne. The situation suggests that Fox was a transitional figure in local politics, the vassal who bridged the short period between the defeat of Chak Tok' Ich'aak and the accession of Spearthrower Owl's child.

The arrival verb at G5 provides a pivot point in the Marcador's narrative, now coming full circle and linking the contemporaneous dedication rite to the transformational history it commemorates. The remaining glyphs of Columns G and H describe the events of 378 in new and important terms. The arrival verb at G5 is, as we have seen, followed by the toponym *mutu'l ch'een* (H5: **MUT-CH'EEN**), "Tikal cave" or "Tikal town." But this is just part of an intriguing sequence of locational references. At Block G6 is once again the place-name seen at E4, "The Five Snowy Mountains *Kaloomte'*." Here, however,

THE TIKAL MARCADOR | 85 |

the toponym is not embedded within an honorific title, but stands juxtaposed with the preceding Tikal emblem. Their grouping after *huley* may give us a direct record of the start and finish of Sihyaj K'ahk's journey. That is, Fox was "the vassal of Sihyaj K'ahk', when . . . had arrived to Tikal-town from the Five Snowy Mountains." Again, this closing section is meant to provide some historical context to the ancestral reference made earlier in the passage, thus establishing a narrative symmetry to the overall narrative.

The subjects of the arrival are specified in the remaining glyphs of Columns G and H, again providing some essential background for understanding the significance of the Marcador's dedication as a continuation of the events of 378. We find a second mention of the *Waxaklajuun Ubaah Chan*, the Teotihuacan War Serpent, who seems to have arrived alongside Sihyaj K'ahk', perhaps as a divine symbol of military might. An alternate view, closely related, would see the "Eighteen Heads of the Snake" reference as a collective term for an armed force, a group of warriors who are the "snake heads." This is highly reminiscent of the term *holkan*, literally meaning "snake's head," used at the time of the conquest as a title for elite soldiers. It is interesting to note that the sign for **CHAN**, "snake," here takes the form of a Teotihuacan-style snake, resembling the forms of Xiuhcoatl from much later Postclassic iconography.

Next in the sequence of personal references comes something a bit more transparent in Block H7, **AL-K'UH-IXIK-?**. I see this as composed of two related terms, *'al*, "child of a woman," and the female honorific term *k'uh(ul) 'ixik*, "holy woman." The following glyph at G8 is a title or honorific term closely related to women, representing the deity GI and his mythical relationship to solar rebirth. It appears to be closely linked to the status of motherhood, as shown by its prominent usage in parentage statements, as for example on Stela 31, as the main title of the mother of Sihyaj Chan K'awiil. It also introduces the name of Lady Sak K'uk', the mother of K'inich Janab Pakal, on the Oval Palace Tablet of Palenque. Its appearance on the Marcador would seem to be another such association between a mother and child, given the accompanying mention of *'al*, "child of a woman."

The identity of this woman is unclear, and no personal name appears with this title. But the implications of the reference are especially important, and they agree with another key detail of the larger Entrada story. We will recall that the year following the arrival of Sihyaj K'ahk' saw the inauguration of Yax Nun Ayiin, the son of Spearthrower Owl, as Tikal ruler. Several lines of evidence strongly point to his being a young child or even an infant at the time of his crowning, when Sihyaj K'ahk' served as regent, the representative of the Teotihuacan ruler. The child-king would have arrived at Tikal only a short time earlier, as indicated by the likely reference to Yax Nun Ayiin's departure from Teotihuacan on one of the inscribed bones from Burial 116, with the date 8.17.2.3.16 4 Cib 14 Ceh, or December 26, 378, nearly a year after the Entrada event (see Figure 31). If this is the case, then it is natural to assume that the child journeyed to the Maya area in the close company of his mother, a spouse or consort of Spearthrower Owl. This would account for their joint "arrival" cited on the rear panel of the Marcador, the child (*'al*) and the mother (*k'uhul ixik*) arriving alongside other military representatives (*waxaklajuun ubaah chan*). Again, to step back from the details for a moment, it is important to note that all of these mentions come as a way to contextualize the dedication of the Marcador stone itself—that it was a like-in-kind event to a similar dedication that occurred around the time of the Entrada, or more precisely when the mother and child arrived on the scene some months later.

The very last glyphs of the Marcador text panel are especially difficult to read. We may have another verb at G9, and multiple references to the term "strike" (**JATZ'**) at H8 and H9. I suspect that these include other personal references of some type, citing others who arrived in the retinue alongside the warriors, the mother, and the child.

The Marcador emerges from these myriad epigraphic details as a memorial of conquest. It also stands as a document attesting to Tikal's close political relationship with Teotihuacan in the late fourth and early fifth centuries CE. The inscription is clear in describing the arrival of 378 as a military defeat (*och ch'een*), and the monument itself was attributed, or commemorated, the ruler we call Spearthrower Owl. Although it has long been described as a "ball court marker" or alternatively as a "battle standard," the form of the sculpture is likely that of a spear or dart thrust into the ground, also with a circular shield attached to its upper section. The form, therefore, may echo a quintessential symbol of war and conquest in Mesoamerica—what the Maya called *took' pakal*, "knife-and-shield," and what the Nahua-speaking peoples of Postclassic Central Mexico called *mitl chimalli*, "arrow-and-shield." This emblematic symbol of conquest is directly and prominently attributed to Spearthrower Owl, whose emblematic hieroglyph is featured on the rosette-like disc atop the monument. Taken together, the evidence points to the possibility that the Marcador was conceived as an iconic representation and testament to the military takeover of Tikal in 378 by Spearthrower Owl and his agent (his "hands") Sihyaj K'ahk'. Its dedication in 414 is cited as a renewal project, perhaps the reconception of some earlier monument erected closer to the time of the Entrada. The monument's own termination and caching around 450 CE, after the turn of the *bak'tun* at 9.0.0.0.0, may represent another significant cultural-historical episode, when ties to Central Mexico were weakened and Tikal's dynasty exerted its independence. As we will discuss in more detail, it is possible that Spearthrower Owl's death in 439, after sixty-five years on the throne, was related to this cultural and political break.

These interpretations refine earlier assessments of the Marcador and its significance and, more importantly, bring the nature of Teotihuacan-Maya interactions into clearer historical context. Proskouriakoff was unable to bring the Marcador into her own prescient discussions on Early Classic history, as it was discovered only a short time before her death in 1986. However, the monument did feature heavily in Schele and Freidel's view that it was a symbolic war banner of a far more localized event, celebrating the defeat of Uaxactun at the hands of Tikal. Their interpretation gave a novel spin to Proskouriakoff's earlier suggestion that the conflict was essentially local in character, with Uaxactun leading a war against Tikal's king, perhaps with the aid of "foreigners as mercenaries" (Proskouriakoff 1993:9). Writing within a decade of its discovery, Schele and Freidel were adamant that the Marcador and other Tikal inscriptions were examples of Mexican imagery used by the Maya for Maya purposes: "this international symbolism, grafted onto orthodox Maya practices, functioned as part of the propaganda that enabled Smoking Frog [Sihyaj K'ahk'] to be installed as usurper king at Uaxactun" (Schele and Freidel 1993:149). My own foray into these discussions came slightly later (Stuart 2000) and offered a new assessment of much of the same data, using the Marcador as a focal point for understanding the roles of Sihyaj K'ahk' and Spearthrower Owl. Elements of earlier interpretations remain true, especially Proskouriakoff's essential point that the 11 Eb episode was an "arrival of strangers." The Marcador helps us to see that this was a violent and disruptive event.

The other revealing titular phrase on the Marcador is a numbered successor title reading *chan tz'akab ajaw*, "the four(th) sequential ruler" (**4-TZ'AK-bu-AJAW**). Such titles are common in Maya historical texts where the number varies according to a ruler's position in a particular dynastic sequence (Riese 1984; Schele 1986b). At Tikal, Spearthrower Owl's own grandson, Sihyaj Chan K'awiil, is known to be "the sixteenth successor" within Tikal's local sequence of kings. Spearthrower Owl's designation as "fourth" must involve an entirely separate ruler count. We have no history of those earlier figures or of the lengths of their reigns, but considering Spearthrower Owl's accession date of 374, we might conclude that the sequence began with a founder who would have been established, by the roughest of measures, sometime around 300 CE. Nielsen and Helmke (2008) make a similar observation about the calculation of these previous reigns. The presence of the successor title indicates that, at least from the perspective of an Early Classic Maya scribe, Spearthrower Owl was the participant in a "dynastic" structure of some sort, or at least the fourth member of a sequence of kings established not long before his crowning. It is tempting to see the changes between the Late Tlamimilolpa and Early Xolalpan phases at Teotihuacan as related to this political transformation. The discernable differences between the Tlamimilolpa and Xolalpan phases, including increased "central authority" and its expansionistic presence in Mesoamerica, might be associated with some new political arrangement.

NOTES

1 *Quauhololli* was the Nahuatl term for a wooden mace-like weapon, usually with a rounded ball at the top of a handle (Hassig 1988:85). Images of such weapons are sparse, making it difficult to draw a direct parallel to the form of the weapon depicted on the Marcador.

2 In her important study of Maya war iconography, Bassie-Sweet (2019:171–176) independently reached a similar interpretation of the Marcador sculpture, making the case that it represents a weapon and a shield. My own views on the Marcador's form were first presented on October 28, 2019, at a public lecture at the Mesoamerican Colloquium Series at the University of Texas at Austin. There I referred to Eagle Striker (Spearthrower Owl) as "Owl Striker," as I was still in the process of refining the translation of the name.

3 A close parallel to this curious lunar statement is on Stela 15 at Nimli Punit, Belize, where a similar two-handed sign appears in the Lunar Series associated with 9.14.10.0.0 5 Ahau 3 Mac. The "hand" signs look similar to the combination we find at Tikal, with the addition of a "percentage" design on the inner **K'AB**(?) hand, perhaps alluding to the death-related head we find in B6 on the Marcador text. On the Nimli Punit stela, it comes after an apparent *huliiy* verb prefixed by "thirteen (days)." This would suggest that the hand-in-hand combination refers to the starting point of the lunar day count—i.e., the new moon thirteen days prior to the Period Ending. Palenque's Temple of the Inscriptions also makes use of a similar phrase, although it does not appear as part of a formal Lunar Series. Near the very end of that very long text, the inscription features the death of K'inich Janab Pakal and uses the day 4 Oc (9.12.11.4.10 4 Oc 3 Ch'en) as an anchor for a Distance Number of 1.8 (twenty-eight days), leading to the ruler's death date. The **AL-K'AB**(?) glyph appears there with the number three as coefficient—an intriguing feature that suggested to Linda Schele that it was simply a unique variant of the month Ch'en (personal communication, 1977). This remains a possibility, but it is also interesting that it again precedes a head with death features (and a lunar crescent postfix?), repeating the pattern seen on A6–B6 of the Marcador text. Once more we have a connection to twenty-eight days, repeating the lunar age recorded on the Marcador in Block B4. It is probably no coincidence that 9.12.11.4.10 occurred on or very near the new moon as well, and on the Palenque text it may have worked simply to state that Pakal's demise came nearly a lunar month after its appearance, a noteworthy astronomical association. In any event, the connections of the "two hands" phrase with the lunar calendar and new moons seem clear, even if its precise function and meaning remain elusive. It may be that the mention of "finger," *y-alk'ab'*, relates to the use of a finger logogram as the numeral one in some rare instances.

4 EAGLES AND EMBLEMS

IN THIS CHAPTER, I EXPAND ON THE IDEA THAT SPEARTHROWER OWL'S ("Eagle Striker's") personal name appears well beyond the historical inscriptions and artworks of the central Peten, occurring with surprising frequency in the Teotihuacan-inspired iconography of other Maya centers in the Late Classic period. The forms and functions of these glyphs and icons overlap considerably with the hieroglyphic names we have discussed in Maya texts, and also rely on the distinctive visual genre of "emblematic writing" that characterized the script of Teotihuacan (Taube 2000, 2011). Or, to state it more precisely, these emblematic or iconic versions reflect Teotihuacan modes of visual communication as presented through a Maya lens, lending them a distinctive, hybrid appearance that has long hindered their investigation. As we have seen at Tikal, retrospective mentions of Spearthrower Owl were made decades and even centuries after the Entrada, in Late Classic contexts, where they are even further removed from the modes and practices of Teotihuacan writing. Their persistence in Maya art, if they are indeed personal references, highlights the importance of the long-deceased Teotihuacan ruler and his profound influence on history.

These "iconic hieroglyphs" occur in headdresses, on shields, and on other insignia that have long been interpreted as elements of what Schele once called the "Tlaloc-Venus War Complex," an amalgam of visual forms thought to exemplify Maya appropriations of Teotihuacan iconography, specifically related to "Venus-regulated warfare" (Schele and Mathews 1998:416; Schele and Miller 1986:213). My discussion here builds on many of the same visual patterns but downplays those earlier astronomical interpretations, preferring to see them in a more historical light given what we now know about the significance of Spearthrower Owl and his allies. The widespread presence of Teotihuacan costume and insignia in Maya art began during the era of his rule and personal influence, in examples we have already discussed at Tikal and elsewhere. Much of the emphasis on eagles, "goggles," darts and obsidian blades of "Tlaloc-Venus War" imagery are, I suspect, direct iconographic allusions to the personal name of this foreign ruler. The question to consider here is whether the "Tlaloc-Venus War Complex" discussed by Schele, Stone (1989), and others in the monuments of Piedras Negras, Palenque, Copan, and elsewhere, has a direct link to early historical references to Spearthrower Owl and to the inflection points of Early Classic history that surrounded the Entrada.

My own leanings in this regard are an outgrowth of earlier research on the art and iconography of Copan, with its repetitious mentions of its distant dynastic founder, K'inich Yax K'uk' Mo', who had his own strong ties to Teotihuacan (Fash and Fash 2000; Sharer 2003, 2004; Stuart 2000). Here was a specific individual of the Early Classic period, who was mentioned and depicted repeatedly in later Copan monuments, up to the very last additions to Copan's acropolis. The Teotihuacan-inspired motifs and messages of late Copan were absorbed into these constant ancestral references, all alluding to the era of the founder and to Teotihuacan itself, the place where K'inich Yax K'uk' Mo' assumed his authority and "took the *k'awiil*," as stated on Altar Q (Stuart 2000). Copan's Temple XXVI, with its imposing Hieroglyphic Stairway, was perhaps a more general recollection of a "foreign past" (Stuart 2005a). But even there I suspect that the uses of a "neo-Teotihuacan" style were far more specific in their scope. As I hope to show here, they can be seen as allusions to the actors and events of Early Classic history and to the ruler who was responsible for the strongest period of interaction and political influence in the late fourth and early fifth centuries. It is important to note that K'inich Yax K'uk' Mo's accession and visitation to the Mexican Highlands occurred in 426 CE, within the documented lifetime of Spearthrower Owl. Other sites and dynasties make ample use of Teotihuacan militarism for their own ideological purposes, yet we should keep in mind the possibility that many are rooted in Spearthrower Owl himself and in his status as a great conqueror in the Maya world.

EMBLEMS AND ICONS

In a series of important works on the writing and communication of Teotihuacan, Karl Taube presented numerous examples of what he called "emblematic" writing at that site (Taube 2000, 2002, 2011) (Figure 66). These are a special subset within the larger Teotihuacan writing system, making use of combinations of large, visually complex elements, in contrast to the simpler-looking forms we find, for example, in the assorted painted glyphs on the floor of La Ventilla (Nielsen and Helmke 2011). Teotihuacan's emblematic writing tends to occur in connection with painted figures, no doubt as proper names of people and places. They would seem to represent a level of visual complexity at one end of a sliding scale, similar perhaps to the range of variation we see at work within the hieroglyphic system of the Maya. Some examples of a hieroglyph can be simple in their presentation while others are exceedingly creative and visually ornate. I suspect that this scalability of complexity was a feature common to all Mesoamerican writing systems and fundamental to their close conceptual relationship to what we often tend to call iconography.

The writing of Teotihuacan still remains difficult to decipher in a systematic way, but it is probably safe to assume that many of its signs are logograms, simply based on their behavior and visual arrangements. I do not necessarily see Teotihuacan script as being Nahuatl, despite some claims made to the contrary (Whittaker 2021:174–193). The Nahuatl attribution first gained some attention in the 1990s, in the wake of my

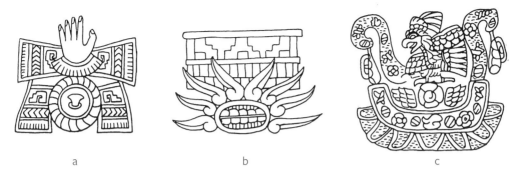

Figure 66 Examples of "emblematic" hieroglyphs in Teotihuacan writing (from Taube 2000:figs. 20f, 20g, 17d). Drawings by Karl Taube.

tentative suggestion of a reading of the glyph **ko-sa-ka**-THRONE on Stela 31 at Tikal, above a portrait of Yax Nun Ayiin (see, for example, Wichmann 2010:439). This syllabic sequence seemed strongly reminiscent of the Nahuatl noun *cozca(tl)*, "jewel," used as a modifier for another sign that resembled an *icpalli* throne, as depicted in Central Mexican manuscripts. However, this particular interpretation now seems unlikely, with the supposed "throne" glyph instead more recognizable as an early variant of a Maya logogram read as **PAS**, "open" (the sign represents a hand opening a woven basket). There is no direct evidence for Nahuatl terms in Early Classic Maya writing, or for any words in a non-Mayan language for that matter. In my view, the question of what language was spoken or written at Teotihuacan remains unresolved, although a few promising options are on the table (see Helmke and Nielsen 2021).

Many emblematic glyphs of the Teotihuacan or neo-Teotihuacan tradition are well integrated into the wider iconographic system, making them nearly indistinguishable from "iconography" and difficult to parse according to our own familiar categories. The stucco panel from the Margarita structure at Copan provides a good example with which to explore these melding notions of text and image (Figure 67a). The two entwined birds and their associated motifs form a complex emblem that is, in essence, the name hieroglyph of K'inich Yax K'uk' Mo', the dynastic founder of Copan. The two solar deities (**K'IN[ICH]**) emerge from the open beaks of birds, each with **YAX** elements atop its head (this is the common placement of **YAX** in other contexts). One bird is a quetzal (**K'UK'**), the other a macaw (**MO'**), providing all of the components of the name, **K'IN(ICH)-YAX-K'UK'-MO'**. Taube (2000:28–29) connected this elaborated hieroglyph to the emblematic tradition of writing from Teotihuacan, suggesting that it may have been inspired by the founder's historical connections to Central Mexico. The name of the king is repeated in the complex designs that flank the doorway of the later temple known as Rosalila, built over the Margarita structure and ultimately over the tomb of the founder (Figure 67b). Here the design is different, and it would not easily be considered "writing" on first sight. A frontally presented quetzal (**K'UK'**) once again has the solar god (**K'IN[ICH]**) emerging from its beak. The bird is once more shown in full-figure, with large flanking serpent-wings. The animate forms of

Figure 67
Emblematic name glyphs of Copan's founder, K'inich Yax K'uk' Mo': a) Margarita structure of Copan; and b) Rosalila structure of Copan. Drawing by Lucia Henderson (a); and drawing by David Stuart (b).

the wings include a macaw's beak, integrated to the upper maw of the serpent. This is the hieroglyphic sign that can routinely serve as a graphic abbreviation of the macaw's head, **MO'** (Stuart 2005b:150). Again, all of the written elements are provided, creating an especially elaborate hieroglyphic form isolated from any textual setting. This is a decidedly Maya design, however, and suggests that some degree of emblematic writing existed in early Maya visual communication as well. The final iteration of Temple XVI showed yet another "hieroglyph" of the founder on its exterior, presented as a central image on the middle outset platform of the central stairway (see Figure 57b). I suggest that all three iconic images from Margarita, Rosalila, and final-phase Temple XVI were functionally equivalent, marking the building with the iconic name of the heroic ancestor. In this last iteration, the solar god assumes a full bodily form, framed by a solar cartouche (**K'IN**) in the form of a rectangular Teotihuacan-style war shield (Fash 2011:65). The solar god's headdress shows a bird that is a combination of a quetzal and a macaw, replicating in three dimensions a form that is otherwise found in conventional Maya writing from the Early Classic period. This then is also a "hieroglyph" of sorts, integrated into the thematic messaging of the temple overall, depicting the founder of Copan as a deceased warrior, and in effect *as* his own name.

These compositions illustrate some of the creative aspects of Maya emblematic writing, as well as the challenges in any attempt to readily distinguish them from what we would otherwise call iconographic forms (the war shield of the last example is not a glyph, yet it is fused with the solar cartouche of **K'IN**, for the name). But such complexity is also rare. Here it is possible that they are even consciously evocative of the system of emblematic script that Taube (2000) described for Teotihuacan, given the long-lasting meanings of this evolving temple as well as the strong historical ties of Copan's founder to Teotihuacan and specifically to Spearthrower Owl (Fash 2011:35–47; Stuart 2005a). The layered temples not only prominently displayed a visual composition of the royal name but did so perhaps within a Teotihuacan mode of presentation. As we will see, Temple XXVI does much the same thing, with a different thematic emphasis.

The Margarita name panel likely repeated on either side of the substructure's staircase (only one was excavated) and points to the existence of earlier uses of iconic or emblematic script in the Maya Lowlands. Their location and framing elements leave no doubt that they occupy the place where we normally see three-dimensional masks, often of enormous size in Preclassic architecture. These modeled faces and heads can sometimes assume very complex forms, and they have been traced back to Middle Formative times as well in the central Maya Lowlands. Some even have clear hieroglyphic elements integrated within their designs. It is possible that many of these designs were names as well, "written" in three dimensions on architecture as a means of labeling their associated identities.

The most frequent appearance of such hieroglyphic forms is on headdresses or integrated with headgear—again connected to the importance of visual names (Kelley 1982). As I have shown in several examples, headdresses routinely display hieroglyphic names or even assume the form of hieroglyphic names. We see this especially well-developed in Early Classic Maya art, at Kaminaljuyu and throughout the Peten. The representation of Yax Nun Ayiin's name as the headdress of the solar deity on Tikal's Stela 31 is an excellent example (see Figure 33), and several others can be mentioned, ranging from the monuments at Naranjo to the ancestral portraits within Pakal's tomb at Palenque.

To these we can also add the portrait on the facade of Tikal's Structure 5D-57, showing a warrior with a distinctive bird headdress (see Figure 46). This we understand to be a portrait of the Late Classic ruler Jasaw Chan K'awiil, shown several days after the defeat of the Kanul ruler Yuknoom Yich'aak K'ahk', holding a prominent captive from that conflict (Schele and Freidel 1993:205–206). As described earlier, his imposing headdress shows an eagle or raptorial bird in flight, its wings extended upward and with its tail feathers morphed visually into the representation of the end of a Teotihuacan-style dart. The idea here is that it penetrates the body of the bird, indicated also by a Teotihuacan-style "bleeding heart" glyph at the very center of the owl's chest, directly above the ruler's face. This form is clearly a Maya version of the Teotihuacan "blood" and "heart" signs, elaborated in Maya fashion (Figure 69).

The "blood" or "heart" element indicates a wound to the stricken eagle or owl, pierced in its chest. Here we should naturally see a connection to the more emblematic name hieroglyphs of Spearthrower Owl. It was Schele who first established the connection between this particular neo-Teotihuacan headdress at Tikal and the "owls" and raptorial birds seen in Early Classic depictions, including those in the personal

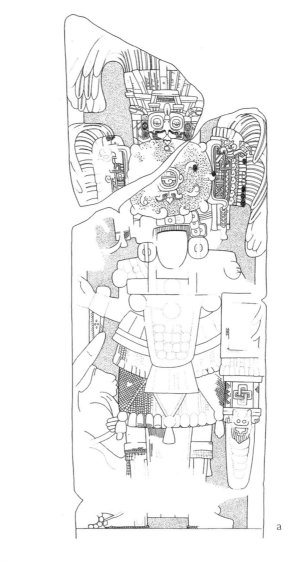

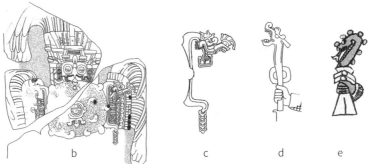

Figure 68 Piedras Negras, Stela 9, and its headdress: a) overall view (after Stuart and Graham 2004:51); b) detail of headdress; c) War Serpent atlatl; d) War Serpent atlatl on Bonampak, Stela 2; and e) serpent atlatl from a portrait of Huitzilopochtli in the Codex Borbonicus. © President and Fellows of Harvard College, Peabody Museum of Archaeology and Ethnology.

name we have discussed at length. Indeed, many of the observations that follow in this chapter build upon that key linkage (Grube and Schele 1994; Schele and Freidel 1993:205; Schele and Grube 1994). In this light, we can see the headdress on the facade of Structure 5D-57 as a name label for the warrior Jasaw Chan K'awiil, showing him *as* Spearthrower Owl, conflating their historical identities and tapping into Tikal's long historical legacy of conquest. And as we have already seen, the closely related narrative of Temple I at Tikal highlights the defeat of the Kanul ruler in 695, as well as Jasaw Chan K'awiil's own parallel identity as an embodiment of Teotihuacan warfare and its ideology (Schele and Freidel 1993:209). The war was precisely 260 years (thirteen *k'atuns*) after the death of Spearthrower Owl, and the facade portrait may make another visual allusion to this key historical connection, to the long-deceased ruler of Teotihuacan as an idealized conqueror par excellence, worthy of remembrance and embodiment. What Schele and others once saw as a compelling example of "Venus-Tlaloc" iconography related to Teotihuacan warfare emerges, in this instance at least, as a more personal connection between two rulers distant in time and place yet linked by family and the sacred duties of war.

Very similar eagle or owl headdresses regularly appear in Late Classic Maya art outside of Tikal, as part of the larger complex of Teotihuacan war imagery and iconography. Many such references abound at Piedras Negras, where several monuments are well-known for their strong visual connections to Teotihuacan and militaristic iconography (Stone 1989). Stela 9 (Figure 68a) shows a warrior with a distinctive "balloon" headdress that represents the body of a raptorial bird shown frontally. Its wings are to either side, animated in the form of curved rattlesnakes that seem closely related to the Teotihuacan War Serpent. These clearly replicate the forms of serpent atlatls shown in Mesoamerican art (Figure 68c–e), including the Xiuhcoatl spearthrowers wielded by Huitzilopochtli in Late Postclassic sources (Bassie-Sweet 2021; Stone 1989; Taube 1992b). We can recall that this weapon was used as a means of writing **JATZ'** ("strike") in the more conventional names of Spearthrower Owl. The juxtaposition of a War Serpent atlatl and the raptorial bird, therefore, offers an unmistakable visual parallel to the personal name. The bird's head is shown frontally with goggles over its eyes, and its tail forms the upper feathered array of the headdress. As on the Tikal facade, the eagle's beak shows a heart sign dangling from the very tip—a small detail repeated in the version of Spearthrower Owl's name as presented on the front of Stela 31 (see Figures 37g and 41a). In the center of the bird's chest, we once more find the Teotihuacan "bleeding heart" sign, indicating a wound. Considering all of these elements, it is difficult not to link this headdress form to Spearthrower Owl's personal name.

The ornate form of the "heart" or "blood" sign in the Stela 9 (Figure 69a) headdress is worthy of a few more comments. It is identical to hearts shown in Teotihuacan art and writing as well as in the Late Classic writing system at Cacaxtla and elsewhere (Helmke and Nielsen 2011) (Figure 69b–c). These and other examples display a Maya sign in their interior that I have previously identified as the syllable **pu,** or as the logogram for **PUH**, "cattail, bulrush," with clear visual connections to depictions of reeds or bulrushes in Maya art (Stuart 2000; Taube 1992b). Why this would be integrated with a representation of a heart or a bloody wound is difficult to know,

EAGLES AND EMBLEMS | 97 |

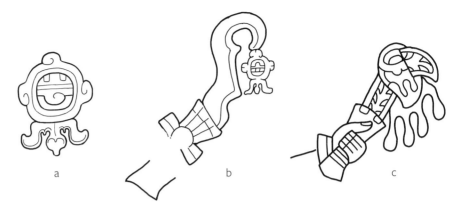

Figure 69 The neo-Teotihuacan "heart" sign: a) detail of headdress from Piedras Negras, Stela 9; b) obsidian blade with heart, from Acanceh facade; and c) Teotihuacan heart on obsidian knife from the Atetelco murals. Drawings by David Stuart.

but one possible explanation comes from an alternate meaning of the root *puh* in lowland Mayan languages. In Yukatekan and Ch'olan, the noun *puh* means "pus," or that which oozes from a wound (*materia de llaga o postema*). In Yukatek, *u puhil kinil* is a "wound" (*herida con materia*) (Barrera Vásquez 1980:671). Alternatively, this visual connection also brings to mind the widespread word in lowland Mayan languages for "heart," *puksik'al*, a loan from Totonacan languages. Whatever the case, it seems possible that on Stela 9, and in related images, the **pu** sign as a Teotihuacan-style "heart" glyph, helping to convey the representation of a stricken, wounded bird with blood or a heart on its breast.

Other monuments from Piedras Negras include rectangular shields emblazoned with similar eagles or owls, some shown frontally (Figure 70). These also include variants of the Teotihuacan "blood" signs as circular elements over the chest, again with the sign **PUH** emphasized. One such shield from Stela 7 (Figure 70b) shows a beak ending with a "blood" or "heart" sign, while other shields show a very strong likeness to the "owl and weapons" hieroglyphs discussed earlier (Langley 2002:294; Stuart 2000; Taube 2002; von Winning 1948). There can be little doubt that all of these images of "bloodied birds" at Tikal and Piedras Negras are related. Whether we can analyze them all as emblematic hieroglyphic names for Spearthrower Owl is open to question, but I am inclined to believe they are, emblazoned on shields and headdresses as personalized references to a ruler of Teotihuacan, not as some more general militaristic symbol.[1]

The most elaborate rectangular shield is found at Piedras Negras, Stela 34 (see Figure 70e). Rather than displaying an eagle or bird, it shows a full-length frontal portrait of a standing Teotihuacan warrior. The shield's overall form and presentation resembles the mosaic depiction of a rectangular shield from Copan, which once adorned the staircase of Temple XVI, where it framed the standing iconographic image of Copan's ancestral founder, K'inich Yax K'uk' Mo' (see Figure 57b). The Stela 34 shield also can be taken as a Late Classic version of the rectangular shield held by Yax Nun Ayiin on Stela 31 of Tikal, with its frontal portrait of a Teotihuacan ruler or warrior with

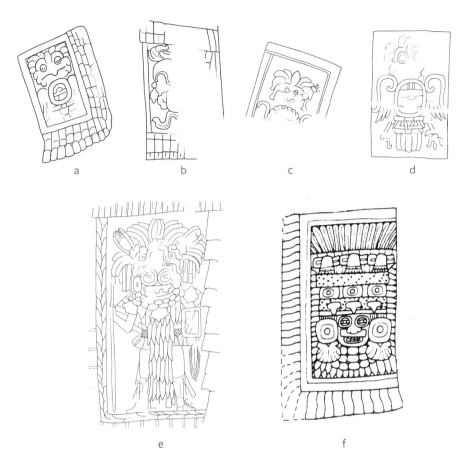

Figure 70 Rectangular shields showing raptorial birds and related hieroglyphic elements: a) Piedras Negras, Panel 2; b) Stela 7; c) Stela 26; d) Stela 32; e) Stela 34; and f) comparable shield from Tikal, Stela 31. Drawings by David Stuart (a–e) and William R. Coe, from Jones and Satterthwaite 1982:fig. 52 (f).

a tassel headdress (Figure 70f). Given the parallels in image and iconography among all of these shields, I suspect the relatively early example from Stela 31 might be seen as a near-contemporaneous image of Spearthrower Owl himself, replicating his presentation on Stela 32 of Tikal. All the identifications of the shields as personalized symbols are speculative, to be sure, but a logical thread unites them, traceable to the hieroglyphic names of Spearthrower Owl.

Why would he be represented at all at Piedras Negras? Although we have no extant references to Spearthrower Owl in the site's historical inscriptions, and nearly all of the texts are Late Classic, it nonetheless is clear that this kingdom had its own strong ties to Teotihuacan, both historically and ideologically. The closest evidence of this comes from Panel 12, dedicated in 514, which depicts a ruler shown in Teotihuacan-style regalia, wearing a distinctive back-fan (Figure 71). The accompanying inscription cites a local ruler as the *y-ajaw ochk'in kaloomte'*, "vassal of the west *kaloomte'*," precisely in the same way that we have seen in other texts, in relation to either Sihyaj K'ahk' or Spearthrower Owl.

EAGLES AND EMBLEMS | 99

Figure 71 Piedras Negras, Panel 12. Photograph by David Stuart.

A similar hierarchical relationship appears in the history recited on the later Panel 2 of Piedras Negras, recounting aspects of the same political interactions from Early Classic history. There we read that in 510, the local lord "receives his helmet" in a ceremony overseen by a foreign actor possibly named Tajoom Uk'ab Tuun, a "west *kaloomte*'" with evident Teotihuacan associations (Martin and Grube 2008; O'Neil 2012:160) (Figure 72). This is probably the same overlord who is cited on Panel 12. He is surely the same person named on an inscribed wooden box from the Piedras Negras region (Anaya H., Mathews, and Guenter 2003). There, Tajoom Uk'ab Tuun is named and also bears the title *winte'naah ajaw*, "lord of *winte'naah*," a building or place I have previously shown to be associated with Teotihuacan history and iconography (Stuart 2000). These citations of a foreign *ochk'in kaloomte'* at Piedras Negras recall patterns we find with Spearthrower Owl, even though they date to over a century later. They may well refer to a successor or to some other foreign representative, or even to a ruler of Teotihuacan again with a Mayan name. If nothing else, this evidence raises the intriguing possibility, if not likelihood, that Teotihuacan was still actively involved in the complex power plays among some Classic Maya kingdoms as late as the early sixth century. By this time, the regional focus may have been more on their lower Usumacinta region rather than the central Peten. Spearthrower Owl's deeper and more marked history in the Maya region during the fourth and fifth centuries may have helped set the stage for these slightly later historical allusions to Teotihuacan in the inscriptions of Piedras Negras. The iconography of Spearthrower Owl seems quite personal and explicit, even if the inscriptions mention other actors and time frames. The backdrop of Teotihuacan's longer-term historical influence in the Peten would go far toward explaining the strong desire by Piedras Negras (and other Maya kingdoms) to evoke ancient Teotihuacan's military might (O'Neil 2012:161).

Returning to the rectangular shields of Piedras Negras, we see how they are not simply representations of eagles or owls but also include distinctive "blood" or "heart"

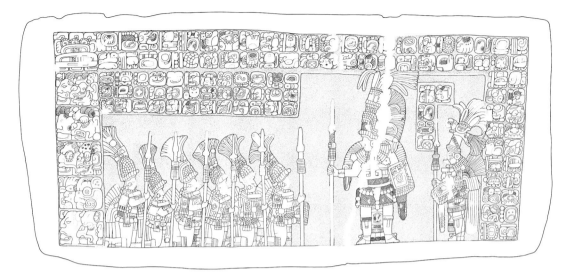

Figure 72 Piedras Negras, Panel 2. Drawing by David Stuart.

elements over the birds' breasts. In one example from Stela 26, a "dart" element can be seen piercing the bird, which would explain the presence of the "blood" or "heart" element—a depiction of a wounded raptorial bird that I argue is the full pictorial representation of the name "Eagle Striker" or Spearthrower Owl (Figure 70c). These are equivalent to the warrior headdresses on Piedras Negras, Stela 9, and on the Tikal facade that we have discussed, providing a good link to the personal name glyphs we can trace in the inscriptions of Tikal and elsewhere.

We also find a related design at Palenque, often in a much more simplified form decorating the so-called incense bags held by court attendants on the platform of Temple XIX (Stuart 2005b) (Figure 73). These are probably hieroglyphs, an interpretation supported by their alternation with more conventional Ahau date glyphs that we find on similar bags at Piedras Negras (examples appear on Stelae 11, 13, and 15). On the small Palenque bags, the Teotihuacan-style glyph appears to be the distinctive trefoil "blood" sign with a piercing instrument set at an angle. This bears a striking resemblance to examples of pierced hearts in Teotihuacan art, some of which seem to have existed as stand-alone hieroglyphs, attested in both Teotihuacan and Maya art (Figures 74 and 75). As a possible reduced composition, this also bears some structural resemblance to the image of the frontal bird on the shield of Piedras Negras, Stela 26, with a large "blood" sign at its breast and an angled dart piercing at its upper right (see Figure 70c).

Variant forms on other incense bags from the Temple XIX relief add yet another detail—a circular or goggled eye with a heavy eyelash (Figure 75a). This includes the "dripping blood" element below, and it looks to be an elaboration on the same theme. It is possible that the circular eye is a much-reduced pars pro toto visual reference to the eagle or owl. This is suggested by a far more elaborate version of the same motif, painted on the vessel K8777, a vase possibly from El Peru (Waka') (Figure 75b). Here we see the addition of a second eye, giving the effect of a frontal face with the

EAGLES AND EMBLEMS | 101

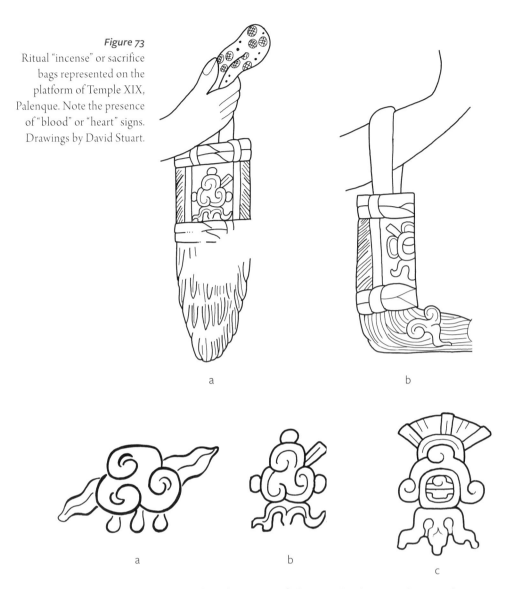

Figure 73
Ritual "incense" or sacrifice bags represented on the platform of Temple XIX, Palenque. Note the presence of "blood" or "heart" signs. Drawings by David Stuart.

Figure 74 Pierced "heart" or "blood" elements: a) design on bowl excavated at La Sufricaya, Guatemala; b) hieroglyph on Temple XIX bag; and c) detail of costume on Cancuen, Stela 2. Drawings by David Stuart.

"dripping blood" element now resembling a fanged mouth. Its Tlaloc-like appearance adds an additional layer to the design's many Teotihuacan references. The "proboscis" of this butterfly-like face also resembles the curved end of an atlatl, repeating a visual metaphor we see elsewhere that equates the bird's beak or proboscis with an obsidian blade. Another vase published by Robicsek and Hales (1981:table 12i) shows a more naturalistic image of a bird with a distinctive eye above the same trilobed "blood" element (Figure 75c). These comparisons provide a good example of how Maya artisans employed a sliding scale of complexity in the representation of a standardized motif or icon, some full and transparent, others highly abstracted and abbreviated. While

Figure 75 "Eyes with blood" designs and their elaborations: a) ritual bag from Temple XIX at Palenque; b) elaborated form on vessel K8777; and c) full bird with blood sign on codex-style vessel. Drawings by David Stuart.

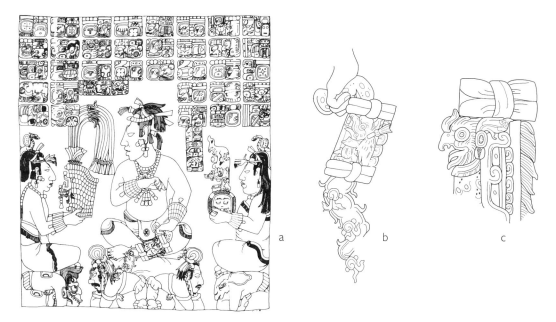

Figure 76 Raptorial birds on ritual bags at Palenque: a) Tablet of the Slaves; b) detail of ritual bag; and c) bag from Temple XIX main panel. Drawing by Linda Schele © David Schele, courtesy Ancient Americas at LACMA (a); and drawings by David Stuart (b–c).

attested in Maya art and epigraphy, such pars pro toto conventions are also found in Teotihuacan's own writing system.

Yet another example of this same motif, now naturalistic in its look, appears on the decorated incense bag shown on Palenque's Tablet of the Slaves (Figure 76), dating to the same time period as the Temple XIX reliefs. In this famous depiction of royal crowning, the Palenque ruler K'inich Ahkal Mo' Nahb receives the militaristic emblems of kingship from his mother and father, including the *took' pakal* glyph of war and a mosaic helmet (Schele 1978; Stuart 2012; Wald 1997). The bag displays another hieroglyph, shown as an owl or eagle whose body is pierced by a Teotihuacan-style

EAGLES AND EMBLEMS | 103

dart. In fact, Schele was the first to equate this particular image to the "Spearthrower Owl" glyphs at Tikal, seeing them as symbols of Teotihuacan warfare (Schele and Freidel 1993:449). But we can probably be more specific in its identification, seeing how it relates to the wider array of raptorial bird images and glyphic forms we have discussed so far, consistently shown with weapons, wounds, or both. K'inich Ahkal Mo' Nahb is also depicted on the large relief panel from Temple XIX at Palenque, where an attendant figure named Yok Ch'ich' Tal holds a very similar ritual bag to what we see on the Tablet of the Slaves (Figure 76c). He is a Yajawk'ahk' of the royal court, a title associated with ritual fires and warfare, and with clear visual associations with Teotihuacan (Stuart 2005b; Zender 2004). The bag he holds is again decorated with an ornate eagle-like bird with goggled eyes. The wings are now far more elaborate, with Teotihuacan "heart" (**pu**) elements. No arrow or dart seems to pierce this bird's body, but in other aspects it is nearly identical to others we have examined. The *k'an*-cross element on its ear is also seen on the bird of Piedras Negras, Stela 9, linking the two in yet another key detail.

As royal accoutrements for K'inich Ahkal Mo' Nahb, the bags with the eagle or owl glyphs may have served a purpose much like the shields of Piedras Negras, as fitting personal references to Teotihuacan and its long-deceased king.[2] It is probably no coincidence that there are hints of Teotihuacan's direct involvement in Palenque's own dynastic affairs during the Early Classic period, around the time of the Entrada. This comes from an image of a goggled Teotihuacan warrior in the site's North Group, as well as a probable reference to Sihyaj K'ahk' in an incomplete stucco text from House D of the Palace (Stuart and Stuart 2008:119–137) (Figure 77). The context for that intriguing textual reference is now lost, but it seems to have been part of a longer mythic-historical narrative conveyed by the stucco piers and facade of House D, dating to the reign of K'inich Janab Pakal. Whatever the case, the Late Classic ideology of warfare that was inspired by Teotihuacan's earlier presence in the Maya world was expressed in several Palenque artworks. That these might have included direct personal references to Spearthrower Owl seems entirely possible.

The avian war-shields of Piedras Negras require an additional comment before we move on to bigger questions. We occasionally see as part of their design the inverted "trapeze-and-ray" element, as it is often called, attached to the bottom of some of the circular heart elements, just above the birds' tails (Figure 70a and d). This appears also on the large Stela 9 headdress, seemingly placed atop the head of the eagle or owl. There it is at the base of the bird's tail once more, shown behind the headdress and with the tail feathers thrust upward, so essentially the same design. The meaning of this "trapeze-and-ray" (or "A-O") motif has long been a thorny and difficult issue in Mesoamerican iconography. In a brilliant study, Nielsen and Helmke (2020) link it to symbols of rulership, and specifically to royal headdresses. It is interesting to note that in one example they cite, from a Maya codex-style vessel, a raptorial bird similar to those we have examined "wears" such a device (Nielsen and Helmke 2020:fig. 11b). It also appeared in an Early Classic context at Tikal, worn on a variant of the "owl and weapons" glyph painted on a tripod lid from Group 6C-XVI (see Figure 52). The "trapeze-and-ray" (or the very similar "Xi glyph," as it is sometimes called) is also routinely found on the tails

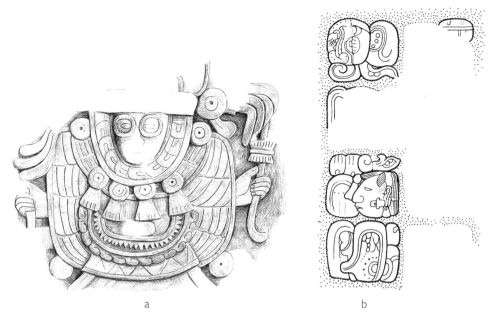

Figure 77 Teotihuacan history at Palenque: a) drawing of stucco sculpture from Temple V of the North Group; and b) a possible reference to Sihyaj K'ahk' from the House D stucco text. Drawings by David Stuart.

of supernatural serpents in Maya and Mexican art, especially on the Teotihuacan War Serpent (Taube 2012). Its close association with weaponry, serpent-tails, and bird-tails seems an important part of its origin and meaning but is still hard to understand. Even so, it suggests a remote possibility that the "trapeze-and-ray" is not always a headdress element but was included as an additional allusion to a deified weapon—the tail of the War Serpent—thrust into the bird's body. The weapon-as-tail of the bird depicted on the Tikal facade headdress may go some way in establishing such an equivalence.

Such an interpretation is also supported by a remarkable ceramic plate in the codex style, first published by Robicsek and Hales (1981:75) (Figure 78). The vessel is Late Classic, from around the mid-eighth century, and like others of its type it was produced in the very northern Peten region of Guatemala or southern Campeche. The plate bears a finely rendered Maya painting, replete with Teotihuacan references and stylistic elements, as discussed by both Stone (1989) and Taube (1992a, 2012). The human figure sits with his knees up, an unusual pose by Maya conventions, known only from a few other depictions of Teotihuacan warriors and figures (examples can be traced to the paintings at La Sufricaya and to the full-figure glyphs of Copan's Temple Inscription) (Scherer, Golden, and Houston 2018:176–179). He holds in his hand an elaborate curved staff depicting the Teotihuacan War Serpent, surely akin to the rattlesnake atlatl device already discussed on Stela 9 at Piedras Negras. Here and in many other depictions, the War Serpent is adorned with protruding "fan"-like elements, sometimes interpreted as butterfly wings (Figure 79a). These are more likely the feathered ends (fletches) of darts or arrows, and they adorn the Teotihuacan War Serpent here and elsewhere to indicate

Figure 78 Codex-style plate bearing a possible portrait of Spearthrower Owl, seated upon his name glyph. Drawing by David Stuart.

Figure 79 The "fan" motif as the depiction of arrow fletching: a) War Serpent from codex-style plate; b–c) details from War Serpent on Yaxchilan, Lintel 25; d) Teotihuacan dart with fletching; and e) Teotihuacan dart with fletching from Copan, Temple Inscription. Drawings by David Stuart.

his basic nature as an animate weapon. The round, downy tuft of the dart's end corresponds to the same feature found on many Teotihuacan darts represented in Maya art (Figure 79d and e). As we will recall, this rounded element may be what came to be abstracted as a spherical form on the "dart shaft" of the Marcador of Tikal. The repeating combinations of down-feather tufts and fletching indicate the rear of a dart that has pierced its target—a fitting design for indicating a weapon of war. As with the "trapeze-and-ray" symbol, its presence on the Teotihuacan War Serpent seems appropriate given how it is ancestral to the Xiuhcoatl of Late Postclassic Central Mexico, also an animated weapon or atlatl (Taube 1992b, 2012).

The seated figure on the codex-style plate appears atop a complex group of elements that by now should seem familiar. At the front is the profile head of the Teotihuacan War Serpent, whose tail is visible as the snake rattles on the other side of the central circle. The end of the rattle is, in turn, adorned by a large bifurcated scroll resembling flames. Part of the tail of the snake is formed also by the "trapeze-and-ray" element, with a tied knot at its base. This specific iconographic feature is very common in Aztec depictions of Xiuhcoatl, including one important depiction cited by Taube, where it forms the animate spear or arrow of Huitzilopochtli piercing the body of Coyolxauhqui (Taube 2018:72). On the plate, the War Serpent is oriented horizontally, passing through the large cartouche just below the seated figure. If we examine this central element more closely, we see it has an elaborated Teotihuacan-style "blood" or "heart" sign at its lower part, with the abstracted trilobe drops below. Above this is a large single, circular eye, repeating a combination we saw on the incense bags of Palenque as well as in other depictions (Figures 75 and 76). The codex-style plate, therefore, shows us an important elaboration on the emblematic forms of the name we have already seen as decorative elements on shields and ritual bags, all bearing Spearthrower Owl's personal name glyph—the wounded or stricken eagle or owl—in emblematic form. It is tempting to interpret this image as a Late Classic portrait of Spearthrower Owl, surrounded by visual allusions to Teotihuacan, his status as a warrior, and to his direct identification using emblematic glyphic forms that by themselves evoke the traditions of Teotihuacan writing.

Finally, another elaborately painted plate from the Tikal region shows a related image of a wounded, rather unhappy bird, with blood flowing out of its body from its talons (Figure 80a). Neo-Teotihuacan elements are incorporated throughout its design, including circular goggle eyes, a Teotihuacan-style collar similar to what is worn by the eagles at Palenque, and images of weapons. The left wing of the bird is decorated with flint knives, with the opposite wing decorated with obsidian blades. Blood gushes out of the center of the eagle's body, adorned with a *k'an* cross. A Late Classic stucco vase (K7221) displays the very same bird, also with Teotihuacan elements (Figure 80b). Significantly, the clear end of a dart or arrow appears directly above his head.

Interpreting the images on these codex-style vessels as personal references to a long-deceased ruler remains highly tentative. It posits a far more narrow and specific function for images and icons that have long been seen as more generalized emblems of warfare and sacrifice. Seeing them as emblematic names, while still only suggestive in my own mind, nevertheless conforms to patterns we know from other codex-style vases. We should recall that many such vases of the Late Classic period recount events and narratives of deep political history, most prominently in the so-called dynasty vases relating the early kings of the Kanul courts (Martin 1997, 2017). Spearthrower Owl may have been evoked and memorialized in a similar way through these courtly vessels, reflecting a deep connection that he may have had with the kingdoms of the Kanul dynasty and their allies. As we have already seen, the inscription on a jade earspool noted that Spearthrower Owl was directly involved in the early political history of the Chatan Winik lords, corresponding to the region where the plate was probably manufactured. A recently unearthed stela at El Achiotal, Guatemala, may also imply

Figure 80 Depictions of Teotihuacan-style raptorial birds: a) plate from the Tikal region; and b) vase from the central Peten (K7221). Drawings by Simon Martin (a) and David Stuart (b).

a political tie between an early holder of the Chatan Winik title and the new political order established in the Early Classic and overseen by Sihyaj K'ahk' at Tikal (Canuto, Auld-Thomas, and Aredondo 2020). The neo-Teotihuacan imagery on codex-style vessels owned by later Chatan Winik lords may allude to this deeper historical connection as well.

Images of eagles also appear as part of the Mexican-style militaristic regalia worn by Maya rulers, as depicted on several monuments of the Río Pasión region, at the sites of Dos Pilas, Aguateca, and Cancuen (Figure 81). There we see their full-winged birds worn about the neck and over other elaborate jade collars, surely late examples of the similar bird we saw worn over the necklace of the Teotihuacan warrior on Tikal, Stela 32 (see Figure 44). The birds wear distinctive collars or jewels of their own, as on the incense bags of Palenque discussed above. I suspect that all such images are related to the large eagles found with some warrior portraits in Early Classic art in Teotihuacan style, as we see on a small travertine (*tecali*) plaque depicting a frontal view of a Teotihuacan warrior holding flaming weapons (recall our discussion above of the hieroglyph *k'ahk'* substituted by a dart in the name of Sihyaj K'ahk') (Figure 82). This remarkable image, supposedly found in the Peten of Guatemala, is one of the most compelling we know of a regal Teotihuacan warrior.[3] The centrally placed eagle with its large X-like cross echoes not only the later chest devices at Aguateca and elsewhere but also the "owl and weapons" hieroglyphs worn over the chest. The abstracted bars of the X certainly recall the placement of the crossed arrows or darts in other examples, although here they have an abstracted form that makes them difficult to identify. I tentatively suggest that some, if not all, of these eagle-like accoutrements and symbols might well serve as labels that make reference to the illustrious foreign ruler and warrior. It is important to keep in mind that the king of Dos Pilas (Mutul) would have been a direct descendant

Figure 81 Eagle pectoral worn by ruler on Aguateca, Stela 2. Photograph of cast by David Stuart.

of Spearthrower Owl, just as were his cousins who ruled at Tikal (also a Mutul court).[4] Such family connections are less secure for the portrait on Cancuen, Stela 2, depicting the local ruler Tajal Chan Ahk as a Teotihuacan warrior with a bird device on his chest. But we do know that the Cancuen dynasty had strong political and familiar ties with that of Dos Pilas (and, therefore, Tikal) in earlier generations (Houston 1993:115).

A final example of a possible "Spearthrower Owl" name emblem from Maya imagery comes from Copan, found among the rich iconographic adornments associated

Figure 82
Teotihuacan warrior with "eagle" hieroglyph on carved travertine (*tecali*) plaque. Drawing by David Stuart.

with the Hieroglyphic Stairway. The balustrades that flank this remarkable monument are formed by repeating representations of curved obsidian blades, each adorned with the visage of a bird with goggled eyes (Figure 83). The entire building, at least in its final phase, was replete with imagery and iconography evoking Teotihuacan (Fash 2011:110; Fash et al. 1992; Fash and Fash 2000; Stuart 2005a). This included life-sized portraits of seated warriors integrated into the steps and the inscription, as well as architectural details of the temple above. As I have argued in a separate analysis (Stuart 2004a), this imposing building from the eighth century served at least in part as an ancestral shrine, focused on the life and dynastic legacy of the founder K'inich Yax K'uk' Mo'. In its earlier iteration, it was also the funerary temple of an expansive, influential ruler named K'ahk'

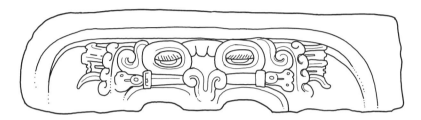

Figure 83
Emblematic bird designs from the balustrades of Copan's Hieroglyphic Stairway. Note the arrow fletching and "blood" signs aside the eyes. Drawings by David Stuart.

Uti' Witz' K'awiil, the twelfth king of the Copan dynasty. In later years, political instability compelled Copan's builders to reframe the stairway monument as a celebration of Copan's militaristic prowess under the reign of the fifteenth king, K'ahk' Yipyaj Chan K'awiil. Both themes contributed to the focus on Teotihuacan, and the balustrades of the stairway are explicit in the imagery of warfare, ancestry, and human sacrifice.

The repeating elements on the stairway balustrades, like similar motifs on the upper temple, represent large obsidian knives whose curved blades were equated with the beaks of raptorial birds. This connection is shown again by the frontal bird faces with goggled eyes that adorn the upper portions of each blade. Flanking the eyes is a combination of the Teotihuacan "heart" or "blood" glyph (at times reduced to repeating curls) as well as the fletching of a dart or arrow—the same "fan" motif or butterfly wing we have already seen in connection to representations of the War Serpent and other Teotihuacan iconography. I argue that the combined image of the projectile and blood indicates a wound, repeating a theme we have encountered elsewhere in neo-Teotihuacan iconography. The goggled bird faces suggest that the fuller designs on the blades refer to wounded, stricken eagles, bringing us to yet another possible emblematic mention of Spearthrower Owl, repeating up and down the Hieroglyphic Stairway.[5] This would be an appropriate reference, physically framing the inscription and Copan's dynastic history, with K'inich Yax K'uk' Mo' as its underlying hero and focus. The founder's own accession in the year 426 was, we will recall, still within Spearthrower Owl's reign, and the text of Altar Q makes it clear that the Copan founder journeyed to Teotihuacan (the *winte'naah*) in order to receive sanction for his authority (*ch'am k'awiil*). We can be confident that Spearthrower Owl played an instrumental role in the founding of a new political and ritual center at Copan, on the frontier of the Maya world, and it seems for this reason he was prominently named around the Hieroglyphic Stairway. Whether he was ever mentioned in the inscription itself is impossible to know, given that the section pertaining to K'inich Yax K'uk' Mo' and Copan's Early Classic history is largely missing.

EAGLES AND EMBLEMS

The interpretation of these iconographic case studies as personalized references to Spearthrower Owl goes beyond the evidence we began with in this study, rooted in history and Peten's dynastic politics. Indeed, much of it should remain tentative. A connection to the more established hieroglyphic names of Spearthrower Owl at Tikal and elsewhere seems strong and suggests an equivalence, as Schele and others noted long ago, yet alternatives are still possible. If we set aside the bird headdresses, shields, incense bags, and ceramic designs and analyze them separately, we have a tightly circumscribed iconographic "complex" that emphasizes some sort of raptorial bird, most likely an eagle, displaying blood and wounds on its body. It remains possible that this was not a name, but a highly specific motif that held some more general significance for the Classic Maya as an allusion to the ideology of Teotihuacan-inspired warfare and sacrifice, maybe something even akin to the "omen of war" discussed by Grube and Schele (1994). Still, the representations of wounded, bleeding birds appear far removed both historically and thematically from the belligerent eagles and eagle warriors that were so important to the militaristic imagery of the Postclassic period. Whatever the case, it was a highly specific icon, fundamental to the Maya understanding of Teotihuacan's legacy and participation in dynastic history. It is this basic truth about the "stricken eagle" that makes a possible allusion to Spearthrower Owl himself so attractive and in need of future revisits and assessments.

SPEARTHROWER OWL IN OAXACA?

Apart from the Maya region, Teotihuacan's influences are also quite visible in the art and writing of other areas of Mesoamerica, most notably in the monumental art of Oaxaca and Guerrero (Marcus 1983; Nielsen et al. 2019; Nielsen and Rivera 2019). At Monte Albán, sculptures from the South Platform show processions of Teotihuacan-style individuals with hieroglyphic names, some with military helmets, others with "tassel headdresses." The plaque known as the Lápida de Bazán also depicts a standing Teotihuacan-style figure in association with a more local personage, clearly indicating a close relationship between the two areas (Millon 1973).

Outside of the Valley of Oaxaca, we find one especially interesting image of a Teotihuacan-style figure on Monument 2 from the site of Cerro de la Tortuga, located near the Pacific coast (Rivera 2011) (Figure 84). This stela is tall, some 2.70 m in height, and shows an image of a standing lord facing to the left, with speech-scrolls emanating from his mouth. Over the center of his body is a large hieroglyphic form consisting of a day sign "8 Earthquake" (Caso's "Glyph E") that is infixed within a "shield and dart" sign, which is, in turn, combined with an emblematic representation of a bird with outstretched wings. Iván Rivera is correct to link this image with the Teotihuacan "owl and weapons" symbol, which we have now seen is a hieroglyphic form that is difficult to distinguish from the personal name glyphs of Spearthrower Owl, in its more Teotihuacan mode of presentation. The placement of a name glyph over the center of the body conforms to patterns we have seen elsewhere on figurines and in sculptures both in Oaxaca and in the Maya region, as just discussed above, and suggests a personal reference (Urcid and Joyce 2001:fig. 22). Its combination here with "8 Earthquake" suggests

Figure 84
Monument 2 from Cerro de la Tortuga, Oaxaca (Rivera 2011:fig. 1). Drawing by Iván Rivera.

Figure 85
Zapotec inscription on cylinder vessel, with *lechuza y armas* sign (Urcid 2003:fig. 3). Drawing by Javier Urcid, with detail by David Stuart.

EAGLES AND EMBLEMS

that the latter may have some sort of function as a calendrical name, complementing the "eagle" hieroglyph. The Cerro de la Tortuga monument would seem to be an intriguing candidate for another portrait of Spearthrower Owl, pointing to his importance in other parts of Mesoamerica in the Early Classic.

Remaining in Oaxaca, we should bring up another possible reference to Spearthrower Owl on an inscribed Zapotec vessel. Urcid (2003) produced an important analysis of this cylindrical vase, now in the collections of the Museo Amparo, which displays a complex assortment of Zapotec hieroglyphs. One prominent glyph, placed directly below a complex year record, is a depiction of a raptorial bird being pierced by Teotihuacan-style darts (Figure 85). Urcid specifically linked this form to the Maya and Teotihuacan images of birds with weapons that we have discussed, although, following Schele and Grube, he analyzed it as a general symbol of warfare. It is perhaps significant that the arrows are shown pointing to the bird, suggesting a form of Spearthrower Owl that is more explicit in the sense of a "Striker of Eagles." I should caution that without any proper context for the hieroglyph, its identification as a name or personal reference remains pure conjecture on my part, although Urcid's own suggestions of such a connection seem reasonable. The dating of this vase is said to be Late Classic, after the fifth century (Urcid 2003:99), making it a possible retrospective mention of the ruler, like many others we have seen.

NOTES

1 Heart and blood imagery at Teotihuacan requires a bit more explanation, given its ubiquity and its ability to employ both simple and complex designs over a long history. We might begin with the most basic element—a trefoil with three or more drops (Figure 69). This heart can sometimes assume a more coherent, circular form in Teotihuacan art, apparently with little distinction. Elaborations on this form show them as more "naturalistic" dripping blood, which are clearly ancestral to the blood signs we find at Cacaxtla, in numerous hieroglyphs that seem to function as titles for warriors (Helmke and Nielsen 2011:22–28). Parallels also exist in the Toltec-style art of Chichen Itza, as the hearts consumed by jaguars and eagles. All of these Central Mexican forms bear a clear resemblance to early Maya "blood" glyphs, read **K'IK'** or **CH'ICH'**, which can be traced back to the Late Preclassic period. In Maya writing, this same "blood" sign served as the basis of all day sign cartouches in Maya hieroglyphic writing (suggesting that the days themselves are in some way individual characterizations of human blood). The "blood" glyph may have had an original prototype among the Middle Preclassic Olmec, from which all of these later forms evolved. It seems another pan-Mesoamerican hieroglyph firmly rooted in the greater visual tradition of the region.

2 It is significant that the bags and shields with similar decoration are closely related to one another, even paired directly in various images of Teotihuacan warriors in Maya art. Stela 9 of Piedras Negras is one of several examples.

3 The small plaque, from a private collection, was first published and described by Hellmuth (1986:45–46). He gave several details about its nature and origin, including the specific statement that "found by a bulldozer operator making a rural road in the Sierra Lacandona area of Peten." If so, it stands as one of the more remarkable examples of Teotihuacan-style art from the Maya area. It is clearly Early Classic, probably dating between 350 and 450 CE. My drawing is solely based on that by Barbara van Huesen, which was, in turn, made from the original stone. I have no information as to its current whereabouts.

4 The specific connection to the Stela 32 of Tikal takes on greater meaning once we understand that the Late Classic ruler of Dos Pilas would be fusing his identity with that of a direct ancestor, Spearthrower Owl. The visual display of the eagle emblem or glyph on the chest is distinct from what we see at Piedras Negras, perhaps due to its own different political or dynastic relationship to Central Mexico in the Early Classic.

5 The prominence of "goggles" on these bird faces deserves further comment. As many students of Maya and Teotihuacan art have noted, these are likely to have their origin in the representations of circular eyes from the natural world. In Teotihuacan art, for example, such rounded eyes have been likened to the pronounced eyes of butterflies and moths, with the accompanying hooked "proboscis" making an even stronger link in many representations (Bassie-Sweet 2021; Headrick 2007:124–145). Images of large circular eyes may also have their origin in the pronounced round eyes of raptorial birds, especially those of eagles and owls. "Goggles" made of shell were a common feature on Central Mexican warriors (García–Des Lauriers 2017), and we might consider their inclusion in military and ritual costume as allusions to butterflies and possibly to eagles, akin to the "eagle warriors" of much later Central Mexico.

5 HINTS OF TEOTIHUACAN HISTORY

THE IDENTIFICATION OF SPEARTHROWER OWL AS A HISTORICAL RULER at Teotihuacan engages directly with the old "thorny problem" regarding the nature of the city's political organization, to use Cowgill's (2015:190) apt description. At first it would seem to agree with those who have advocated for some sort of a centralized, even autocratic form of rule, more or less in keeping with familiar patterns of authority from elsewhere in Mesoamerican history. But opinions regarding Teotihuacan's sociopolitical organization vary greatly, based on differing inferences from the material record, the city's urban layout, and the site's distinctive and supposedly "impersonal" visual culture (Carballo 2020; Cowgill 1997; Pasztory 1988). For some, the lack of written history and the relative invisibility of kings in the city's art imply a form of governance that may be more collective in nature or decentralized, far different from the systems of centralized rulership found elsewhere in Mesoamerica. It should, therefore, not be surprising that the idea of Spearthrower Owl as a Teotihuacan ruler was met with some skepticism after it was first proposed. After all, his existence arose unexpectedly from Maya written records, not from Teotihuacan itself, where "history" has had no significant role to play in the formation of interpretive models.

Ideas of a collective or non-centralized political system at Teotihuacan have been advocated for decades. Several archaeologists working at Teotihuacan and its environs have proposed a system of governance involving multiple rulers, a collective political arrangement with a group of two or more leaders. Manzanilla (1992, 2002) has long advocated for this view and specifically sees evidence for four ruling lineages coexisting, and in some way sharing power, at Teotihuacan (see also Froese, Gersenson, and Manzanilla 2014). Taking a perspective from art history, Pasztory (1992, 1997) claimed that the "impersonal" art of Teotihuacan indicates the city's unique role in Mesoamerica as an "egalitarian" community. Later, she emphasized Teotihuacan's supposed contrast with other Mesoamerican visual cultures, particularly the Maya, noting that the abstract art of Teotihuacan "rejected the politically instituted representations of rulers and captives" (Pasztory 1988:50). In her view, Teotihuacan represented itself as a "utopian state" and "was opposed to the dynastic cult, individualism, naturalistic art style, and public inscriptions on monuments of the other great cultures in Mesoamerica" (Pasztory

1992:314). Pasztory has been highly influential in her view of Teotihuacan art as a radical shift away from visual cultures found elsewhere in Mesoamerica, developing what she called "an entirely new set of artistic conventions . . . that departed from the southern tradition of Olmec and later Monte Alban and Maya art" (Pasztory 1997:49). These conventions reflected a turn toward "a society that did not glorify any specific aristocratic individuals, but the community as a whole. Its art expresses values that are impersonal, corporate and communal" (Pasztory 1997:50). It is this characterization that Graeber and Wengrow (2021) drew upon to develop their ideas and arguments, using Teotihuacan as a singular case study of a large urban area with what they see as having little direct evidence of centralized rule or kingship.

Pasztory's characterizations of a Teotihuacan "utopia" were met with strong criticism from other Teotihuacan specialists (for example, Millon 1992:371). Cowgill (2015:191) questioned the assumptions that grew out of Teotihuacan's supposed "impersonal" art, noting that "the apparent low profile of Teotihuacan rulers is not unambiguous evidence that their power was restricted." In comparison, one might characterize much of Olmec iconography as "impersonal" as far back as the Middle Formative period, as it was rooted in the conventions of high-level abstraction that are not too different from what we see at Teotihuacan itself. (I suspect that much of Teotihuacan's sense of the abstract derives from this Preclassic precedent, in fact.) Moreover, drawing inferences of political structure from artistic conventions and negative evidence—in this case, the lack of royal portraits and monuments—seems highly problematic. We might also point to the Postclassic visual culture of the Mexica, who saw ancient Teotihuacan as a culture well worthy of emulation (López Luján 1989). In the Aztec tradition, portraits of rulers are also extremely rare, with only a handful of examples attested. Many of those that we do know have often proved difficult to identify, or are fused with complex religious iconography.[1] Yet the preponderance of religious iconography and non-personal themes in the monumental sculpture of Tenochtitlan could, by similar logic, be seen as an indication of some less authoritarian system of rule.

None of these doubts about "collective" authority would advocate for any strong parallels between Teotihuacan and Maya systems of rulership. Major differences in both scale and structure obviously existed. But it is also important to remember that Teotihuacan's general urban features and art styles were well established before the late fourth century; the current proposal that an individual named Spearthrower Owl ("Eagle Striker") was a ruler says nothing of the *nature* of the institution of Teotihuacan authority or rulership (or lack thereof) before the Early Xolalpan period. Put simply, the "either/or" nature of these ongoing debates may cloud the possibility of multiple types of governance being present at different eras, some conforming to historical parallels in Mesoamerica with others remaining radically different. And without written history, archaeological and artistic evidence will always be limited in their ability to address these larger questions of political organization and historicity. The hints of history described in these pages, I hope, will spur much more discussion and debate on the matter, with the realization that there were named persons of authority at Teotihuacan, at least from a Maya perspective.

The representation of rulers is rare in Teotihuacan's figural art, but symbols of elite authority may be common. Sugiyama emphasized this in relation to the iconography of the Temple of the Feathered Serpent, where a large tomb may have once existed alongside the many sacrificial burials recovered within the principal structure (Sugiyama 1992:220, 2005, 2013). Headrick (2001, 2007) has discussed the issue of rulership at length, and from an art historical perspective that stands in significant contrast to that of Pasztory. Following the earlier suggestion by Schele (1995:111–112), Headrick (2007) interprets the array of standing figures depicted in the murals of Atetelco as representations of Teotihuacan rulers, although recently Carballo (2020:70) has offered a number of counterpoints to this view. Nielsen and Helmke (2020) present a compelling case that many Teotihuacan headdresses should be viewed as royal symbols, much like the symbol of the headband found in other Mesoamerican cultures (Stuart 2015). I agree with Nielsen's (2014:12) assessment that it is "plausible that the strong individual rulers were probably there all along in the history of Teotihuacan, but rather than being downplayed, they may in fact be present in the murals and sculpture in a degree that we scholars have been slow to recognize."

There is clearly room for middle ground in these debates as well, along the lines of René Millon's (1976) suggestion that Teotihuacan might have been organized as an "oligarchic republic," in the sense that rulers probably existed, but did not necessarily operate within the centralized and personalized structures of kingship seen elsewhere in Mesoamerica. Whatever the case, it is probable that Spearthrower Owl, if he was any sort of "dynastic ruler," performed his role within a complex authoritative structure that was very different from what we find in the Maya Lowlands.

The suggestion of a named, historical ruler of Teotihuacan has other important ramifications. When characterizing my early speculations on Teotihuacan-Maya history, Millon (2002:776) stated that "it seems clear that there is a potential here for a breakthrough of far-reaching significance for Teotihuacan studies of all kinds." The newer evidence strengthens those previous arguments, and perhaps might even allow us to begin interpreting aspects of Teotihuacan's archaeological record in historical terms. For example, Spearthrower Owl's lengthy reign may be indirectly tied to a well-known transition in Teotihuacan's chronology. His reign of sixty-five years (374–439 CE) generally corresponds to an important time in Teotihuacan's own development during the Early Xolalpan phase, widely seen as Teotihuacan's apogee, when the city reached its greatest expansion as a hegemonic power, its greatest architectural splendor, and its maximum population (Angulo V. 1998:114; Cowgill 2003:329).

Spearthrower Owl's title on the Marcador as "fourth sequential ruler" is significant here, for it points to a beginning of some new arrangement not long beforehand, perhaps around 300 CE. As noted, the phrase used on the Marcador is identical to numbered dynastic titles in other Maya texts. It would be premature to characterize Teotihuacan political structures based on one hieroglyph, but the clue is nevertheless important. Given what we know of dynastic structures of rulership in highland Mexico, Oaxaca, and the Maya Lowlands, it is plausible that a sequence of authorities or rulers also characterized a part of Teotihuacan's complex political history. Its apparent timing approximates an important shift visible in Teotihuacan's own archaeological record. It was at this time, in the transition from the Late Tlamimilolpa into the Early Xolalpan period (300–530 CE), when Teotihuacan saw what many perceive to be a radical political and ideological change, perhaps even the violent rejection of one political system for another (Carballo 2020; Cowgill 1983, 1992, 1997, 2015:148; R. Millon 1976, 1988:112; Sugiyama 1992:221). This is indicated most vividly in the Ciudadela complex, with the intentional burning of the Temple of the Feathered Serpent and the covering of its front by a large *adosada* platform. What emerged out of this shift, according to some, was a more centralized system of government that controlled many aspects of the city's economic production and distribution. Militarism was also a dominant feature of this new arrangement, reflected at Teotihuacan (Sugiyama 1992, 2002, 2005) as well as through evidence of Teotihuacan's presence and influence throughout much of southern Mesoamerica, including the Maya region (Bove and Medrano Busto 2003). These changes may have been associated with what we can historically infer from Tikal's Marcador, that the years 300–350 CE saw the establishment of a new succession of rulers, one of whom was Spearthrower Owl, a significant agent for a militaristic ideology that was novel for its time.

In light of these patterns, I argue that Spearthrower Owl was "a" ruler of Teotihuacan, as either a participant in a new system or perhaps as one among a group of rulers, reflecting a complex governing arrangement that echoes Millon's "oligarchic" model mentioned earlier. Both options are possible. All we know from history is that Spearthrower Owl was installed as what the Maya called an *ajaw*, much like any other prominent dynast. And whereas researchers remain uncertain of what existed before (or after) this particular political arrangement, I suggest that the case of Spearthrower Owl provides a key insight into one particular time period of Teotihuacan's history—the Late Tlamimilolpa and Early Xolalpan phases, if not later—when the city may have been governed by a new system, disruptive locally and from a considerable geographical distance. My own preference is to see Teotihuacan ruled by a series of powerful individuals after ca. 300, conforming more or less to what we know as "dynasties" from a comparative Mesoamerican perspective.

Speculations on the nature of Spearthrower Owl's own political situation, or on the political or economic power he wielded, would require evidence and an expertise falling well beyond the scope of this study, focused as it is more on his history and references in epigraphy and iconography. The inscriptions at Tikal say nothing directly of what motivated the Entrada and the disruption of the political order that was in place prior to 378 CE. The two regions had bonds well before this time, and it is safe to assume that the Entrada episode, however else we might understand it, was a flash point in the long-developing and evolving relationship between two elite communities and two (for a time) close-knit families. Spearthrower Owl engaged militarily with Tikal very soon after assuming the throne, suggesting that his own inauguration may have rapidly set certain forces in motion, leading to the journey of Sihyaj K'ahk' toward Tikal. Spearthrower Owl's young son was soon thereafter "prepped" to rule over much of the central Maya Lowlands, journeying to Tikal with his mother, possibly a royal woman of Tikal, and later marrying into a powerful Maya dynasty in order to strengthen a long-term connection. Did Spearthrower Owl have other sons who would inherit rule at Teotihuacan? Presumably, but we know nothing of other dramatis personae of the time.

Spearthrower Owl's death in 439 corresponds to a downturn in Teotihuacan's conspicuous influence at Tikal and in the Maya Lowlands. It was a relatively sudden change, apparently visible in Tikal's own archaeological record, with the intentional burial of Group 6C-XVI, where Spearthrower Owl's Marcador was once erected, under 4–5 m of fill (Laporte and Fialko 1990). Laporte dates this termination to about 450 CE. I see these as related events, and the timing corresponds to what seems like a fairly abrupt end to Teotihuacan's widespread political contact and influence in the Maya region over the previous two or more generations, all apparently under Spearthrower Owl's oversight.

One final point should be addressed regarding Spearthrower Owl and his place of origin. While not developed in the original proposal, I had considered Kaminaljuyu as an alternate locale, given that site's proximity to the Maya Lowlands and its well-known associations with Teotihuacan during its Esperanza phase, the beginning of which comes after the middle of the fourth century and before the middle of the fifth century (Braswell 2003b:98–99), at precisely the same time as we have historical evidence in the Peten. Coggins (1975) had earlier speculated that Yax Nun Ayiin came to Tikal from Kaminaljuyu, an interpretation with no historical evidence but which reflected a general discomfort at that time in seeing direct ties between Tikal and far more distant Teotihuacan. But we now know that Kaminaljuyu may not show quite so dominant a Teotihuacan presence in the Esperanza phase as once believed, given limitations in the ceramic data and general ambiguities in the distributions of architectural influence (Braswell 2003b). Given the preponderance of evidence, we can be sure that Teotihuacan was the focal point of Tikal's foreign references. I argue that this is especially clear now, given the traceable movement of Sihyaj K'ahk' from the west on his journey toward Tikal in 378, passing through El Peru. And the texts are especially revealing in their characterization of the ensuing arrival of a "western authority" (*ochk'in k'awiil*), and in their use of Spearthrower Owl's own title on at least one occasion, "the west *kaloomte'*."

This emphasis on the "west" resonates with important historical evidence from Copan as well. Although the main actors and events of the Entrada were concentrated in the central Peten, Copan played a key role in the ensuing decades as a place of intensive Teotihuacan influence and presence (Fash and Fash 2000; Sharer 2003, 2004; Stuart 2000, 2005a, 2005b; Taube 2004a). As noted, Altar Q seems to bear a historical mention of a long-distance journey by the founder K'inich Yax K'uk' Mo' to "receive *k'awiil*," almost surely at Teotihuacan itself. His accession in the highlands took place nearly fifty years after the Entrada, in 426, still at a time when Spearthrower Owl would have been alive (recall that Spearthrower Owl's last known mention as a historical actor comes from El Peru's Stela 51, when he "witnessed" or sanctioned the taking of power of a local El Peru lord in 432). The central event of Altar Q's narrative is not the accession of K'inich Yax K'uk' Mo', however, but rather his own arrival back to Copan the following year, on February 9, 427 (8.19.11.0.13 5 Ben 11 Muan). This is featured by its centered position in the middle columns of the text. The event is described as the "resting of the leg (*hil ook*) of *k'awiil*, the west *kaloomte'*," a statement that combines a number of the terms we have already encountered in the titles of Spearthrower Owl and in the narratives of the Entrada. We might characterize the 427 arrival of K'inich Yax K'uk' Mo' as Copan's "local Entrada," in some ways a historical offshoot of the earlier events of 378. Analysis of his physical remains show that the Copan founder had his origins in the central Peten before residing in Copan (Buikstra et al. 2004; Price et al. 2010).

Whatever the case, the authority of Copan's founding dynast was explicitly sanctioned by (and at) Teotihuacan, and I argue by Spearthrower Owl himself. Again, this is the key event of Copan's own history that would have led to the specific citation of Spearthrower Owl in the iconographic motifs of the balustrades of Temple XXVI and the Hieroglyphic Stairway. That pyramid, along with the ancestral shrine of K'inich Yax K'uk' Mo' at Temple XVI, where Altar Q was placed, both face westward toward Teotihuacan and to the source of the political ideology that was central to their iconography and historical messaging (Taube 2004a).

CONCLUSION

In recent years, we have refined our knowledge of Maya history in unexpected ways, including by shedding light on political connections with Central Mexico during the late fourth and early fifth centuries CE. One pivotal event in that relationship, as we have seen, was the conquest of Tikal in 378 CE, creating what amounted to a new political order in the central lowlands of the Peten, and possibly even beyond. Here I have provided historical context for a singular individual who was behind it all, a person possibly named Spearthrower Owl ("Eagle Striker"), who I argue reigned as ruler at Teotihuacan from 374 to 439 CE. He was the conqueror of Tikal, acting through his local agent and representative, Sihyaj K'ahk', who, in turn, ruled over Tikal and the central lowlands for many years.

His hieroglyphic name was long interpreted as a much more generic reference, such as a "war" or "lineage" symbol. Using what we know of Maya grammar and iconographic conventions, I see little option but to see it as a personal reference. Whether this function can be extended to the assorted headdresses, shields, and other iconographic examples is more difficult to confirm, but I have tried to point out a direct line connecting all of them, seeing them all as variations on one name, either as hieroglyphic forms or as "emblems," employing a spectrum of conventions that bridged the Maya and Teotihuacan writing systems. This would include Teotihuacan's "owl and weapons" motif, likely a hieroglyphic name.

Earlier interpretations of the "owl and weapons" as a military insignia were based on outmoded and even vague ideas about the presence and nature of writing at Teotihuacan. Von Winning's first discussion of it over seventy years ago came at a time when Teotihuacan writing was barely even perceived, yet those earlier ideas have long persisted. At Teotihuacan, as in the Maya area, it is evident that "eagle" and "weapons" elements appear together as two juxtaposed or superimposed hieroglyphic signs. Given that most other attested Teotihuacan hieroglyphs are personal names, it follows that the "owl and weapons" would have this function as well. At the same time, it is also important to recognize that our categories of "name" and "insignia" may not be so mutually exclusive in ancient Mesoamerican writing systems. In both Central Mexico and the Maya area, as we have repeatedly seen, many personal name glyphs assume almost iconic status as costume elements or architectural decoration.

The earlier years of Spearthrower Owl's reign correspond roughly to the onset of the Early Xolalpan phase of Teotihuacan's chronology, not long after the appearance of conspicuous evidence of political and/or religious change in that city's own material record. Drawing from this temporal correlation, it has long appeared likely that Teotihuacan developed a new political order around that time, corresponding to heightened militarism and expansionistic connections throughout Mesoamerica (Sugiyama 2002, 2005). Spearthrower Owl was the fourth in a sequence of rulers or dynasts who were important players in these developments. As yet no other Teotihuacan rulers can be identified using Early Classic Maya sources, although, as we have seen, there are hints in the inscriptions of Piedras Negras of a much later ruler, another "west *kaloomte'*," from the early 500s.[2]

Many of the conspicuous traces of Teotihuacan's presence in the Maya Lowlands have been interpreted as local adoptions of Teotihuacan symbolism, repurposed within Maya ideology and messaging (Borowicz 2003; Millon 1992:354; Schele and Freidel 1993; Stone 1989). This was certainly the case, up to a point, throughout much of Late Classic Maya history, when Maya rulers made direct reference to Central Mexico as an important component of their own visual ideology, hearkening back to the political realities and influences of the past (Stuart 2005a). But the adaptation of Central Mexican imagery by later Maya kings should also be understood as acts of cultural and social memory, evoking a specific history of long regional interaction that was punctuated by the conquest of Tikal in 378 CE. And because he fathered a Tikal ruler and was a predecessor of later lords, Spearthrower Owl served as an inspiring ancestor in the art and ideology of ancient Tikal and beyond. In the end, he seems not so much a "stranger king" but an active and even familiar participant in Maya elite affairs of the era, even after the Maya of the Peten had a long and conspicuous presence at Teotihuacan. In his own lifetime, he was at once "of" and "apart from" Tikal and its dynastic politics, giving rise to a complex dynamic of interaction and cultural allusion between the two regions.

The recently discovered evidence of a large-scale Maya presence at Teotihuacan offers a fascinating balance to the long-debated indications of "Mexican foreigners" among the Maya. Excavations in the Temple of the Columns area has revealed numerous fragments of murals in a Maya style, deliberately destroyed around 350–450 CE. Skeletal remains from the complex hint at a possible violent episode where a number of Maya individuals were killed around the same time period (Sugiyama et al. 2020). An elaborate cache offering from the same area of Teotihuacan, dating to about 250–300 CE, included a sacrificed spider monkey from the Maya region (most likely the Pacific coast)—a compelling indication of a long history of "multilateral and fluid ritual exchange with Maya dignitaries" (Sugiyama et al. 2022). This recent data shows that the Maya were directly engaged with Teotihuacan for an extended period leading up to the reign of Spearthrower Owl and the Entrada, perhaps even involving intermarriage among elites of the two cities. This last point resonates nicely with the history of

Yax Nun Ayiin, as described above. While it is beyond the scope of this study to frame this new archaeological evidence in historical terms, a marked disruption of the Maya presence at Teotihuacan certainly must be related to the rapid changes we see later in the distant Peten. One must wonder if the violent end of a Maya elite community at Teotihuacan led to the events of 378, when Spearthrower Owl and Sihyaj K'ahk' were proactive in influencing Maya power dynamics and political factionalism. Spearthrower Owl's period of rule, however we interpret it, was very outward looking from his center of power and directly engaged with Maya dynasties.

Teotihuacan's influence in the Maya region did not begin with Spearthrower Owl or the Entrada that he oversaw, but it intensified greatly during his long reign from 374 to 439 CE. Most of the material expressions of Central Mexican influence and "presence" are attributable to this period, including the founding of the Copan dynasty. This acute period of interaction seems to have ended abruptly around the time of Spearthrower Owl's death at an elderly age, when we find the intentional burying and termination of his associated architectural complex at Tikal (Laporte and Fialko 1990). Over the subsequent centuries, Maya monuments and artworks continued to evoke Teotihuacan and Spearthrower Owl more specifically, integrating him into the memorials of dynastic ancestors and their associated ideologies. His numerous appearances in the art and ideology of both Teotihuacan and the lowland Maya might even suggest that he developed into a sort of deified culture hero, a transcendent hero-figure reminiscent of other venerated rulers throughout Mesoamerican history (McAnany 2007; Nicholson 2001; Willey 1976).

One important question to address is whether we should characterize Teotihuacan's authority in the central Maya Lowlands—what Tikal's scribes called the *ochk'in k'awiil*—as an expression of "empire," a word sometimes used to describe to the highland city's widespread influence and hegemony in Mesoamerica during the Early Classic period.[3] Whether or not this is a useful descriptor is a debate best left for others, given the political, economic, and social complexities that it implies. Nevertheless, I sense that "empire" is too strong a framework for understanding Spearthrower Owl's focused role in the Maya region. Tikal's overthrow seems to have targeted a specific dynasty among many and was likely an event that grew out of preexisting social and even familial connections, to the extent that Spearthrower Owl himself was an active protagonist within Tikal's dynastic affairs. The generation or two of close political oversight by Teotihuacan also clearly involved some degree of participation and buy-in among a number of surrounding Maya courts and city-states. If we were to call Teotihuacan's control "imperial," we should always recognize that it was a pinpointed conquest at first, planting a political and ideological movement that was adopted among more local client states or provinces. Perhaps the best means of envisioning the shifting political arrangement after the Entrada is to view it through a Maya lens. The overthrow of Tikal can be seen as a dramatic flash point within a long-standing relationship, a "power-grab" perhaps instigated by perceived disturbances or personal conflicts within a preexisting patron-client arrangement, something less acute than an empire. Hierarchical relations built on person-focused power dynamics were ubiquitous in Maya history, and, in fact, formed the armatures of many political-alliance networks over the centuries, playing out on a smaller geographical scale (Martin 2020). I suspect that Teotihuacan's relationship to Tikal may have been conceived along similar and (literally) familiar structural lines, only far longer in geographical scope.

In my original publication on Spearthrower Owl and the Entrada, I noted how Mayanists had tended to view the presence of Teotihuacan art and imagery in the Maya area in one of two ways—either as evidence of direct external engagement, or as evidence of an internal Maya appropriation of foreign symbolism for their own ideological purposes (Stuart 2000). In the 1980s and 1990s, the more "internalist" model was the dominant framework. In Maya art, neo-Teotihuacan elements and motifs were grouped under the term "Tlaloc-Venus War Complex," a foreign-inspired iconography of warfare developed by Maya rulers mostly in the Late Classic period (Schele 1986a). The emergence of a detailed historical background to these phenomena now allows us to see both outside and inside dynamics at work. The Entrada of the Early Classic period was an external intrusion from afar, perhaps brought about by issues of political and interfamily conflict among far-flung yet related elites. The power structures that the Entrada developed over the ensuing decades, during Spearthrower Owl's long reign, created a new framework for militaristic ideology in the Peten region and beyond. From the fifth through ninth centuries, Maya kings at Tikal, Piedras Negras, Copan, and elsewhere made direct reference to the legacy of Teotihuacan and even to its great ruler, reframing Teotihuacan's specific ideology and visual culture for their own purposes. Evoking the long-deceased hero-king of Teotihuacan was, I argue, part of that mix, showing that both "externalist" and "internalist" viewpoints are correct, depending on time, place, and context.

Historical and archaeological details pertaining to these issues will continue to be refined and expanded through future discoveries and epigraphic insights, much as we have seen in the two decades since Spearthrower Owl's role as a Teotihuacan ruler was first proposed. We need only be reminded of this by the recent discovery of El Peru (Waka'), Stela 51, with its surprising new reference to Spearthrower Owl as a Tikal *ajaw* and as a "witness" to the accession of a local king, most likely from afar. Current excavations at Teotihuacan and the discovery of Maya paintings and ceramics in the Plaza de las Columnas are also revealing a number of exciting finds, their implications yet to be fully absorbed and analyzed. And the situation becomes even more intriguing with the excavation (ongoing even as I write these words) of Teotihuacan-style paintings at Tikal, on a miniature *talud-tablero* platform on Group 6D-XV, near the Ciudadela complex and the group where the Marcador was unearthed forty years ago (Edwin Román-Ramirez, personal communication 2023). Adding to the near constant flow of new discoveries, I am convinced that the historical record of the Classic Maya will continue to provide occasional clues, both direct and indirect, regarding the politics and history of the Entrada and its aftermath. Maya sources may continue to shed an indirect light on ancient Teotihuacan during the late fourth and early fifth centuries, at least as represented through a Maya perspective. Such refinements should bring Spearthrower Owl and his role into better focus, both as a key figure in Teotihuacan's once opaque history and as an influential actor in Classic Maya politics.

NOTES

1 The Aztec Piedra del Sol, or Calendar Stone, may provide a case study of this interpretive blind spot. Ever since the days of Eduard Seler (Nicholson 1993), it has been traditionally interpreted as a straightforward image of the Mexica solar deity Tonatiuh. However, as I recently argued, the central face can be best seen as a hybrid image, the portrait of the ruler Moteczomah II in the guise of the patron deity Huitzilopochtli, who are, in turn, identified as the sun and its many cosmological components (Stuart 2021). What for so long has been seen as a quintessential example of purely religious or mythological iconography is, in fact, rooted in historical and political messaging, with a Mexica ruler at its center.

2 I have pointed out how Panel 2 from Piedras Negras mentions another possible foreign ruler who oversaw an important military or ritual of military investiture in the year 510. His name, as best we can determine, was Tajoom Uk'ab Tuun, and he bears the familiar title *ochk'in kaloomte'*, referencing the west. There is a stated hierarchical relationship between him and his Piedras Negras vassal, possibly named Yaht Ahk, an early namesake for the much later Ruler 7. The discovery of the wooden box bearing Tajoom's name, and a record of the very same event, provides compelling evidence of his own close Teotihuacan associations (Anaya H., Mathews, and Guenter 2003). The box text includes a Distance Number to an earlier event, possibly a journey to or from highland Mexico, not unlike the narrative on Altar Q of Copan.

3 For critical assessments of Teotihuacan's role as a regional empire, see Smith and Montiel (2001) and Smith (2020).

APPENDIX 1

Key Dates of the Entrada and Early Classic Peten History (250–450 CE)

SOURCE	MAYA DATE	584286 CORR.	EVENT
Tikal, Stela 29	8.12.14.8.15 13 Men 3 Zip	July 9, 292	? (early Yax Nun Ayiin ruler?)
Uaxactun, Stela 9	8.14.5.12.16 9 Cib 14 Kayab	April 19, 328	accession?
Uaxactun, Stela 19	8.16.0.0.0 3 Ahau 8 Kankin	February 3, 357	Period Ending by "Tz'ak Vulture"
Tikal, Marcador	8.16.17.9.0 11 Ahau 3 Uayeb	May 5, 374	accession of Spearthrower Owl ("Eagle Striker")
Tikal, Stela 39	8.17.0.0.0 1 Ahau 8 Ch'en	October 21, 376	Period Ending by Chak Tok Ich'aak, "Tz'ak Vulture" captive
Tikal, Monument 34	8.17.0.15.7 9 Manik 10 Xul (?)	August 21, 377	"descent" (departure?) of Sihyaj K'ahk'
El Peru, Stela 15	8.17.1.4.4 3 Kan 7 Mac	January 8, 378	arrival of Sihyaj K'ahk' to El Peru
Naachtun, Stela 24	8.17.1.4.10 9 Oc 13 Mac	January 14, 378	?
Naachtun, Stela 24	8.17.1.4.11 10 Chuen 14 Mac	January 15, 378	?
Tikal, Stela 31	8.17.1.4.12 11 Eb 15 Mac	January 16, 378	arrival of Sihyaj K'ahk' to Tikal
Tikal, Marcador	8.17.1.4.12 11 Eb 15 Mac	January 16, 378	arrival of Sihyaj K'ahk' to Tikal
Uaxactun, Stela 5	8.17.1.4.12 11 Eb 15 Mac	January 16, 378	arrival of Sihyaj K'ahk' to Tikal
Uaxactun, Stela 22	8.17.1.4.12 11 Eb 15 Mac	January 16, 378	arrival of west *k'awiil* to Tikal
El Peru, Stela 51	8.17.1.4.12 11 Eb 15 Mac	January 16, 378	arrival of Sihyaj K'ahk' to Tikal
La Sufricaya, Mural 7	8.17.1.4.12 11 Eb 15 Mac	January 16, 378	arrival of *k'awiil* to Tikal
Tikal, Monument 35	8.17.2.3.16 4 Cib 14 Ceh?	December 26, 378	"descent" (departure?) of Yax Nun Ayiin
La Sufricaya, Mural 7	8.17.2.4.16 11 Cib 14 Mac	January 15, 379	building dedication (one-year anniversary)
El Zapote, Stela 4	8.17.2.5.3 5 Akbal 1 Kankin	January 22, 379	accession of Sihyaj K'ahk' vassal?
Achiotal, Stela 1	8.17.2.12.12 11 Eb 5 Zip (implied)	June 20, 379	accession of Sihyaj K'ahk' vassal

| 127 |

SOURCE	MAYA DATE	584286 CORR.	EVENT
Tikal, Stela 31	8.17.2.13.15 8 Men 8 Zotz' (?)	July 30, 379	"ascent" of Yax Nun Ayiin?
Tikal, Stela 4	8.17.2.16.17 5 Caban 10 Yaxkin	September 13, 379	accession of Yax Nun Ayiin, Sihyaj K'ahk' vassal
Bejucal, Stela 2	8.17.4.16.18 11 Etz'nab 1 Yaxkin	September 3, 381	accession of Sihyaj K'ahk' vassal
Río Azul, Stela 1	8.17.16.12.3 11 Akbal 11 Kayab (?)	March 29, 393	accession of Sihyaj K'ahk' vassal?
Bejucal, Stela 2	8.17.17.0.0 11 Ahau 3 Tzec	July 24, 393	Period Ending by local ruler
Tikal, Stela 4	8.18.0.0.0 12 Ahau 8 Zotz'	July 8, 396	Period Ending by Yax Nun Ayiin
Uaxactun, Stela 4	8.18.0.0.0 12 Ahau 8 Zotz'	July 8, 396	Period Ending by "Sky Raiser"
Tres Islas, Stela 1	8.18.0.0.0 12 Ahau 8 Zotz'	July 8, 396	Period Ending
Tikal, Hombre	8.18.7.3.5 10 Chicchan 18 Tzec	August 6, 403	unknown
Tikal, Stela 31	8.18.8.1.2 2 Ik 10 Zip (?)	June 18, 404	death of Yax Nun Ayiin?
Tikal, Hombre	8.18.10.1.1 6 Imix 19 Uo	June 7, 406	second arrival of Sihyaj K'ahk' to Tikal?
Tikal, Hombre	8.18.10.1.10 2 Oc 8 Zip	June 16, 406	arrival of ?
Tikal, Hombre	8.18.10.8.12 1 Eb 10 Yax	November 4, 406	seating event with Yax Nun Ayiin
Tikal, Stela 31	8.18.15.11.0 3 Ahau 13 Zac (?)	November 27, 411	accession of Sihyaj Chan K'awiil?
Tikal, Marcador	8.18.17.14.9 12 Muluc 12 Kankin	January 24, 414	dedication of Marcador
Tres Islas, Stela 1	8.18.18.13.14 6 Ix 12 Mac (?)	January 4, 415	?
El Peru, Stela 15	8.19.0.0.0 10 Ahau 13 Kayab	March 25, 416	Period Ending by K'inich Bahlam
Tres Islas, Stela 1	8.19.0.0.0 10 Ahau 13 Kayab	March 25, 416	Period Ending
Tikal, Stela 31	8.19.10.0.0 9 Ahau 3 Muan	February 1, 426	Period Ending by Sihyaj Chan K'awiil?
El Peru, Stela 51	8.19.16.16.12 5 Eb seating of Ceh	November 28, 432	accession of ruler; Speathrower Owl ("Eagle Striker") "sees it"
Tikal, Stela 31	9.0.0.0.0 8 Ahau 13 Ceh	December 11, 435	Period Ending by Sihyaj Chan K'awiil
El Peru, Stela 51	9.0.0.0.0 8 Ahau 13 Ceh	December 11, 435	Period Ending by local ruler
El Zapote, Stela 5	9.0.0.0.0 8 Ahau 13 Ceh	December 11, 435	Period Ending by Sihyaj Chan K'awiil
Tikal, Stela 31	9.0.3.9.18 12 Etz'nab 11 Zip	June 11, 439	death of Speathrower Owl ("Eagle Striker")
Tikal, Stela 31	9.0.10.0.0 7 Ahau 3 Ceh	October 19, 445	Period Ending by Sihyaj Chan K'awiil
Uaxactun, Stela 31	9.0.10.0.0 7 Ahau 3 Ceh	October 19, 445	Period Ending by Baahte' K'inich

REFERENCES CITED

Adams, Richard E. W.

1999 *Río Azul: An Ancient Maya City.* University of Oklahoma Press, Norman.

Anaya H., Armando, Peter Mathews, and Stanley Guenter

2003 A New Inscribed Wooden Box from Southern Mexico. Online publication, http://mesoweb.com/reports/box/text.html.

Angulo V., Jorge

1998 El desarrollo sociopolítico como factor de cambio cronológico cultural. In *Los ritmos de cambio en Teotihuacán: Reflexciones y discusiones de su cronología*, edited by Rosa Brambila and Rubén Cabrera, pp. 103–128. Instituto Nacional de Antropología e Historia, Mexico City.

Appiah, Kwame Anthony

2021 Digging for Utopia. *The New York Review of Books*, December 16.

Arroyo, Barbara, Takeshi Inomata, Gloria Ajú, Javier Estrada, Hiroo Nasu, and Kazuo Aoyama

2020 Refining Kaminaljuyu Chronology: New Radiocarbon Dates, Bayesian Analysis, and Ceramics Studies. *Latin American Antiquity* 31(3):477–497.

Aveleyra Arroyo de Anda, Luis

1963a *La estela teotihuacana de La Ventilla.* Museo Nacional de Antropología, Instituto Nacional de Antropología e Historia, Mexico City.

1963b An Extraordinary Composite Stela from Teotihuacan. *American Antiquity* 29(2):235–237.

Ayala Falcón, Maricela

1987 La estela 39 de Tikal, Mundo Perdido. In *Memorias de Primer Coloquio Internacional de Mayistas, 5–10 de agosto de 1985*, pp. 599–654. Universidad Nacional Autónoma de México, Instituto de Investigaciones Filológicas, Centro de Estudios Mayas, Mexico City.

Barrera Vásquez, Alfredo

1980 *Diccionario maya Cordemex: Maya–español, español–maya.* Cordemex, Mérida.

Bassie-Sweet, Karen

2019 A Portrait of Sihyaj K'ahk'. Unpublished paper, https://www.academia.edu/41482544/A_Portrait_of_Sihyaj_Kahk.

2021 *Maya Gods of War.* University Press of Colorado, Louisville.

Beliaev, Dmitri

2017 Río Azul Dynasty and Polity: New Epigraphic Evidence. Paper presented at the 3rd Annual Workshop for the Textdatenbank und Wörterbuch des Klassischen Maya, Bonn University, Bonn.

Beliaev, Dmitri, and Stephen D. Houston

2019 A Sacrificial Sign in Maya Writing. *Maya Decipherment*, https://mayadecipherment.com/2020/06/20/a-sacrificial-sign-in-maya-writing.

Beliaev, Dmitri, David Stuart, and Camilo Luin

2017　Late Classic Maya Vase with the Mention of Sihyaj K'ahk' from the Museo VICAL, Casa Santo Domingo, Antigua Guatemala. *Mexicon* 39(1):1–4, 28.

Beliaev, Dmitri, Alexandre Tokovinine, Sergey Verpetskii, and Camilo Luin

2013　Los monumentos de Tikal. In *Proyecto atlas epigráfico de Petén, fase 1*, pp. 37–170. Centro de Estudios Maya Yuri Knorosov, Guatemala City.

Beliaev, Dmitri, and Sergei Verpetskii

2018　Los monumentos de Itsimte (Petén, Guatemala): Nuevos datos e interpretaciones. *Arqueología Iberoamericana* 38:3–13.

Berlo, Janet Catherine

1984　*Teotihuacan Art Abroad: A Study of the Metropolitan Style and Provincial Transformation in Incensario Workshops.* 2 vols. BAR International Series, Oxford.

Berrin, Kathleen (editor)

1988　*Feathered Serpents and Flowering Trees: Reconstructing the Murals of Teotihuacan.* Fine Arts Museums of San Francisco, San Francisco.

Black, Stephen L.

1990　The Carnegie Uaxactun Project and the Development of Maya Archaeology. *Ancient Mesoamerica* 1(2):257–276.

Boot, Erik

2010　Loanwords, "Foreign Words," and Foreign Signs in Maya Writing. In *The Idea of Writing: Play and Complexity*, edited by Alexander J. de Voogt and Irving L. Finkel, pp. 129–138. Brill, Leiden.

Borowicz, James

2003　Images of Power and the Power of Images: Early Classic Iconographic Programs of the Carved Monuments of Tikal. In *The Maya and Teotihuacan: Reinterpreting Early Classic Interaction*, edited by Geoffrey E. Braswell, pp. 217–234. University of Texas Press, Austin.

Bove, Fredrick J., and Sonia Medrano Busto

2003　Teotihuacan, Militarism, and Pacific Guatemala. In *The Maya and Teotihuacan: Reinterpreting Early Classic Interaction*, edited by Geoffrey E. Braswell, pp. 45–80. University of Texas Press, Austin.

Braswell, Geoffrey E.

2003a　Introduction: Reinterpreting Early Classic Interaction. In *The Maya and Teotihuacan: Reinterpreting Early Classic Interaction*, edited by Geoffrey E. Braswell, pp. 1–43. University of Texas Press, Austin.

2003b　Dating Early Classic Interaction between Kaminaljuyu and Central Mexico. In *The Maya and Teotihuacan: Reinterpreting Early Classic Interaction*, edited by Geoffrey E. Braswell, pp. 81–104. University of Texas Press, Austin.

Buikstra, Jane E., T. Douglas Price, James H. Burton, and Lori E. Wright

2004　Tombs from Copan's Acropolis: A Life History Approach. In *Understanding Early Classic Copan*, edited by Ellen E. Bell, Marcello A. Canuto, and Robert J. Sharer, pp. 191–212. University of Pennsylvania Museum of Archaeology and Anthropology, Philadephia.

Canuto, Marcello, Luke Auld-Thomas, and Ernesto Aredondo

2020　Teotihuacan and Lowland Maya Interactions: Characterizing a Mesoamerican Hegemony. In *Teotihuacan: The World Beyond the City*, edited by Kenneth G. Hirth, David M. Carballo, and Barbara Arroyo, pp. 371–408. Dumbarton Oaks Research Library and Collection, Washington, D.C.

Carballo, David M.

2020　Power, Politics, and Governance at Teotihuacan. In *Teotihuacan: The World Beyond the City*, edited by Kenneth G. Hirth, David M. Carballo, and Barbara Arroyo, pp. 57–96. Dumbarton Oaks Research Library and Collection, Washington, D.C.

Carmack, Robert M., and James L. Mondloch

1983 *El Titulo de Totonicapán: Texto, traducción y comentario*. Universidad Nacional Autónoma de México, Instituto de Investigaciones Filológicas, Centro de Estudios Mayas, Mexico City.

Carter, Nicholas P., Yeny M. Gutiérrez Castillo, and Sarah Newman

2018 Border Lords and Client Kings: El Zotz and Bejucal in the Late Classic Period. In *An Inconstant Landscape: The Maya Kingdom of El Zotz, Guatemala*, edited by Thomas G. Garrison and Stephen D. Houston, pp. 93–115. University Press of Colorado, Louisville.

Caso, Alfonso

1972 Dioses y signos teotihuacanos. In *Teotihuacán: XI Mesa Redonda,* pp. 249–279. Sociedad Mexicana de Antropología, Mexico City.

1984 *Reyes y reinos de la Mixteca*. 2 vols. Fondo de Cultura Económica, Mexico City.

Clayton, Sarah C.

2005 Interregional Relationships in Mesoamerica: Interpreting Maya Ceramics at Teotihuacan. *Latin American Antiquity* 16(4):427–448.

Coggins, Clemency Chase

1975 Painting and Drawing Styles at Tikal. PhD dissertation, Harvard University, Cambridge, Mass.

Cojti Ren, Iyaxel

2021 The *Saqirik* (Dawn) and Foundation Rituals among the Ancient K'iche'an Peoples. In *The Myths of the Popol Vuh in Cosmology, Art, and Ritual*, edited by Holley Moyes, Allen J. Christenson, and Frauke Sachse, pp. 77–92. University Press of Colorado, Louisville.

Colas, Pierre Robert

2004 *Sinn und Bedeutung Klassischer Maya-Personennamen: Typologische Analyse von Anthroponymphrasen in den Hieroglyphen-Inschriften der Klassischen Maya-Kultur als Beitrag zur Allgemeinen Onomastik*. Acta Mesoamericana 15. Verlag Anton Saurwein, Markt Schwaben.

Cowgill, George L.

1983 Rulership and the Ciudadela: Political Inferences from Teotihuacan Architecture. In *Civilization in the Ancient Americas: Essays in Honor of Gordon R. Willey*, edited by Richard M. Leventhal and Alan L. Kolata, pp. 313–344. University of New Mexico Press, Albuquerque.

1992 Toward a Political History of Teotihuacan. In *Ideology and Pre-Columbian Civilizations*, edited by Arthur A. Demarest and Geoffrey W. Conrad, pp. 87–114. School of American Research Press, Santa Fe.

1997 State and Society at Teotihuacan, Mexico. *Annual Review of Anthropology* 26(1):129–161.

2003 Teotihuacan and Early Classic Interaction: A Perspective from Outside the Maya Region. In *The Maya and Teotihuacan: Reinterpreting Early Classic Interaction*, edited by Geoffrey E. Braswell, pp. 45–80. University of Texas Press, Austin.

2015 *Ancient Teotihuacan: Early Urbanism in Central Mexico*. Cambridge University Press, New York.

Culbert, T. Patrick

1993 *The Ceramics of Tikal: Vessels from the Burials, Caches and Problematic Deposits*. Tikal Reports no. 25, pt. A. University of Pennsylvania Museum of Archaeology and Anthropology, Philadelphia.

Culbert, T. Patrick (editor)

1991 *Classic Maya Political History: Hieroglyphic and Archaeological Evidence*. Cambridge University Press, Cambridge.

Davletshin, Albert, and Stephen D. Houston

2021 Maya Creatures VI: A Fox Cannot Hide Its Tail. *Maya Decipherment*, https://mayadecipherment.com/2021/01/08/maya-creatures-vi-a-fox-cannot-hide-its-tail/

Edmonson, Munro S.

1965 *Quiche-English Dictionary*. Middle American Research Institute, Tulane University, New Orleans.

Estrada-Belli, Francisco, and Alexandre Tokovinine

2016 A King's Apotheosis: Iconography, Text, and Politics from a Classic Maya Temple at Holmul. *Latin American Antiquity* 27(2):149–168.

Estrada-Belli, Francisco, Alexandre Tokovinine, Jennifer M. Foley, Heather Hurst, Gene A. Ware, David Stuart, and Nikolai Grube

2009 A Maya Palace at Holmul, Peten, Guatemala, and the Teotihuacan "Entrada": Evidence from Murals 7 and 9. *Latin American Antiquity* 20(1):228–259.

Fahsen, Federico

1988 A New Early Classic Text from Tikal. *Research Reports on Ancient Maya Writing,* no. 17. Center for Maya Research, Washington, D.C.

Fash, Barbara W.

2011 *The Copan Sculpture Museum: Ancient Maya Artistry in Stucco and Stone.* Peabody Museum Press, Harvard University, Cambridge, Mass.

Fash, William L., and Barbara W. Fash

2000 Teotihuacan and the Maya: A Classic Heritage. In *Mesoamerica's Classic Heritage: From Teotihuacan to the Aztecs*, edited by David Carrasco, Lyndsay Jones, and Scott Sessions, pp. 433–463. University Press of Colorado, Boulder.

Fash, William L., Alexandre Tokovinine, and Barbara W. Fash

2009 The House of New Fire at Teotihuacan and Its Legacy in Mesoamerica. In *The Art of Urbanism: How Mesoamerican Kingdoms Represented Themselves in Architecture and Imagery,* edited by William L. Fash and Leonardo López Luján, pp. 201–229. Dumbarton Oaks Research Library and Collection, Washington, D.C.

Fash, William L., Richard V. Williamson, Carlos Rudy Larios, and Joel Palka

1992 The Hieroglyphic Stairway and Its Ancestors: Investigations of Copan Structure 10L-26. *Ancient Mesoamerica* 3(1):105–115.

Fialko, Vilma

1988 El marcador del juego de pelota de Tikal: Nuevas referencias epigráficas para el período clásico temprano. *Mesoamerica* 9(15):117–135.

Fitzsimmons, James L.

2009 *Death and the Classic Maya Kings.* University of Texas Press, Austin.

Freidel, David A., Hector L. Escobedo, and Stanley P. Guenter

2007 A Crossroads of Conquerors: Waka' and Gordon Willey's "Rehearsal for the Collapse" Hypothesis. In *Gordon R. Willey and American Archaeology: Contemporary Perspectives*, edited by Jeremy A. Sabloff and William L. Fash, pp. 187–208. University of Oklahoma Press, Norman.

Freidel, David A., and Linda Schele

1988a Kingship in the Late Preclassic Maya Lowlands: The Instruments and Places of Ritual Power. *American Anthropologist*, n.s., 90(3):547–567.

1988b Symbol and Power: A History of the Lowland Maya Cosmogram. In *Maya Iconography*, edited by Elizabeth P. Benson and Gillett G. Griffin, pp. 44–93. Princeton University Press, Princeton.

Froese, Tom, Carlos Gersenson, and Linda R. Manzanilla

2014 Can Government Be Self-Organized? A Mathematical Model of the Collective Social Organization of Ancient Teotihuacan, Central Mexico. *PloS One* 9(10): e109966, https://doi.org/10.1371/journal.pone.0109966.

Garcia Cháves, Raúl

2002 La relación entre Teotihuacan y los centros provinciales del clásico en la cuenca de México. In *Ideología y política a través de materiales, imágenes y símbolos: Memoria de la Primera Mesa Redonda de Teotihuacan*, edited by María E. Ruiz Gallut, pp. 501–527. Universidad Nacional Autónoma de México, Mexico City.

García–Des Lauriers, Claudia

2017 The Regalia of Sacred War: Costume and Militarism at Teotihuacan. *Americae: European Journal of Americanist Archaeology* 2:83–98.

Garrison, Thomas G., Stephen D. Houston, Andrew K. Scherer, David del Cid, Jose Luis Garrido López, Ewa Czapiewskea-Halliday, and Edwin Róman

2016 A Royal Maya Country House: Archaeology at Bejucal, Guatemala. *Journal of Field Archaeology* 41(5):532–549.

Graeber, David, and David Wengrow

2021 *The Dawn of Everything: A New History of Humanity*. Farrar, Straus and Giroux, New York.

Graham, Ian

1986 *Corpus of Maya Hieroglyphic Inscriptions*, vol. 5, pt. 3, *Uaxactun*. Peabody Museum of Archaeology and Ethnology, Harvard University, Cambridge, Mass.

Greene, Virginia, and Hattula Moholy-Nagy

1966 A Teotihuacan-Style Vessel from Tikal: A Correction. *American Antiquity* 31(3):432–434.

Grube, Nikolai

1990 Die Errichtung von Stelen: Entzifferung einer Verbhieroglyphie auf Monumentun der klassischen Mayakultur. In *Circumpacifica: Festscrift für Thomas S. Barthel*, edited by Bruno Illius and Matthias Samuel Laubscher, pp. 189–215. Peter Lang, Frankfurt am Main.

2004 El origen de la dinastía Kaan. In *Los cautivos de Dzibanché*, edited by Enrique Nalda Hernández, pp. 117–131. Instituto Nacional de Antropología e Historia, Mexico City.

Grube, Nikolai (editor)

1995 *The Emergence of Lowland Maya Civilization: The Transition from the Preclassic to the Early Classic*. Verlag Anton Saurwein, Möckmühl.

Grube, Nikolai, and Maria Gaida

2006 *Die Maya: Schrift und Kunst*. SMB DuMont, Berlin.

Grube, Nikolai, and Linda Schele

1994 Kuy, the Owl of Omen and War. *Mexicon* 16(1):10–17.

Guenter, Stanley

2014 The Epigraphy of El Perú-Waka'. In *Archaeology at El Perú-Waka': Ancient Maya Performances of Ritual, Memory, and Power*, edited by Olivia C. Navarro-Farr and Michelle Rich, pp. 147–166. University of Arizona Press, Tucson.

Hassig, Ross

1988 *Aztec Warfare: Imperial Expansion and Political Control*. University of Oklahoma Press, Norman.

Headrick, Annabeth

2001 Merging Myth and Politics: The Three Temple Complex at Teotihuacan. In *Landscape and Power in Ancient Mesoamerica*, edited by Rex Koontz, Kathryn Reese-Taylor, and Annabeth Headrick, pp. 169–195. Westview Press, Boulder, Colo.

2007 *The Teotihuacan Trinity: The Sociopolitical Structure of an Ancient Mesoamerican City*. University of Texas Press, Austin.

Hellmuth, Nicholas M.

1975 *The Escuintla Hoards: Teotihuacan Art in Guatemala*. F.L.A.A.R. Progress Reports 2, no 2. Foundation for Latin American Anthropological Research, Guatemala City.

1986 *Ballgame Iconography and Playing Gear: Late Classic Maya Polychrome Vases and Some Sculpture of Peten, Guatemala*. Foundation for Latin American Anthropological Research, Culver City, Calif.

1988 Early Maya Iconography on an Incised Cylindrical Tripod. In *Maya Iconography*, edited by Elizabeth P. Benson and Gillett G. Griffin, pp. 152–174. Princeton University Press, Princeton.

Helmke, Christophe

2013 Mesoamerican Lexical Calques in Ancient Maya Writing and Imagery. *The PARI Journal* 14(2):1–15.

Helmke, Christophe, and Jaime Awe

2016 Sharper than a Serpent's Tooth: A Tale of the Snake-head Dynasty as Recounted on Xunantunich Panel 4. *The PARI Journal* 17(2):1–22.

Helmke, Christophe, and James E. Brady

2014 Epigraphic and Archaeological Evidence of Cave Desecration in Ancient Maya Warfare. In *A Celebration of the Life and Work of Pierre Robert Colas*, edited by Christophe Helmke and Frauke Sachse, pp. 195–227. Acta Mesoamericana 27. Verlag Anton Saurwein, Munich.

Helmke, Christophe, and Jesper Nielsen

2011 *The Writing System of Cacaxtla, Tlaxcala, Mexico.* Boundary End Archaeology Research Center, Barnardsville, N.C.

2021 Teotihuacan Writing: Where Are We Now? *Visible Language* 55(2):29–73.

Houston, Stephen D.

1993 *Hieroglyphs and History at Dos Pilas: Dynastic Politics of the Classic Maya.* University of Texas Press, Austin.

2008 A Classic Maya Bailiff? *Maya Decipherment*, https://maya decipherment.com/2008/03/10 /a-classic-maya-bailiff/.

Houston, Stephen D., Thomas G. Garrison, and Omar Alcover Firpi

2019 Citadels and Surveillance: Conflictive Regions and Defensive Design in the Buenavista Citadels of Guatemala. *Contributions to New World Archaeology* 13:9–36.

Houston, Stephen D., and Peter Mathews

1985 *The Dynastic Sequence of Dos Pilas, Guatemala.* Pre-Columbian Art Research Institute, San Francisco.

Houston, Stephen D., John Robertson, David Stuart, et al.

2000 The Language of Classic Maya Inscriptions. *Current Anthropology* 41(3):321–356.

Houston, Stephen D., Edwin Román Ramírez, Thomas G. Garrison, David Stuart, Héctor Escobedo Ayala, and Pamela Rosales

2021 A Teotihuacan Complex at the, Classic Maya City of Tikal, Guatemala. *Antiquity* 95:1–9.

Houston, Stephen D., and David Stuart

1996 Of Gods, Glyphs, and Kings: Divinity and Rulership among the Classic Maya. *Antiquity* 70:289–312.

Houston, Stephen D., David Stuart, and Karl A. Taube

2006 *The Memory of Bones: Body, Being, and Experience among the Classic Maya.* University of Texas Press, Austin.

Hull, Kerry

2016 *A Dictionary of Ch'orti' Mayan–Spanish–English.* University of Utah Press, Salt Lake City.

Jones, Christopher

1977 Inauguration Dates of Three Late Classic Rulers at Tikal, Guatemala. *American Antiquity* 42(1):28–60.

Jones, Christopher, and Linton B. Satterthwaite

1982 *The Monuments and Inscriptions of Tikal: The Carved Monuments.* Tikal Reports 33, part A. University Museum, University of Pennsylvania, Philadelphia.

Kelley, David H.

1982 Costume and Name in Mesoamerica. *Visible Language* 16(1):39–48.

Kettunen, Harri

2017 Uk'ay Ajbuj: Otherworldly Owls in the Mundo Maya. In *Into the Underworld: Landscapes of Creation and Conceptions of the Afterlife in Mesoamerica*, edited by Jarosław Źrałka and Christophe Helmke, special issue, *Contributions in New World Archaeology* 10:113–148.

Kidder, Alfred V., Jesse D. Jennings, and Edwin M. Shook

1946 *Excavations at Kaminaljuyu, Guatemala.* Carnegie Institution of Washington 561. Carnegie Institution of Washington, Washington, D.C.

Klein, Cecelia F.

1976   *The Face of the Earth: Frontality in Two-Dimensional Mesoamerican Art.* Garland, New York.

Kováč, Milan, and Ramzy R. Barrois

2012   El papel de Sihyaj K'ahk' en Uaxactun y el Petén central. In *Maya Political Relations and Strategies*, edited by Jarosław Źrałka, Wiesław Koszkul, and Beata Golińska, special issue, *Contributions in New World Archaeology* 4:113–126.

Kováč, Milan, Dmitri Beliaev, Jakub Špoták, and Alexander Safronov

2019   Uaxactun after the Conquest by Teotihuacanos as Told by the Mural of Palace B-XIII. *Contributions in New World Archaeology* 13:37–66.

Kubler, George

1967   *The Iconography of the Art of Teotihuacan.* Dumbarton Oaks, Trustees for Harvard University, Washington, D.C.

Lacadena, Alfonso, and Søren Wichmann

2004   On the Representation of the Glottal Stop in Maya Writing. In *The Linguistics of Maya Writing*, edited by Søren Wichmann, pp. 100–164. University of Utah Press, Salt Lake City.

Langley, James C.

1986   *Symbolic Notation of Teotihuacan: Elements of Writing in a Mesoamerican Culture of the Classic Period.* BAR, Oxford.

1992   Teotihuacan Sign Clusters: Emblem or Articulation? In *Art, Ideology, and the City of Teotihuacan*, edited by Janet Catherine Berlo, pp. 247–280. Dumbarton Oaks Research Library and Collection, Washington, D.C.

2002   Teotihuacan Notation in a Meso-american Context: Likeness, Concept and Metaphor. In *Ideología y política a través de materiales, imágenes y símbolos: Memoria de la Primera Mesa Redonda de Teotihuacan*, edited by María E. Ruiz Gallut, pp. 275–301. Universidad Nacional Autónoma de México, Mexico City.

Laporte, Juan Pedro

1987   El grupo 6C-XVI, Tikal, Peten: Un centro habitacional del clásico temprano. In *Memorias del Primer Coloquio Internacional de Mayistas*, pp. 221–244. Universidad Nacional Autónoma de México, Instituto de Investigaciones Filológicas, Centro de Estudios Mayas, Mexico City.

Laporte, Juan Pedro, and Vilma Fialko

1990   New Perspectives on Old Problems: Dynastic References for the Early Classic at Tikal. In *Vision and Revision in Maya Studies*, edited by Flora S. Clancy and Peter D. Harrison, pp. 33–66. University of New Mexico Press, Albuquerque.

Laporte, Juan Pedro, and Carlos Herman

2003   Trabajos no divulgados del Proyecto Nacional Tikal, Parte 3: Más información sobre la exploración de la Zona Norte (3D-43). In *XVI Simposio de Investigaciones Arqueológicas en Guatemala, 2002*, edited by Juan Pedro Laporte et al., pp. 359–380. Ministerio de Cultura y Deportes, Instituto de Antropología e Historia, and Asociación Tikal, Guatemala City.

Lincoln, Charles E.

1985   Ceramics and Ceramic Chronology. In *A Consideration of the Early Classic Period in the Maya Lowlands*, edited by Gordon R. Willey and Peter Mathews, pp. 55–94. Institute for Mesoamerican Studies, State University of New York, Albany.

Linné, Sigvald

1934   *Archaeological Researches at Teotihuacan, Mexico.* Oxford University Press, London.

López Luján, Leonardo

1989   *Le recuperación mexica del pasado teotihuacano.* Instituto Nacional de Antropología e Historia, Proyecto Templo Mayor, Mexico City.

Lounsbury, Floyd

1984   Glyphic Substitutions: Homophonic and Synonymic. In *Phoneticism in Mayan Hieroglyphic Writing*, edited by John S. Justeson and Lyle

Campbell, pp. 167–184. Institute for Mesoamerican Studies, State University of New York, Albany.

Manzanilla, Linda R.

1992 The Economic Organization of the Teotihuacan Priesthood. In *Art, Ideology, and the City of Teotihuacan*, edited by Janet Catherine Berlo, pp. 321–333. Dumbarton Oaks Research Library and Collection, Washington, D.C.

2002 Gobierno corporativo en Teoti-huacan: Una revisión del concepto "palacio" aplicado a la gran urbe prehispánica. *Anales de antropología* 35(1):157–190.

Marcus, Joyce

1976 *Emblem and State in the Classic Maya Lowlands*. Dumbarton Oaks, Trustees for Harvard University, Washington, D.C.

1983 Teotihuacan Visitors on Monte Alban Monuments and Murals. In *The Cloud People: Divergent Evolution of the Zapotec and Mixtec Civilizations*, edited by Kent V. Flannery and Joyce Marcus, pp. 175–181. Academic Press, New York.

Martin, Simon

1993 Tikal's "Star War" Against Naranjo. In *Eighth Palenque Round Table,* edited by Martha J. Macri and Jan McHargue, pp. 223–236. Pre-Columbian Art Research Institute, San Francisco.

1997 The Painted King List: A Commentary on Codex-Style Dynastic Vases. In *The Maya Vase Book: A Corpus of Rollout Photographs*, by Justin Kerr, vol. 5, pp. 846–867. Kerr Associates, New York.

2002 The Baby Jaguar: An Exploration of Its Identity and Origins in Maya Art and Writing. In *La organización social entre los mayas prehispánicos, coloniales y modernos*, edited by Vera Tiesler, Rafael Cobos, and Merle Greene Robertson, vol. 1, pp. 49–78. Conaculta–INAH, Mexico City.

2003 In the Line of the Founder: A View of Dynastic Politics at Tikal. In *Tikal: Dynasties, Foreigners and*

Affairs of State, edited by Jeremy A. Sabloff, pp. 3–46. School of American Research Press, Santa Fe.

2016 Ideology and the Early Maya Polity. In *The Origins of Maya States*, edited by Loa P. Traxler and Robert J. Sharer, pp. 507–544. University of Pennsylvania Museum of Archaeology and Anthropology, Philadelphia.

2017 Secrets of the Painted King List: Recovering the Early History of the Snake Dynasty, *Maya Decipherment*, https://mayadecipherment.com /2017/05/05/secrets-of-the-painted -king-list-recovering-the-early -history-of-the-snake-dynasty/.

2020 *Ancient Maya Politics: A Political Anthropology of the Classic Period, 150–900 CE*. Cambridge University Press, New York.

Martin, Simon, and Nikolai Grube

2000 *The Chronicle of Maya Kings and Queens: Deciphering the Dynasties of the Ancient Maya*. Thames and Hudson, London.

2008 *The Chronicle of Maya Kings and Queens: Deciphering the Dynasties of the Ancient Maya*. 2nd ed. Thames and Hudson, London.

Martin, Simon, and Joel Skidmore

2012 Exploring the 584286 Correlation between the Maya and European Calendars. *The PARI Journal* 13(2):3–16.

Mathews, Peter

1985 Maya Early Classic Monuments and Inscriptions. In *A Consideration of the Early Classic Period in the Maya Lowlands*, edited by Gordon R. Willey and Peter Mathews, pp. 5–54. Institute for Mesoamerican Studies, State University of New York, Albany.

Matteo, Sebastián, and Céline Gillot

2022 Sihyaj K'ahk': A New Portrait on a Late Classic Vase in the Collections of the Montreal Museum of Fine Arts. *Mexicon* 44(2):47–55.

Maxwell, Judith M., and Robert M. Hill II (translators)

2006 *Kaqchikel Chronicles: The Definitive Edition*. University of Texas Press, Austin.

McAnany, Patricia

2007 Culture Heroes and Feathered Serpents: The Contribution of Gordon Willey to the Study of Ideology. In *Gordon R. Willey and American Archaeology: Contemporary Perspectives*, edited by Jeremy A. Sabloff and William L. Fash, pp. 208–231. University of Oklahoma Press, Norman.

Michelon, Oscar (editor)

1976 *Diccionario de San Francisco*. Akademische Druck und Verlagsanstalt, Graz.

Millon, Clara

1973 Painting, Writing and Polity at Teotihuacan, Mexico. *American Antiquity* 38(3):294–314.

1988 A Reexamination of the Teotihuacan Tassel Headdress Insignia. In *Feathered Serpents and Flowering Trees: Reconstructing the Murals of Teotihuacan*, edited by Kathleen Berrin, pp. 114–134. Fine Arts Museums of San Francisco, San Francisco.

Millon, René

1976 Social Relations in Ancient Teotihuacan. In *The Valley of Mexico: Studies in Pre-Hispanic Ecology and Society*, edited by Eric R. Wolf, pp. 205–248. University of New Mexico Press, Albuquerque.

1988a The Last Years of Teotihuacan Dominance. In *The Collapse of Ancient States and Civilizations*, edited by Norman Yoffee and George L. Cowgill, pp. 102–164. University of Arizona Press, Tucson.

1988b Where Do They All Come From? The Provenance of the Wagner Murals from Teotihuacan. In *Feathered Serpents and Flowering Trees: Reconstructing the Murals of Teotihuacan*, edited by Kathleen Berrin, pp. 78–113. Fine Arts Museums of San Francisco, San Francisco.

1992 Teotihuacan Studies: From 1950 to 1990 and Beyond. In *Art, Ideology, and the City of Teotihuacan*, edited by Janet Catherine Berlo, pp. 339–429. Dumbarton Oaks Research Library and Collection, Washington, D.C.

2002 Comentarios finales. In *Ideología y política a través de materiales, imágenes y símbolos: Memoria de la Primera Mesa Redonda de Teotihuacan*, edited by María E. Ruiz Gallut, pp. 761–797. Universidad Nacional Autónoma de México, Mexico City.

Moholy-Nagy, Hattula

2008 *The Artifacts of Tikal: Ornamental and Ceremonial Artifacts and Unworked Material*. Tikal Reports 27, part A. University of Pennsylvania Museum of Archaeology and Anthropology, Philadelphia.

Morley, Sylvanus G.

1937– *The Inscriptions of Petén*. Carnegie
1938 Institution of Washington, Washington, D.C.

Murakami, Tatsuya, and Claudia García–Des Lauriers

2021 Introduction: Teotihuacan and Early Classic Mesoamerica. In *Teotihuacan in Early Classic Mesoamerica: Multiscalar Perpectives on Power, Identity, and Interregional Relations*, edited by Claudia Garcia–Des Lauriers and Tatsuya Murakami, pp. 3–45. University Press of Colorado, Louisville.

Navarro-Farr, Olivia, Griselda Pérez Robles, Mary Kate Kelly, Juan Carlos Pérez, and David Freidel

2022 Nuevos acontecimientos del Clásico temprano en El Perú-Waka': Hallazgos recientes en la estructura cívico-ceremonial M13-1. Paper presented at the 2022 Simposio de Arqueología de Guatemala, Guatemala City.

Nicholson, Henry B.

1993 The Problem of the Identification of the Central Image of the Aztec Calendar Stone. In *Current Topics in Aztec Studies: Essays in Honor of Dr. H. B. Nicholson*, edited by Alana

Cordy-Collins and Douglas Sharon, pp. 3–15. San Diego Museum of Man, San Diego.

2001 *Topiltzin Quetzalcoatl: The Once and Future Lord of the Toltecs.* University Press of Colorado, Boulder.

Nielsen, Jesper

2014 Where Kings Once Ruled? Consideration on Palaces and Rulership at Teotihuacan. In *Palaces and Courtly Culture in Ancient Mesoamerica*, edited by Julie Nehammer Knub, Christophe Helmke, and Jesper Nielsen, pp. 7–22. Archaeopress, Oxford.

Nielsen, Jesper, and Christophe Helmke

2008 Spearthrower Owl Hill: A Toponym at Atetelco, Teotihuacan. *Latin American Antiquity* 19(4):459–474.

2011 Reinterpreting the Plaza de los Glifos, La Ventilla, Teotihuacan. *Ancient Mesoamerica* 22(2):345–370.

2014 House of the Serpent Mat, House of Fire: The Names of Buildings in Teotihuacan Writing. In *Meso-american Writing Systems*, edited by Christophe Helmke and Jarosław Źrałka, special issue, *Contributions in New World Archaeology* 7:113–140.

2020 Crowning Rulers and Years: Interpreting the Year Sign Headdress at Teotihuacan. *Ancient Mesoamerica* 31(2):1–16.

Nielsen, Jesper, Christophe Helmke, Fiorella Fenoglio Limón, and Juan Carlos Saint-Charles Zetina

2019 *The Early Classic Murals of El Rosario, Queretaro.* Boundary End Archaeological Research Center, Barnardsville, N.C.

Nielsen, Jesper, and Iván Rivera

2019 Across the Hills, Toward the Ocean: Teotihuacan-Style Monuments in Guerrero, Mexico. In *Interregional Interaction in Mesoamerica*, edited by Joshua D. Englehardt and Michael D. Carrasco, pp. 176–209. University Press of Colorado, Boulder.

Nondédéo, Philippe, Juan Ignacio Cases, and Alfonso Lacadena

2019 Teotihuacanos y mayas en la "Entrada" de 11 Eb' (378 d.C.):

Nuevos datos de Naachtun, Petén, Guatemala. *Revista española de antropología americana* 49:53–75.

O'Neil, Megan E.

2012 *Engaging Ancient Maya Sculpture at Piedras Negras, Guatemala.* University of Oklahoma Press, Norman.

Pasztory, Esther

1988 A Reinterpretation of Teotihuacan and Its Mural Painting Tradition. In *Feathered Serpents and Flowering Trees: Reconstructing the Murals of Teotihuacan*, edited by Kathleen Berrin, pp. 45–77. Fine Arts Museums of San Francisco, San Francisco.

1992 Abstraction and the Rise of a Utopian State at Teotihuacan. In *Art, Ideology, and the City of Teotihuacan*, edited by Janet Catherine Berlo, pp. 281–320. Dumbarton Oaks Research Library and Collection, Washington, D.C.

1997 *Teotihuacan: An Experiment in Living.* University of Oklahoma Press, Norman.

Polian, Gilles

2020 Tseltal-Spanish Multidialectal Dictionary. Online publication, https://dictionaria.clld.org/contributions/tseltal.

Prager, Christian M.

2002 Die Inschriften von Pusilha: Epigraphische Analyse und Rekonstruktion der Geschichte einer klassischen Maya-Stätte. Master's thesis, University of Bonn, Bonn.

2021 A Logogram for **WAX**, "Grey Fox," in Maya Hieroglyphic Writing. *Research Reports on Maya Hieroglyphic Writing* 64. Boundary End Archaeological Research Center, Barnardsville, N.C.

Price, T. Douglas, James H. Burton, Robert J. Sharer, Jane Buikstra, Lori E. Wright, Loa P. Traxler, and Katherine A. Miller

2010 Kings and Commoners at Copan: Isotopic Evidence for Origins and Movement in the Classic Maya Period. *Journal of Anthropological Archaeology* 29(1):15–32.

Proskouriakoff, Tatiana

1993 *Maya History*. University of Texas Press, Austin.

Quenon, Michel, and Genevieve Le Fort

1997 Rebirth and Resurrection in Maize God Iconography. In *Maya Vase Book: A Corpus of Rollout Photographs of Maya Vases*, vol. 5, pp. 884–902. Kerr Associates, New York.

Ricketson, Oliver G., and Edith B. Ricketson

1937 *Uaxactun, Guatemala. Group E, 1926–1931*. Carnegie Institution of Washington, Washington, D.C.

Riese, Berthold

1984 Hel Hieroglyphs. In *Phoneticism in Mayan Hieroglyphic Writing*, edited by John S. Justeson and Lyle Campbell, pp. 263–286. Institute of Mesoamerican Studies, State University of New York, Albany.

Rivera, Iván

2011 Cerro de la Tortuga: Un sitio arqueológico con iconografía teotihuacana en la región chatina, Costa de Oaxaca. In *Monte Albán en la encrucijada regional y disciplinarian: Memoria de la Quinta Mesa Redonda de Monte Albán*, edited by Nelly Robles García and Ángel I. Rivera, pp. 429–444. Instituto Nacional de Antropología e Historia, Mexico City.

Robb, Matthew H. (editor)

2017 *Teotihuacan: City of Water, City of Fire*. Fine Arts Museums of San Francisco, San Francisco.

Robicsek, Francis, and Donald M. Hales

1981 *The Maya Book of the Dead, The Ceramic Codex: The Corpus of Codex Style Ceramics of the Late Classic Period*. University of Virginia Art Museum, Charlottesville.

Safronov, Alexander, and Dmitri Beliaev

2017 La epigrafía de Uaxactun después de un siglo, 1916–2016. In *XXX Simposio de Investigaciones Arqueológicas en Guatemala, 2016*, edited by Bárbara Arroyo, Luis Méndez Salinas, and Gloria Ajú ÁIvarez, pp. 515–528. Ministerio de Cultura y Deportes, Instituto de Antropología e Historia, Asociación Tikal, Guatemala City.

Safronov, Alexander, Dmitri Beliaev, Milan Kovač, and Jakub Špotak

2022 La primera guerra maya: Evidencias epigráficas sobre el conflicto entre Tikal y Uaxactun en el Clásico Temprano. Paper presented at the XXXIV Simposio de Investigaciones Arqueológicas en Guatemala. Ministerio de Cultura y Deportes, Instituto de Antropología e Historia, Asociación Tikal, Guatemala City.

Sanders, William T., and Susan Toby Evans

2005 Rulership and Palaces and Teotihuacan. In *Palaces and Power in the Americas: From Peru to the Northwest Coast*, edited by Jessica Joyce Christie and Patricia Joan Sarro, pp. 256–284. University of Texas Press, Austin.

Sanders, William T., and Joseph W. Michels (editors)

1977 *Teotihuacan and Kaminaljuyu: A Study in Prehistoric Culture Contact*. Pennsylvania State University Press, University Park.

Saturno, William A.

2009 Centering the Kingdom, Centering the King. In *The Art of Urbanism: How Mesoamerican Kingdoms Represented Themselves in Architecture and Imagery*, edited by William L. Fash and Leonardo López Luján, pp. 111–134. Dumbarton Oaks Research Library and Collection, Washington, D.C.

Schele, Linda

1978 Genealogical Documentation on the Tri-Figure Panels at Palenque. In *Proceedings of the Tercera Mesa Redonda de Palenque, June 11–18, 1978: A Conference on the Art, Hieroglyphics, and Historic Approaches of the Late Classic Maya*, edited by Merle Greene Robertson and Donnan Call Jeffers, pp. 41–70. The Pre-Columbian Art Research Center, Palenque.

1986a The Tlaloc Complex in the Classic Period: War and the Interaction between the Lowland Maya and Teotihuacan. Unpublished manuscript, Mesoamerica Center, University of Texas, Austin.

1986b The Founders of Lineages at Copan and Other Maya Sites. *Copan Notes*, no. 6. Copan Mosaics Project, Copan.

1992 The Founders of Lineages at Copan and Other Maya Sites. *Ancient Mesoamerica* 3(1):135–144.

1995 The Olmec Mountain and the Tree of Creation in Mesoamerican Cosmology. In *The Olmec World: Ritual and Rulership*, pp. 105–117. The Art Museum, Princeton University, Princeton.

Schele, Linda, and David Freidel

1993 *A Forest of Kings: The Untold Story of the Ancient Maya*. William Morrow, New York.

Schele, Linda, and Nikolai Grube

1994 Tlaloc-Venus Warfare: The Peten Wars. Notebook for the XVIIIth Maya Hieroglyphic Workshop, March 12–13, 1994. University of Texas, Austin.

Schele, Linda, and Matthew G. Looper

2005 Seats of Power at Copán. In *Copán: The History of an Ancient Maya Kingdom*, edited by E. Wyllys Andrews and William L. Fash, pp. 345–372. School of American Research Press, Santa Fe.

Schele, Linda, and Peter Mathews

1998 *The Code of Kings: The Language of Seven Sacred Maya Temples and Tombs*. Scribner, New York.

Schele, Linda, Peter Mathews, and Floyd Lounsbury

n.d. Parentage and Spouse Expressions from Classic Maya Inscriptions. Unpublished manuscript.

Schele, Linda, and Mary E. Miller

1986 *The Blood of Kings: Dynasty and Ritual in Maya Art*. Kimbell Art Museum, Fort Worth.

Scherer, Andrew K.

2015 *Mortuary Landscapes of the Classic Maya: Rituals of Body and Soul*. University of Texas Press, Austin.

Scherer, Andrew K., Charles Golden, and Stephen D. Houston

2018 True People, Foreigners, and the Framing of Maya Morality. In *Bioarchaeology of Pre-Columbian Mesoamerica: An Interdisciplinary Approach*, edited by Cathy Willermet and Andrea Cucina, pp. 159–191. University Press of Florida, Gainsville.

Seler, Eduard

1998 *Collected Works in Mesoamerican Linguistics and Archaeology*. 6 vols. Labyrinthos, Lancaster, Calif.

Sharer, Robert

1992 The Preclassic Origin of Lowland Maya States. In *New Theories on the Ancient Maya*, edited by Elin C. Danien and Robert J. Sharer, pp. 131–136. University Museum, University of Pennsylvania, Philadelphia.

2003 Founding Events and Teotihuacan Connections at Copán, Honduras. In *The Maya and Teotihuacan: Reinterpreting Early Classic Interaction*, edited by Geoffrey E. Braswell, pp. 143–166. University of Texas Press, Austin.

2004 External Interaction at Early Classic Copan. In *Understanding Early Classic Copan*, edited by Ellen E. Bell, Marcello A. Canuto, and Robert J. Sharer, pp. 297–318. University of Pennsylvania Museum of Archaeology and Anthropology, Philadelphia.

Smith, Mary Elizabeth

1973 *Picture Writing from Ancient Southern Mexico: Mixtec Place Signs and Maps*. University of Oklahoma Press, Norman.

Smith, Michael E.

2020 Teotihuacan and Its Distant Neighbors: Models of Interaction. In *Teotihuacan: The World Beyond the City*, edited by Kenneth G. Hirth, David M. Carballo, and Barbara Arroyo, pp. 463–478. Dumbarton Oaks Research Library and Collection, Washington, D.C.

2022 Early Cities in *The Dawn of Everything*: Shoddy Scholarship in Support of Pedestrian Conclusions. *Cliodynamics: The Journal of Quantitative History and Cultural Evolution* 2:1–13.

Smith, Michael E., and Lisa Montiel

2001 The Archaeological Study of Empires and Imperialism in Pre-Hispanic Central Mexico. *Journal of Anthropological Archaeology* 20(3):245–284.

Smith, Robert E.

1955 *Ceramic Sequence at Uaxactun, Guatemala*. 2 vols. Middle American Research Institute, Tulane University, New Orleans.

Stone, Andrea

1989 Disconnection, Foreign Insignia, and Political Expansion: Teotihuacan and the Warrior Stelae of Piedras Negras. In *Mesoamerica After the Decline of Teotihuacan*, edited by Richard A. Diehl and Janet Catherine Berlo, pp. 153–172. Dumbarton Oaks Research Library and Collection, Washington, D.C.

Stuart, David

1985 A New Child-Father Relationship Glyph. *Research Reports on Ancient Maya Writing*, no. 2. Center for Maya Research, Washington, D.C.

1987 Ten Phonetic Syllables. *Research Reports on Ancient Maya Writing*, no. 14. Center for Maya Research, Washington, D.C.

1993 Historical Inscriptions and the Maya Collapse. In *Lowland Maya Civilization in the Eighth Century A.D.*, edited by Jeremy A. Sabloff and John S. Henderson, pp. 321–354. Dumbarton Oaks Research Library and Collection, Washington, D.C.

1997 Kinship Terms in Maya Inscriptions. In *The Language of Maya Hieroglyphs*, edited by Martha J. Macri and Anabel Ford, pp. 1–12. Pre-Columbian Art Research Institute, San Francisco.

1998a "The Arrival of Strangers": Teotihuacan and Tollan in Classic Maya History. *PARI Online Publications* 25, July 1998, http://www.mesoweb .com/pari/publications/news_ archive/25/strangers/strangers.html.

1998b "The Fire Enters His House": Architecture and Ritual in Classic Maya Texts. In *Function and Meaning in Classic Maya Architecture*, edited by Stephen D. Houston, pp. 373–426. Dumbarton Oaks Research Library and Collection, Washington, D.C.

2000 The "Arrival of Strangers": Teotihuacan and Tollan in Classic Maya History. In *Mesoamerica's Classic Heritage: From Teotihuacan to the Aztecs*, edited by David Carrasco, Lyndsay Jones, and Scott Sessions, pp. 465–514. University Press of Colorado, Boulder.

2002 Glyphs for "Right" and "Left"? Online publication, https://www .mesoweb.com/stuart/notes/ RightLeft.pdf.

2003 On the Paired Variants of **TZ'AK**. Online publication, www.mesoweb. com/stuart/notes/tzak.pdf.

2004a The Beginnings of the Copan Dynasty: A Review of the Hieroglyphic and Historical Evidence. In *Understanding Early Classic Copan*, edited by Ellen E. Bell, Marcelli A. Canuto, and Robert J. Sharer, pp. 215–248. University of Pennsylvania Museum, Philadelphia.

2004b La concha decorada de la tumba del Templo del Búho, Dzibanché. In *Los cautivos de Dzibanché*, edited by Enrique Nalda, pp. 133–140. Instituto Nacional de Antropología e Historia, Mexico City.

2005a A Foreign Past: The Writing and Representation of History on a Royal Ancestral Shrine at Copan. In *Copan: The History of an Ancient Maya Kingdom*, edited by E. Wyllys Andrews and William L. Fash, pp. 373–394. School of American Research Press, Santa Fe.

2005b *The Inscriptions of Temple XIX at Palenque*. Pre-Columbian Art Research Institute, San Francisco.

2011 Some Working Notes on the Text of Tikal Stela 31. Online publication, https://www.mesoweb.com/stuart /notes/Tikal.pdf.

2012 The Name of Paper: The Mythology of Crowning and Royal Nomenclature on Palenque's Palace Tablet. In *Maya Archaeology 2*, edited by Charles Golden, Stephen D. Houston, and Joel Skidmore, pp. 116–142. Precolumbia Mesoweb Press, San Francisco.

2013 The Name of Paper: The Mythology of Crowning and Royal Nomenclature on Palenque's Palace Tablet. In *Maya Archaeology 2*, edited by Charles Golden, Stephen D. Houston, and Joel Skidmore, pp. 116–142. Precolumbia Mesoweb Press, San Francisco.

2014 Naachtun's Stela 24 and the Entrada of 378. *Maya Decipherment,* https://mayadecipherment.com/2014/05/12/naachtuns-stela-24-and-the-entrada-of-378/.

2015 The Royal Headband: A Pan-Mesoamerican Hieroglyph. *Maya Decipherment*, https://mayadecipherment.com/2015/01/26/the-royal-headband-a-pan-mesoamerican-hieroglyph-for-ruler/.

2020 Yesterday's Moon: A Decipherment of the Classic Mayan Adverb *ak'biiy*. *Maya Decipherment*, https://mayadecipherment.com/2020/08/01/yesterdays-moon-a-decipherment-of-the-classic-mayan-adverb-akbiiy/

2021 *King and Cosmos: An Interpretation of the Aztec Calendar Stone*. Precolumbia Mesoweb Press, San Francisco.

Stuart, David, and Ian Graham

2004 *Corpus of Maya Hieroglyphic Inscriptions*, vol. 9, pt. 1, *Piedras Negras*. Peabody Museum of Archaeology and Ethnology, Harvard University, Cambridge, Mass.

Stuart, David, and Stephen D. Houston

2018 Cotton, Snow, and Distant Wonders. *Maya Decipherment*, https://mayadecipherment.com/2018/02/09/cotton-snow-and-distant-wonders/.

Stuart, David, and George Stuart

2008 *Palenque: Eternal City of the Maya*. Thames and Hudson, New York.

Sugiyama, Nawa, William L. Fash, Barbara Fash, and Saburo Sugiyama

2020 The Maya at Teotihuacan? New Insights into Teotihuacan–Maya Interactions from Plaza of the Columns Complex. In *Teotihuacan: The World Beyond the City*, edited by Kenneth G. Hirth, David M. Carballo, and Barbara Arroyo, pp. 139–171. Dumbarton Oaks Research Library and Collection, Washington, D.C.

Sugiyama, Nawa, Saburo Sugiyama, Clarissa Cagnato, Christine A. M. France, Atsuki Irishi, Karissa S. Hughes, Robin R. Singleton, Erin Thornton, and Courtney A. Hofman

2022 Earliest Evidence of Primate Captivity and Translocation Supports Gift Diplomacy between Teotihuacan and the Maya. *Proceedings of the National Academy of Sciences* 119(47): e2212431119, https://doi.org/10.1073/pnas.2212431119.

Sugiyama, Saburo

1992 Rulership, Warfare and Human Sacrifice at the Cuidadela: An Iconographic Study of Feathered Serpent Representations. In *Art, Ideology, and the City of Teotihuacan*, edited by Janet Catherine Berlo, pp. 205–230. Dumbarton Oaks Research Library and Collection, Washington, D.C.

2002 Militarismo plasmado en Teotihuacan. In *Ideología y política a través de materiales, imágenes y símbolos: Memoria de la Primera Mesa Redonda de Teotihuacan*, edited by María E. Ruiz Gallut, pp. 185–209. Universidad Nacional Autónoma de México, Mexico City.

2005 *Human Sacrifice, Militarism and Rulership: Materialization of State Ideology at the Feathered Serpent Pyramid, Teotihuacan, Mexico*. Cambridge University Press, Cambridge.

2013 Creation and Transformation of Monuments in the Ancient City of Teotihuacan. In *Constructing, Deconstructing, and Reconstructing Social Identity: 2,000 Years of*

Monumentality in Teotihuacan and Cholula, Mexico, edited by Saburo Sugiyama, Shigeru Kabata, Tomoko Taniguchi, and Etsuko Niwa, pp. 1–10. Aichi Prefectural University, Cultural Symbiosis Research Institute, Aichi.

Taube, Karl A.

1992a   The Iconography of Mirrors at Teotihuacan. In *Art, Ideology, and the City of Teotihuacan*, edited by Janet Catherine Berlo, pp. 169–204. Dumbarton Oaks Research Library and Collection, Washington, D.C.

1992b   The Temple of Quetzalcoatl and the Cult of Sacred War at Teotihuacan. *Res: Anthropology and Aesthetics* 21:53–87.

2000   *The Writing System of Teotihuacan.* Ancient America 1. Boundary End Archaeological Research Center, Barnardsville, N.C.

2002   The Writing System of Ancient Teotihuacan. In *Ideología y política a través de materiales, imágenes y símbolos: Memoria de la Primera Mesa Redonda de Teotihuacan*, edited by María E. Ruiz Gallut, pp. 331–370. Universidad Nacional Autónoma de México, Mexico City.

2004a   Structure 10L-16 and Its Early Classic Antecedents: Fire and the Evocation and Resurrection of K'inich Yax K'uk' Mo'. In *Understanding Early Classic Copan*, edited by Ellen E. Bell, Marcello A. Canuto, and Robert J. Sharer, pp. 265–295. University of Pennsylvania Museum of Archaeology and Anthropology, Philadelphia.

2004b   Flower Mountain: Concepts of Life, Beauty, and Paradise among the Classic Maya. *Res: Anthropology and Aesthetics* 45:69–98.

2011   Teotihuacan and the Development of Writing in Early Classic Central Mexico. In *Their Way of Writing: Scripts, Signs, and Pictographies in Pre-Columbian America*, edited by Elizabeth Hill Boone and Gary Urton, pp. 77–109. Dumbarton Oaks

Research Library and Collection, Washington, D.C.

2012   The Symbolism of Turquoise in Ancient Mesomerica. In *Turquoise in Mexico and North America: Science, Conservation, Culture and Collections*, edited by J. C. H. King, Max Carocci, Caroline Cartwright, Colin McEwan, and Rebecca Stacey, pp. 117–134. Archetype Publications, in association with the British Museum, London.

2018   Introduction to *Studies in Ancient Mesoamerican Art and Architecture: Selected Works by Karl Andreas Taube*, vol. 1, pp. 13–75. Precolumbia Mesoweb Press, San Francisco.

Tokovinine, Alexandre

2013   *Place and Identity in Classic Maya Narratives.* Dumbarton Oaks Research Library and Collection, Washington, D.C.

Traxler, Loa P., and Robert J. Sharer (editors)

2016   *The Origins of Maya States.* University of Pennsylvania Museum of Archaeology and Anthropology, Philadelphia.

Trik, Aubrey

1963   The Splendid Tomb of Temple I at Tikal, Guatemala. *Expedition* 6(1):2–18.

Urcid, Javier

2003   Conquista por el Señor 1 Muerte: Inscripción zapoteca en un cilindro cerámico. In *Escritura zapoteca: 2500 años de historia*, edited by María de los Angeles Romero Frizzi, pp. 95–142. INAH–CIESAS, Mexico City.

Urcid, Javier, and Arthur A. Joyce

2001   Carved Monuments and Calendrical Names: The Rulers of Río Viejo, Oaxaca. *Ancient Mesoamerica* 12(2):199–216.

Valdés, Juan Antonio, Federico Fahsen, and Gaspar Muñoz Cosme

1997   *Estela 40 de Tikal: Hallazgo y lectura.* Instituto de Antropología e Historia de Guatemala, Guatemala City.

Vázquez López, Veronica, Felix Kupprat, Rogelio Valencia Rivera, and Hugo García Capistrán

2016 The Social Function of the Title "K'uhul Chatahn Winik." Paper presented at the 81st Annual Meeting of the Society for American Archaeology, Orlando.

von Winning, Hasso

1948 The Teotihuacan Owl and Weapon Symbol and Its Association with "Serpent Head X" at Kaminaljuyu. *American Antiquity* 14(2):129–132.

1987 *La iconografía de Teotihuacan: Los dioses y los signos.* 2 vols. Universidad Nacional Autónoma de México, Mexico City.

Wald, Robert

1997 Politics of Art and History at Palenque: Interplay of Text and Iconography on the Tablet of the Slaves. *Texas Notes on Precolumbian Art, Writing, and Culture*, no. 80. University of Texas at Austin, Austin.

Wengrow, David

2022 The Roots of Inequality: An Exchange. *The New York Review of Books*, January 13.

Whittaker, Gordon

1986 The Mexican Names of Three Venus Gods in the Dresden Codex. *Mexicon* 8(3):56–60.

2012 The Names of Teotihuacan. *Mexicon* 34(3):55–58.

2021 *Deciphering Aztec Hieroglyphs: A Guide to Nahuatl Writing.* University of California Press, Oakland.

Wichmann, Søren

2010 Comment on Kaufman and Justeson, "The History of the Word Cacao in Ancient Mesoamerica." *Ancient Mesoamerica* 21(2):437–441.

Willey, Gordon R.

1976 Mesoamerican Civilization and the Idea of Transcendence. *Antiquity* 50:205–215.

1985 The Early Classic in the Maya Lowlands: An Overview. In *A Consideration of the Early Classic Period in the Maya Lowlands*, edited by Gordon R. Willey and Peter Mathews, pp. 5–54. Institute for Mesoamerican Studies, State University of New York, Albany.

Willey, Gordon R., and Peter Mathews (editors)

1985 *A Consideration of the Early Classic Period in the Maya Lowlands.* Institute for Mesoamerican Studies, State University of New York, Albany.

Williams, Robert Lloyd

2013 *The Complete Codex Zouche-Nutall: Mixtec Lineage Histories and Political Biographies.* University of Texas Press, Austin.

Wright, Lori

2005 In Search of Yax Nuun Ayiin I: Revisiting the Tikal Project's Burial 10. *Ancient Mesoamerica* 16(1):89–100.

Zender, Marc

2004 Glyphs for "Handspan" and "Strike" in Classic Maya Ballgame Texts. *The PARI Journal* 4(4):1–9.

DAVID STUART is the David and Linda Schele Professor of Mesoamerican Art at the University of Texas, Austin. He received his PhD in anthropology from Vanderbilt University in 1995. He taught at Harvard University before arriving at the University of Texas, Austin, in 2004, where he now teaches in the Department of Art and Art History. His interests in the traditional cultures of Mesoamerica are wide-ranging, but his primary research focuses on the archaeology and epigraphy of ancient Maya civilization. For the past three decades, he has been very active in the decipherment of Maya hieroglyphic writing, with his major research centering on the art and epigraphy at Copan, Palenque, La Corona, and San Bartolo. More recently, he has been active in the study of Aztec art and hieroglyphs. Stuart's early work on the decipherment of Maya hieroglyphs led to a MacArthur Fellowship in 1984. In 2012, he received a Guggenheim Fellowship and a UNESCO Lifetime Achievement Award. His books include *Palenque: Eternal City of the Maya* (2008), *The Order of Days: Unlocking the Secrets of the Ancient Maya* (2012), and *King and Cosmos: An Interpretation of the Aztec Calendar Stone* (2021).

INDEX

A

accession, of rulers: Chak Tok Ich'aak I date of, 20; date indicator for ruler, 47–48; glyphs at Tikal Marcador, 54, 81; K'inich Yax K'uk' Mo' date of, 121; Sihyaj K'ahk' and Yax Nun Ayiin, 23; Sihyaj K'ahk' missing date and, 22; Spearthrower Owl date of, 47–48; Tikal Marcador glyphs indicating, 54, 75, 81; Yax Nun Ayiin, 25, 34

El Achiotal, Guatemala, 51, 107–108

Aguateca, 108, 109

ajaw (lord), 3, 47, 54, 88, 125; "Eleven at Ajaw" glyph, 81; fourth sequential form of, 83; *kaloomte'* and, 99; *k'uhul ajaw*, 3; "lord of" prefix, 51; *Mutul Ajaw* (lord of Tikal), 14, 43n5; personal reference attached to, 84; Teotihuacan history and Mayan term of, 120; *wiinte'naah*, 100

alligator, in ruler name, 30

Antigua vessels, 29–31

"arrives by foot" (*hul-ookaj*), 19, 44n7

art: figural, 119; impersonal, 117–118

Atetelco murals, 66, 67, 98, 119

atlatl, 34

atlatl-cauac variant, 14

B

bak'tun monument, 13–14, 25, 87

Bejucal, 23, 25, 51; Stela 2, 25, 26

Belize, 51, 89n3

birds: beaks of, 93; bird with "shield-and-darts" sign, 66; "Five Small-bird Mountain," 81; heart and blood imagery, 95–98, 115n1; Hieroglyphic Stairway, 111; unhappy, 107; on war-shields, 104–105

"Born-in-Fire," Sihyaj K'ahk' and, 11

Braswell, Geoffrey E., x

C

Caban (day name in "10 Caban"), Sihyaj K'ahk' and error of, 23, 44n9

Carnegie Institution of Washington, 6

"cauac" head, 60, 81, 84

"cauac shield," 48–50, 60

Cerro de la Tortuga, 112–114

Chak Tok Ich'aak I, 8, 9, 13, 22, 39, 43n8, 47, 52, 85; accession date for, 20; death of, 20; stone raised by, 17–18; Tikal overthrow and, 20–21

chatan winik title, 51, 107–108

Ciudadela complex, 120, 125

Classic Maya, xi. *See also* Early Classic Maya

Codex Mendoza, 73, 82

Copan, Honduras, ix, 4, 5, 14, 36, 51, 73, 91–92, 98, 105–106, 121–122, 124, 125, 126; dynastic founder of, 92, 93–95; Hieroglyphic Stairway of, 92, 109–111, 122

Coyotlatelco period, 71–72

D

darts, 11, 29, 73; "dart shaft" of Tikal Marcador, 106; eagles with, 59; fire and, 13; raptorial birds with shields and, 66; shields and, 112; Spearthrower Owl names and, 57, 60; variants, 41

Davletshin, Albert, 60

death, poetic expression for, 20, 44n8

deities, 5, 11, 38, 39, 66–67, 77, 94. *See also individual deities*

Dos Pilas, 73, 108–109, 115n4

dynasts, Maya: direct descendants of Spearthrower Owl, 108–109; dress, 14; early dynasts of Tikal, 8; honorific titles, 12; institution beginning, 2–3; names and images of, 4; names of central Peten dynasts, 3, 43n1; in Proto-Classic period, 4

Dzibanche, 3, 4–5, 15

147

E

eagles and emblems: eagle consuming human hearts, 59; eagle pectoral worn by Aguateca ruler, 109; "Eagle Striker" and, 91, 101, 118; eagle warriors, x; eagle with shield, 64, 69n3; emblems and icons, 92–112; goggled eyes in, 101, 107, 110, 111, 115n5; heart and blood imagery, 95–98, 115n1; iconic hieroglyphs and, 91–92; in militaristic regalia of Maya rulers, 108–109, 115n4; at Palenque, 107; ritual bags with, 103–104; stricken, 95, 111, 112; Teotihuacan War Serpent, 44n13, 57, 105–106; warrior with flaming weapons and, 108, 115n3

"Eagle Striker," ix, 47, 66, 89n2, 91, 101, 118, 122

Early Classic Maya, xiii, 51, 53; power dynamics and, 47–48; site map, 2

Early Classic Peten: dates of, 1; earliest Period Ending dates and, 7, 8, 17; K'inich Bahlam ruler of, 13; Long Count dates, 5, 7, 10; names of early dynasts of, 3; research absence assertion for, 1; research questions and sources, 1–2; Tikal importance in, 3, 43n1

Early Xolalpan phase, xi, 88, 118–120, 123

Ehb Xook (Yax Ehb Xook), 3, 43n1

"Eighteen Heads of the Snake," 86

Ekholm, Gordon, 28

El Zapote, 23, 25, 44n10, 59; Stela 1, 25; Stela 4, 23, 25; Stela 5, 25, 54, 60

emblems and icons, Teotihuacan influence on Mayan: on bags and shields, 103, 115n2; codex-style vessels and, 105–108; "fan" motif, 106; heart and blood imagery, 95–98, 111, 115n1; Hieroglyphic Stairway of Copan, 109–111; Late Classic warfare and, 104; Maya "emblematic" writing and, 92–95; in Oaxaca, 112–114; "shield and dart," 112; Teotihuacan War Serpent, 80, 105–107; "trapeze-and-ray," 104–105; warrior with eagle and flaming weapons, 108, 115n3. *See also* raptorial birds

Entrada of 378, xiii; Chak Tok Ich'aak accession date and, 20; detailed passages on, 17–20; Early Classic Peten and, 1–9; El Peru connection, 9, 11, 13–14; El Peru Stela 15 highlighting, 9; "he arrived" word and, 9–10; key source, 13–14; Late Classic vessels depicting, 30–31; from Tikal Marcador Tikal pillar, 20–21; Peten inscriptions supporting, 9; records outside of Tikal on, 14; reference and title, 14, 43n5; "shield with darts" motif, 13; "Sihyaj 'Dart'" inscription, 11; Sihyaj K'ahk' and, 11–12, 13, 19; Sihyaj K'ahk' role and history, 21–31; Spearthrower Owl mentions long after, 91; "Storm God" with date of, 74; Sufricaya Mural on, 14, 15; three-verb sequence on, 18–20; Tikal Marcador text on, 76–80; Tikal overthrow revealed in, 20–21; Uaxactun and, 10, 15–16; "western authority" inscription, 15, 17, 43n6, 121; Yax Nun Ayiin as boy-king of Tikal, 31–42. *See also* Sihyaj K'ahk', role and history

Esperanza phase, 1, 121

F

"fan" motif, 99, 105, 106, 111

"Feathered Snake" (Quetzalcoatl), 62, 119, 120

feminine names, prefix for, 39

Fialko, Vilma, 71

Fields, Virginia, 55

fire, 11; "darts" and, 13; "Fire is the Mouth of the Owl," 59; "Fire Mountain" (volcano peak), 38, 45n14; Sihyaj K'ahk' and, 43n4

five mountains, 81, 82, 85–86

Foliated Ahau, 4, 5, 8

"foot-ending," 19, 44n7

G

goggled eyes, 101, 104, 107, 110, 111, 115n5

governance, of Teotihuacan: debates over, x–xi, 117–119, 120; history and, 117; impersonal art and, 117–118; oligarchic republic view of, 119

Great Jaguar Place, 56

Guatemala, 38, 44n10, 44n13. *See* El Achiotal, Guatemala; Antigua vessels; Peten, Group 6C-XVI discoveries and; La Sufricaya, Guatemala

Guerrero, 112

H

hand signs, 13, 89n3

headdresses: detached, 52; iconic hieroglyphs on, 91–92, 95; as name glyph, 58; Piedras Negras, 96–97, 98; royal symbols view of, 119; tassel, 55, 64, 65; "trapeze-and-ray" and, 105; Yax Nun Ayiin, 53

"he arrived" (*huliiy*), 9–10, 11, 14, 77, 89n3

heart and blood imagery, birds and, 95–97, 102, 111, 115n1; *puhil kinil* (wound) and, 98; Teotihuacan War Serpent and, 107

"he cave-enters" (*och-ch'een*), 20, 79–80

"he continues the work of" (*[u] tz'akbu u kabij*), 84

"he was encircled" (*joy[-aj] ti ajaw*), 81

"he water-entered" (*ochha'aj*), 20, 44n8

Hieroglyphic Stairway, Copan, 92, 109–111, 122

Hombre de Tikal, 11, 25, 29, 40–42

Honduras. *See* Copan, Honduras

honorific titles, 12. *See also* kaloomte' (honorific title)

huliiy ("he arrived"), 9–10, 11, 14, 77, 89n3

hul-ookaj ("arrives by foot"), 19, 44n7

Huun Bahlam ("Paper Jaguar"), 8, 43n3

I

incense bags, from Palenque temple, 101–104, 115n2

"it was erected" (*tz'ahpaj*), 20, 29, 74, 83

J

Jaguar God of the Underworld, 38

jaguars, 8, 40, 43n3, 56, 115n1

Jasaw Chan K'awiil, 36, 56–58, 95, 97

jatz, 60–61, 62, 64; heart element and, 68; "striker" and, 84

Jester God, 5

joy(-aj) ti ajaw ("he was encircled"), 81

K

K'ahk' Tiliw Chan Chahk, 34

kaloomte' (honorific title), 12, 19, 36, 42, 50, 62, 77; at Bejucal, 25; five mountains, 85; at Piedras Negras, 123; second arrival and, 41–42; Sihyaj K'ahk' as *ochk'in kaloomte*, 15, 17, 19, 36; variants, 23, 77; western, 13, 15–16, 50, 99, 100, 121–122, 126n2. *See also* Sihyaj K'ahk'

K'an Chitam, 54

K'ante'el, 17–18

Kanul dynasty, 3, 5, 14–15, 107

k'atun (ending date), 4, 8, 18, 75–76, 83; boy-king and, 34, 38–39; maize name and, 53; thirteenth, 56; Tikal Marcador position, 76–77

K'inich Ahkal Mo' Nahb (Palenque ruler), 103–104, 115n2

K'inich Bahlam, 13, 14

K'inich Janab Pakal, 51, 86, 89n3, 104

K'inich Yax K'uk' Mo', 14, 36, 51, 73, 92, 93–95, 98, 110–111; accession date, 121; local Entrada view of, 122

Kubler, George, 67

L

Lápida de Bazán plaque, 112

Laporte, Juan Pedro, 71, 121

La Sufricaya, Guatemala, 9, 23, 77, 102, 105; Mural 7, 14, 15

Late Tlamimilolpa phase, 88, 120

La Ventilla, 71, 72, 92

M

mace-like weapon, Nahuatl term for, 89n1

maize, 51–53

Maize God, 20, 44n8, 77

Marcador. *See* Tikal Marcador

Maya Lowlands, 95, 119; "conquest" of, 20; earliest dated monuments of, 6–7; Preclassic dynast centers, 3; site map, 2; son of Spearthrower Owl and, 120; Spearthrower Owl death and, 121; Yax Nun Ayiin and, 33–34. *See also* Early Classic Peten; Peten, Group 6C-XVI discoveries and

Maya region: dynastic culture beginnings, 2–3. *See also* emblems and icons, Teotihuacan influence in Mayan; *specific topics*

military conquest, 73, 86; eagle imagery and, 108–109, 115n4; term for, 20

Millon, Clara, 55, 58

Millon, René, 58, 119

El Mirador, 2–3

Monte Albán, Oaxaca, 112, 118

Morley, Sylvanus, 6, 9, 43n6

mountains. *See* five mountains

Mundo Perdido, 8–9, 18, 69n3, 71

Mutul: court, 10, 14, 22, 77, 109; king of Dos Pilas, 108–109; Lord of Tikal identification, 14, 43n5

Mutul Ajaw (lord of Tikal), 14

N

Naachtun, 8, 25, 26, 44n11; Stela 24, 27

Nahuatl script, 89n1, 92–93

Nakbe, 2, 51

Namaan court, 59

names and variants, of Spearthrower Owl, ix, x, 48–62; accession glyphs, 54, 81; ancestral reference, 57; atlatl-cauac, 14; blood and heart symbols, 57; "cauac shield," 48–50, 60; "Curl Snout," 48; drawings of, 49; "Feathered Snake," 62, 119, 120; headdress as name glyph, 58; hierarchy statements, 52; jatz, 60–61, 62, 64; maize, 51–53; in Maya iconography and texts, 48–58; militaristic interpretation of, 48–49; "owl and weapons" motif, 58, 63, 64, 67; owl as eagle correction, 58–59; owl identification origins, 58, 59; parentage statements and, 49–50; raptorial birds and, 57–59, 62, 69n1; "stone-in-hand" sign, 60, 69n2; "Striker Owl," 61–62; Teotihuacan iconography and, 58; Uaxactun "weapon complex" and, 61. *See also* emblems and icons, Teotihuacan influence on Mayan; *kaloomte'*; titles

Nanahuatzin (deity), 11

Naranjo, 3, 11, 13, 34, 51, 52, 80, 95

O

Oaxaca, Spearthrower Owl in, 112–114

och-ch'een ("cave-enters"), 20, 79–80

ochha'aj ("he water-entered") (death), 20, 44n8

"owl and weapons" motif, 48, 63; on cylinder tripod ceramics, 64; owl with atlatl mural, 67; with people, 67; personal name interpretation from, 67; in Teotihuacan writing, 66; "trapeze-and-ray" with, 104–105

P

Palace of Quetzalpapalotl, 68

Palenque: K'inich Ahkal Mo' Nahb ruler of, 103–104; ritual bags of, 101–104, 115n2; Tablet of the Slaves, 73, 103–104; Tablet of the Sun, 73; Teotihuacan history at, 105

"Paper Jaguar" (Huun Bahlam), 8, 43n3

Pasztory, Esther, 117–118, 119

El Peru, ix, 9, 11, 14, 41, 101, 121; dedication of, 13–14; patron deity of, 44n7; Sihyaj K'ahk' sculpted portrait in, 28–29; Stela 15, 9, 11–12, 13, 14, 29, 41; Stela 16, 28–29; Stela 51, 9, 12, 13, 14, 121, 125

Peten, Group 6C-XVI discoveries and, xii. *See also* Early Classic Peten

Piedras Negras, 96, 99–101; bags and shields, 103, 115n2; birds on war-shields of, 104–105; headdress with heart sign from, 98; Stela 9, 96–98, 101, 104, 105, 115n2; western *kaloomte'* at, 123

Plaza de las Columnas, xii, 21, 125

Postclassic Central Mexico, myths of, 11

"power being born," 13, 43n4

Proskouriakoff, Tatiana, ix, 9, 10, 33, xivn1

Proto-Classic period, dynasts and, 4

Proyecto Arqueológico Naachtun, 25, 43n5

puh (pus), 97–98

puhil kinil (wound), 98

Pusilha, 4

Q

quauhololli (mace-like weapon), 72, 89n1

Quetzalcoatl, 62

Quetzalpapalotl palace, 68

R

raptorial birds: bird with "shield-and-darts" sign (drawing), 66; depictions of Teotihuacan-style, 108; eagle with shield motif, 64, 69n3; mistaken variant and, 69n1; personal references and, 112; prevalence in Teotihuacan writings, 62–64; rectangular shields showing, 98–99; on ritual bags at Palenque, 103; Spearthrower Owl variants and, 57–59, 62; Tikal Marcador, 84; warfare link with, 104

"Right-hand of the Sun." *See* Unohk'ab K'inich

Río Azul, 20, 23, 51, 58; Stela 1, 26

Río Pasión, 108

ritual incense bags, from Palenque, 101–104, 115n2

Rivera, Iván, 112

rulers, 103–104, 109, 120; accession date indicator of, 47–48; alligator in name, 30; figural art and, 119; "fourth sequential," 83, 119; hierarchy of overseers and, 23; Late Classic Tonina, 34; "seeing" of, 14. *See also* accession, of rulers; *ajaw*; *kaloomte'*; titles; *specific rulers*

S

Safronov, Alexander, 7–8

serpents and snakes, 40, 80; "Feathered Snake," 62, 119, 120; snake's head symbolism, 86; Teotihuacan War Serpent, 80, 105–106, 107

shields: bags and, 103, 115n2; cauac, 48–50, 60; with darts, 13, 112; eagle with, 64, 69n3; earliest Spearthrower Owl name glyph on, 68; rectangular shields of raptorial birds, 98–99; Tikal Marcador as weapon and, 72–74, 89nn1–2; war, 104–105

Sihyaj Chan K'awiil (grandson), 14, 25, 32, 39, 40, 42, 48, 52, 54, 55, 86, 88; headdress held by, 54; in Tikal Marcador narrative, 84–85; wife of, 44n10

Sihyaj K'ahk': as agent or representative, 47, 79, 86; arrival in Tikal, 12, 13, 75; "arrives by foot," 19, 44n7; authority and, 15, 47; "Born-in-Fire" reference to, 11; "descents" of Yax Nun Ayiin and, 36, 37, 44nn12–13; eastern movement of, 11–12, 13; El Peru stelae names of, 12; embedded verb in, 11; "Fire" and, 43n4; *kaloomte'* with Spearthrower Owl and, 12, 51; K'inich Bahlam as aid to, 13; latest mentions of Yax Nun Ayiin and, 40; *ochk'in kaloomte* title and, 15, 17, 19, 36; Palenque possible reference to, 105; second arrival of, 41–42; Spearthrower Owl as higher rank than, 20, 47; in three-verb passage at Stela 31, 19; Tikal left by, 42; in Tikal Marcador narrative, 74, 76–80, 85; as "western authority," 15, 17, 19, 43n6, 121

Sihyaj K'ahk', role and history, 21–31, 43n4; accession date missing for, 22; Bejucal reference to, 25; Caban error and, 23, 44n9; Early Classic Peten significance of, 21; elusive aspects of, 21–22, 29; El Zapote mention of, 25; last mention of, 25; outsider status of, 22–23; as overseer (overlord), 23, 25; portraits of, 28–30; principal charge of, 31–32; shell object with *kaloomte'* and, 28; titles, 30; Uaxactun Stela 4 reference to, 26–28; vases indicating, 30; Yax Nun Ayiin accession and, 23

"Sky Raiser," 10, 26, 28, 51

snake's head, symbolism of, 86

solar ancestors, 33

solar god, 94

Spearthrower Owl: accession date, 47–48; Chatan Winik lords and, 107–108; death of, 42, 55, 121; Early Xolapan phase and, 119; El Peru Stela 15 reference to, 14; erection of monument of, 84; as established nickname, ix; first mention of, 78–79; governance issue and, 118; "grandfathers" and, 84–85; grandson of, 14, 25, 84–85; historical identities conflated with, 97; installation of son of, 22; king of Dos Pilas as direct descendant, 108–109; name variants, ix, x; in Oaxaca, 112–114; as owner of, 84; personal name references to, 30, 91; post-Entrada mentions of, 91; power speculations about, 120; rank as higher than Sihyaj K'ahk', 20; Sihyaj K'ahk' *kaloomte'* and, 12, 51; son of, 31, 120; Tikal Marcador references to personal name of, 74; time of demise, xii; time of life and reign of, xi; 2000 paper on, x; unknown predecessor and, 85; wife of, 34–36; witnessing ("seeing"), 14. *See also* Eagle Striker; names and variants, of Spearthrower

Owl; titles, of Spearthrower Owl; Yax Nun Ayiin; *specific topics*

Spearthrower Owl, interpreting: contemporary portrait of, 55; death record at Tikal, 54; earliest shield bearing name glyph of, 68; Early Classic power dynamics and, 47–48; evidence for Teotihuacan ruler status of, 47–48; first hieroglyph identifying, 48–49; iconographic equivalents of glyphs of, 64–65; length of reign, 48, 54; nickname prompt, 49; tassel headdress worn by, 55; in Teotihuacan writing, 62–68, 69n3; Tikal Marcador accession glyphs, 54, 75, 81

"stone-in-hand" sign, 60, 69n2

Storm God, 38, 51, 72, 74, 83–84

"Striker Owl," 61–62

T

Tablet of the Slaves, 103

Tablet of the Sun, 73

Tajoom Uk'ab Tuun, 100, 126n2

tassel headdress, 55, 64, 65

Taube, Karl, 58, 72, 92, 93, 95, 105–107

Techinantitla murals, 66

Temple of the Feathered Serpent, 119, 120

Temple of the Sun, 36

Teotihuacan: apogee, 119; centralized rule and "rejection" assertion, xi; enclave, xii; governance debates, x–xi, 117–119, 120; headdress, 52; hieroglyphic writing of, 12; new discoveries, xii; Temple of the Sun, 36. *See also* emblems and icons, Teotihuacan influence in Mayan

Teotihuacan-Maya interactions: Entrada of 378 inscriptions and, 17; glyphs-iconography overlap and, 63–64, 91, 93; history and, 119; Maya appropriations of Teotihuacan iconography, 91–92; Tikal dynasty and, xii. *See also* emblems and icons, Teotihuacan influence in Mayan

Teotihuacan War Serpent, 44n13, 57, 80, 86, 97, 105–107

Teotihuacan writing: deity reference view of, 66–67; drawings of glyphs, 63, 65, 66, 67; eagle-and-dart in, 65; emblematic hieroglyphs in (drawings), 93; emblems and icons in, 92–112; glyphs-iconography overlap and, 63–64, 91, 93; "owl and weapons" in, 66, 67; raptorial birds with weapons in, 62–68; shield motif in, 64; Spearthrower Owl in, 62–68, 69n3. *See also* emblems and icons, Teotihuacan influence in Mayan

Tetitla floor paintings, 63

Tikal, ix, 55, 120, xivn1; arrival of authority to, 15; Early Classic Peten and, 3, 43n1; early dynasts of, 8; historical parallelism, 57; historical records at, xi; Hombre de, 11, 25, 29, 40–42; inscriptions supporting ruler status of Spearthrower Owl, 47–48; later kings, 8; Lintels 3 and 2, Temple I, 56–57; major shift in, xi; Maya-Teotihuacan interaction and, xii; Miscellaneous Text 34, 36–37; Miscellaneous Text 35, 37; as Mutul

court, 10, 14, 22, 77, 109; overthrow, 20–21; prior king, 8, 9, 13; Proskouriakoff on date of foreign conquest of, ix, xivn1; Stela 1, 8, 34–35, 60; Stela 4, 11, 14, 23–24, 34, 36, 38; Stela 10, 25, 44n11; Stela 18, 23–24, 34, 36, 38; Stela 29, 5–6, 8, 43n2; Stela 31, x, 8–9, 11, 12, 14, 17–20, 21–23, 28, 32–34, 38–39, 40–42, 44n7, 48, 49–52, 54, 55, 58, 64, 84, 86, 93, 95, 97, 98–99; Stela 32, 55, 64, 99, 108, 115n4; Stela 39, 7, 8–9, 17–18, 43n3; Stela 40, 44n10, 53–54; stelae of Uaxactun and, 5–8; texts from outside, 51; war between Uaxactun and, 8, 9; Yax Nun Ayiin headdress on, 95. *See also* Entrada of 378; Yax Nun Ayiin, as possible boy-king of Tikal

Tikal Marcador, 9, 20–21, 54; accession glyphs, 54, 75, 81; back text: dedication and remembrance, 80–87; carving on back panel of, 75; classification challenge, 71–72; as conquest memorial, 87–88; "dart shaft" of, 106; dedication of, 74, 75, 80–87; design style, 72; discovery, 71; earlier assessments of, 87; form of, 71; front and rear views, 72; front text: arrival and conquest, 76–80; inscription detailing four events, 74–76; "it was erected" self-reference of, 83; last texts of, 87; lunar statement on, 77, 89n3; sides and narrative structure, 74–88; Spearthrower Owl glyphs of, 49, 54; as weapon and shield, 72–74, 89nn1–2. *See also* Sihyaj K'ahk'; Spearthrower Owl

titles, of Spearthrower Owl, 34; *ajaw* and, 3, 14, 120, 125; *chatan winik*, 51, 107–108; "fourth sequential ruler," 83, 119; honorific, 12; local lord, 85, 86; Lord of Tikal, 14, 43n5. *See also* kaloomte'

Tlaloc-Venus War Complex, 91–92, 125

tz'ahpaj ("was erected"), 29, 74, 83

U

Uaxactun: Entrada described at, 15–16; foreign warrior on, 10; Stela 4, 26–28, 51; Stela 5, 9–10, 12, 14, 28, 61; Stela 9, 5–7; Stela 18, 6; Stela 19, 6, 7; Stela 22, 15, 16, 19, 43n6; Tikal victory over, 9; "weapon complex," 61

Uaxactun, Tikal and, 1, 9–10; selected early stelae from, 6; war between, 8, 9

Unohk'ab K'inich ("Right-hand of the Sun"), 3

(u) tz'akbu u kabij ("he continues the work of"), 84

V

"Venus-Tlaloc" iconography, 97

W

war and conquest, 25; famous Teotihuacan warrior image, 55; Late Classic, 104; symbol of, 87; Teotihuacan War Serpent, 44n13, 57, 80, 86, 97, 105–107; term for conquest, 20; Tlaloc-Venus War Complex, 91–92; Uaxactun-Tikal, 8, 9; warrior with eagle and flaming weapons, 108, 115n3; war shields, 73–74, 104–105; wounded birds and, 112. *See also* military conquest

weapons: with personal names/references, 73; Tikal Marcador shield and, 72–74, 89nn1–2

western authority, *kaloomte'* and, 15–16, 99, 100, 121–122, 126n2; clue to eastern movement of Sihyaj K'ahk', 13; personal reference indicator of, 50

"White Owl Jaguar," 40

wife, of Spearthrower Owl, 34–36

wiinte'naah glyph, 36, 37, 44n12, 100

X

Xiuhcoatl, 80, 86, 97, 106–107

Xunantunich, Entrada records at, 14–15

Y

Yax Nun Ayiin (son of Spearthrower Owl), 8, 14, 22, 43n2; accession, 25, 34; death of, 55; grandson, 54; headdress, 53, 95; inauguration of, 23, 86; latest mentions of, 40; portraits of, 32–33; solar ancestor iconography, 33; son of, 32–33; Tikal Marcador and, 86; Tikal statements on child-father relationship, 50

Yax Nun Ayiin, as possible boy-king of Tikal, 31–42; "baby" hieroglyph, 35; ceremonial act, 38, 45n14; death date, 38–39; "descent" of, 36, 37, 44nn12–13; ethnicity question, 33–34; mother's identity, 34–35, 44n10; portraits of, 32–33, 38; reign duration, 38–39; "seating" of, 41; supernatural identity, 40–41; title of age texts, 34; unexpected demise of, 42; wife of, 39

STUDIES IN PRE-COLUMBIAN ART AND ARCHAEOLOGY
PUBLISHED BY DUMBARTON OAKS, WASHINGTON, D.C.

The Studies in Pre-Columbian Art and Archaeology series publishes monographs focused on a specific theme or body of material that merits in-depth treatment. These highlight current research drawing on archaeological, art historical, and ethnohistorical approaches to the Pre-Columbian past in Mesoamerica, Central America, and the Andes.

1 *An Early Stone Pectoral from Southeastern Mexico*, by Michael D. Coe

2 *Three Maya Relief Panels at Dumbarton Oaks*, by Michael D. Coe and Elizabeth P. Benson

3 *Thoughts on the Meaning and Use of Pre-Hispanic Mexican Sellos*, by Frederick V. Field

4 *The Iconography of the Art of Teotihuacan*, by George Kubler

5 *Two Aztec Wood Idols: Iconographic and Chronologic Analysis*, by H. B. Nicholson and Rainer Berger

6 *The Olmec Paintings of Oxtotitlan Cave, Guerrero, Mexico*, by David C. Grove

7 *A Study of Olmec Iconography*, by Peter David Joralemon

8 *An Olmec Figure at Dumbarton Oaks*, by Elizabeth P. Benson

9 *A Possible Focus of Andean Artistic Influence in Mesoamerica*, by Mino Badner

10 *Izapan-Style Art: A Study of Its Form and Meaning*, by Jacinto Quirarte

11 *Human Decapitation in Ancient Mesoamerica*, by Christopher L. Moser

12 *The Thread of Life: Symbolism of Miniature Art from Ecuador*, by Johannes Wilbert

13 *A Further Exploration of the Rowe Chavín Seriation and Its Implications for North Central Coast Chronology*, by Peter G. Roe

14 *A Man and a Feline in Mochica Art*, by Elizabeth P. Benson

15 *The Iconography of the Teotihuacan Tlaloc*, by Esther Pasztory

16 *Seven Matched Hollow Gold Jaguars from Peru's Early Horizon*, by Heather Lechtman, Lee A. Parsons, and William J. Young

17 *Ecology and the Arts in Ancient Panama: On the Development of Social Rank and Symbolism in the Central Provinces*, by Olga F. Linares

18 *Aspects of Classic Maya Rulership on Two Inscribed Vessels,* by George Kubler

19 *The Danzantes of Monte Albán,* by John F. Scott

20 *State and Cosmos in the Art of Tenochtitlan,* by Richard F. Townsend

21 *The Burial Theme in Moche Iconography,* by Christopher B. Donnan and Donna McClelland

22 *The Origins of the Chavín Culture,* by Chiaki Kano

23 *A Study of Olmec Sculptural Chronology,* by Susan Milbrath

24 *Chacs and Chiefs: The Iconology of Mosaic Stone Sculpture in Pre-Conquest Yucatán, Mexico,* by Rosemary Sharp

25 *The Mirror, the Rabbit, and the Bundle: "Accession" Expressions from the Classic Maya Inscriptions,* by Linda Schele and Jeffrey H. Miller

26 *Four Lienzos of the Coixtlahuaca Valley,* by Ross Parmenter

27 *Izapa Relief Carving: Form, Content, Rules for Design, and Role in Mesoamerican Art History and Archaeology,* by Virginia G. Smith

28 *The Origins of Maya Art: Monumental Stone Sculpture of Kaminaljuyu, Guatemala, and the Southern Pacific Coast,* by Lee Allen Parsons

29 *The House of the Bacabs, Copan, Honduras,* edited by David Webster

30 *Axe-Monies and Their Relatives,* by Dorothy Hosler, Heather Lechtman, and Olaf Holm

31 *The Frieze of the Palace of the Stuccoes, Acanceh, Yucatan, Mexico,* by Virginia E. Miller

32 *The Major Gods of Ancient Yucatan,* by Karl Taube

33 *Classic Maya Place Names,* by David Stuart and Stephen D. Houston

34 *Zapotec Hieroglyphic Writing,* by Javier Urcid Serrano

35 *Sandals from Coahuila Caves,* by Walter W. Taylor

36 *Script and Glyph: Pre-Hispanic History, Colonial Bookmaking, and the Historia Tolteca-Chichimeca,* by Dana Leibsohn

37 *Place and Identity in Classic Maya Narratives,* by Alexandre Tokovinine

38 *Holes in the Head: The Art and Archaeology of Trepanation in Ancient Peru,* by John W. Verano, with contributions by Bebel Ibarra Asencios, David Kushner, Mellisa Lund Valle, Anne R. Titelbaum, and J. Michael Williams

39 *Painted Words: Nahua Catholicism, Politics, and Memory in the Atzaqualco Pictorial Catechism,* by Elizabeth Hill Boone, Louise M. Burkhart, and David Tavárez

40 *The Archaeology of Mural Painting at Pañamarca, Peru,* by Lisa Trever, with contributions by Jorge Gamboa, Ricardo Toribio, and Ricardo Morales

41 *Spearthrower Owl: A Teotihuacan Ruler in Maya History,* by David Stuart